Jenny

Jenny

A sequel to Natasha

Jane Waters

authorHOUSE®

AuthorHouse™ LLC
1663 Liberty Drive
Bloomington, IN 47403
www.authorhouse.com
Phone: 1-800-839-8640

This is a work of fiction. All of the characters, names, incidents, organizations, and dialogue in this novel are either the products of the author's imagination or are used fictitiously.

Published by AuthorHouse 10/16/2013

ISBN: 978-1-4918-1744-5 (sc)
ISBN: 978-1-4918-1743-8 (e)

Any people depicted in stock imagery provided by Thinkstock are models, and such images are being used for illustrative purposes only. Certain stock imagery © Thinkstock.

This book is printed on acid-free paper.

Because of the dynamic nature of the Internet, any web addresses or links contained in this book may have changed since publication and may no longer be valid. The views expressed in this work are solely those of the author and do not necessarily reflect the views of the publisher, and the publisher hereby disclaims any responsibility for them.

IN APPRECIATION

I want to thank the birth mothers and adoptive parents who have allowed me to be a part of your experiences, pain, and healing. I am honored to have worked with you and I have learned much from you about courage and faith.

I want to thank the director of Crisis Pregnancy Outreach, Cheryl Bauman, for inviting me over two decades ago to be involved with this outstanding non-profit, Christian agency. Thank you for your friendship and for trusting me with the care of our clients. May God bless you richly for all you have done for CPO.

Additionally, I want to thank all the hundreds of volunteers for CPO who give tirelessly of themselves. Your rewards are awaiting you in Heaven.

I especially want to thank my husband, Chris, for his editing, constant encouragement, and faith in me. You are my hero.

Where would I be without the love and support of my family, friends, and church family! Your prayers, thoughts, emails, and continual faith in me have inspired me to be more than who I thought I would be.

Finally, I want to thank my Heavenly Father for trusting me with this story. This was Your inspiration and I hope I told it well. Thank You for being the perfect Father who loves us beyond what we can imagine. I pray that this will offer hope to someone in need of Your healing touch.

With much love,
Janey

Note: The characters in this book are completely fictional, though realistic. It is my desire to honor those whose pain I have heard in my twenty-nine years' experience as a therapist. All names are fictitious except for Cheryl Bauman, who is the director of Crisis Pregnancy Outreach in Jenks, OK. Otherwise, any resemblance to actual persons, living or dead, events, or locale is purely coincidental.

CHAPTER 1

Christmas was fast approaching. And, for a welcome change, the weather was perfect: bitingly cold with a wintry mix of ice and snow, turning mostly to snow by the end of Christmas Eve.

Weather in the windy state of Oklahoma was always unpredictable. It could be seventy degrees one day and twenty the next. On some days, the winds would curl in from the south producing a balmy, tropical atmosphere only to have the winds shift from the north, driving in the harsh cold winds. Dressing in several layers was the key to survival in this state.

But, this Christmas Eve, the weather cooperated with her wish. Jenny loved the snow, especially since she was on winter break from school. She and her four younger brothers had plenty of opportunities to make snowmen, build forts, make angels on the ground, and drink plenty of steamy, hot chocolate.

Everything seemed in place. Her father and brothers had hand-selected the perfect eight-foot tall, Douglas fir tree from a farm in the country earlier in the week. The family had spent hours decorating the tree with strings of white, blinking lights and dotting it with huge, shiny, red balls hanging with gold threads from the branches.

Scads of beautifully decorated presents were stacked in uneven patterns covering the homemade Christmas tree skirt while the aroma of oven-cooked, honeyed ham and newly baked dill bread filled every crevice of the house.

This would be a perfect evening offering all the ingredients for a memorable holiday. Family and relatives gathered in the kitchen while Jenny warmed herself at the glowing fire in the huge, white-stoned fireplace in the living room.

Christmas Eve! The time of excitement for all children. The best time of the entire year! Or, should be, anyway.

But, not for Jenny. At least, not this year.

Something was missing and it bothered Jenny that she couldn't quite put her finger on the source of her unrest. Was it some*thing*? Or, some*one*? And, why did she feel so burdened with unsolicited feelings such as anger, guilt, and sadness. She was only eleven years old, but those small shoulders of hers seemed to carry a burden large enough to weigh down an ox.

Based on the last five years, Jenny knew she had every reason in the world to anticipate a great holiday this year. The last few Christmases had been vastly different than the first six she had spent with her birth mother, Natasha. So, why was she so sad? What was so wrong? Jenny pondered these things while sitting cross-legged on the brown, billowy loveseat in the living room, staring at the tree.

Her adoptive parents, Cathey and Randy Abbott, knew something was troubling Jenny, and when they asked her if she was feeling ill, she repeatedly told them that everything was just fine. But, they knew better. Especially Cathey, who had always paid close attention to Jenny's facial expressions. To her, Jenny's face was an open book and would, more often than not, betray her words.

So, why, why, why was she so down this Christmas Eve? She was grateful to be safe, secure, and surrounded by loved ones who adored her and her siblings. They had continuous electricity and warmth, no strange people banging at their door in the middle of the night, and their house was filled with laughter and affection. And, food? They had such a variety of prepared foods. And, not only food for the holidays, but food year round!

When she'd lived with Natasha, Jenny had dreaded listening to her siblings' growling stomachs. And, her own. But, the Abbott family ate like royalty, complete with chicken casseroles, hamburger dishes, occasional steaks, salads, crackers and cheese, and any flavor of jello they wanted. They could eat anytime, except before dinner, and could have as much as they wanted.

She had the perfect life. At eleven years of age, Jenny had read books depicting families who lived comfortable and happy lives. She called them *book families*. Never in her earlier years would she have ever hoped to have been part of a book family! And, now she and her brothers were!

Pondering what had stolen her joy that night, Jenny eyes began to water.

It hit her like a frozen snowball stinging her face. Not *everyone* would be here for Christmas. Randy and Cathey's extended family had brought presents for the children and side dishes for their meal, but one person would be missing this year—not only from this family occasion, but from Jenny's life itself, or so it seemed.

Natasha, her birth mother—her first mother—had disappeared. Natasha was gone.

Again.

CHAPTER 2

This sudden realization triggered a watershed of tears running down Jenny's cheeks. Her heart echoed emptiness and her stomach clinched tightly as she thought about her birth mother somewhere out on the streets. She had not heard from Natasha in weeks. No one had. And, though Jenny was only eleven, she knew that when they didn't hear from her for an extended period of time, it usually meant disaster.

Though Jenny could be a fairly outspoken young girl, she usually kept her feelings hidden deep within her heart. A learned response, really. Not genetic. Came by it honestly from years of having to care for her younger siblings when Mom was "running errands," as Natasha called them. Jenny was never invited to go with her on those occasions. *It's no place for a child,* her mother said.

Before the Abbott's, no adult in Jenny's life had ever been dependable, so life insisted that she set aside her own needs and rely on herself when others' needs arose. Men, especially, oozed mistrust to this little one. She had never before met her birth father, so how could she trust someone who had abandoned her before birth? Nor had she met any of the birth fathers of her brothers. And, none of Natasha's male "friends" had ever showed a healthy interest in, or kindness towards, them. Though Jenny never understood why, she had always assumed that something was wrong with *her*. Otherwise, wouldn't they have been friendlier towards her?

So many questions about those early years! And, this Christmas Eve, memories flooded Jenny's mind.

Scores of feelings swirled around in her heart, much like a crocodile wildly thrashing about in water. Hurt. Fear. Panic. Sadness. And, if she were honest with herself, anger. It was still so difficult for Jenny to feel anger towards her mother. She hated it when her mother got mad, especially when it was aimed at her. Worse, she had come to hate the half-ton load of responsibility she felt for her mother's bad moods. She had genuinely tried to make her mom happy, but could never do enough to change her dark moods.

Even as young as four or five years old, Jenny had tried several ways to make her laugh, like drawing funny pictures, dancing on the couch, and keeping the boys from making so much noise when her mom was sleeping. Sometimes, her methods worked, but not often enough.

Keeping the toys picked up in their small apartment was a never-ending job, as was trying to search for things to feed her brothers' empty tummies when her mother was out. It seemed as if they were always hungry. In an odd way, Jenny felt as though she had co-parented during the times when Natasha was "absent." Somebody had to step in where her mother had left off. There was a job vacancy, and she was the only one available.

Natasha had come to rely on Jenny's ability, creativity, and willingness to pick up the slack when she didn't feel well after a long night of having stayed out. And, over time, Jenny had become used to her absences for long periods of time, but hated it when she was gone all night.

Sometimes, at night, her brothers would awaken needing a drink of water or comfort from a nightmare. Yearning for their mother's comfort, the children had been repeatedly left unsettled. However, slowly, they had become accustomed to Jenny's care for them. Her young, sweet voice and delicate touch to their faces had been far better than having received nothing at all. But, where was the source of Jenny's comfort? Too often she had been left alone at night, her own fears unsoothed.

Eventually, the boys had come to prefer their sister's care over their mother's because she had become more irritable than nurturing, more depressed than energizing, and more selfish than mothering. They had rarely been able to distinguish if their mother had been gone at night or just too tired to get up with them. Jenny thought it was better that they did not know.

Always the helper, Jenny had been glad to be of assistance to her mom anytime. Well, as long as it didn't interfere with coloring on paper at the kitchen table. Coloring had brought her such joy! She loved to create her own drawings on paper, coloring books, or even grocery sacks when she could find nothing else. Coloring had been the way in which Jenny could escape to her own fantasy world—a place where she had not been expected to take care of anyone except herself. And, sing? Oh, how Jenny had loved to sing! The combination of drawing and singing had been enough to lift her tiny, six-year-old spirit when she had felt low.

Though Jenny could only remember one or two Christmases with Natasha, it bothered her that she had few memories attached to such a supposedly joy-filled season, and too many of the pain-afflicted ones.

Surviving the early years had made Jenny mad, but she knew better than to express her anger towards her mother. She had learned that lesson the hard way. There was a price which had to be paid for that mistake, and the debt was usually paid with swiftly-delivered slaps to the face or hits to her backside. Jenny had often thought that, for being such a tired woman, her mother could sure pack a wallop. Natasha was at her strongest when she was angriest, that's for sure.

Jenny had taken more than her fair share of hits, but she never regretted the punishment taken for her brothers. It used to make Jenny's stomach churn when her mother headed for the boys with her hand cocked and loaded. Most of the time, she had been able to distract her mother by knocking over her glass of milk or screaming at the top of her lungs so that Sam, their neighbor, might hear and come check on them. That had been the best case scenario.

Sam had been nice, though, even if he was in his thirties. Sometimes, when her mother was out for the evening, Sam had bought them pizza —real pizza from a pizza store—and had waited with them until her mother returned. Nights with him had been fun, and he never seemed to get irritated with them—not really. Mostly, he had seemed to be mad at her mother for letting the house get so dirty. Sam hated the bugs which crawled on the countertops, but Jenny hadn't minded much. She had actually named a few, but she could never tell if they were the same bugs or new ones which came around, so she had finally given up and called all of them "Pepper" because they were so black.

Her brothers had liked Sam, too. Everyone had, except her mother, that is. Natasha had known that he was the one who had called the police on her several times. Social services had come to check on them a couple of times and had threatened to take the kids away if she didn't make some much needed changes. Sadly, she didn't, which is how they came to be taken and placed with the Abbott's.

For several years after the adoption, Natasha had done quite well with turning her life around. Sure, there had been setbacks and relapses, but they had been relatively short-lived—usually a few days, maximum of a week.

It had taken Jenny the same number of years to feel less anxious about Natasha's safety. Having been adopted by Cathey and Randy meant that

Jenny didn't have to worry about having to keep her brothers calm and secure. They were all well fed regardless of where Natasha was or what she was doing. And, Jenny didn't have to wake up in the middle of the night to comfort her brothers. Actually, they had stopped awakening with nightmares soon after moving in with the Abbott's. Everyone seemed to be getting more sleep, especially since the baby had grown older.

When Natasha had been pregnant with David, the last member of the sibling group, she had prematurely gone into labor with pre-eclampsia and had to be rushed to the hospital. Having had a C-section, and as a result of blood tests, Natasha had been found with high levels of THC in her system. Pot was her first drug of choice, and her second was men. The test results, coupled with the previous investigations from Social Services, lined up the perfect storm for all of the children to be removed from Natasha's care immediately.

Fortunately, in accordance with God's perfect Plan, Crisis Pregnancy Outreach had been able to stand in the gap before the Department of Social Services was called, which allowed the children to be placed with a loving, Christian family. And, because CPO's adoptions have always been *open*, the children have been able to have an on-going relationship with Natasha. The Abbott's had always included Natasha on family occasions, birthdays, soccer games, and piano performances. Natasha had attended most, but there were many times she was absent. She had given reasons which sounded logical and truthful, like having to study for tests or just general clashes in schedules. However, sometimes she gave no excuse at all for why she had not attended.

As a result, disappointment had been a close friend of Jenny's—a friend which had been nearly impossible to scrape off for any length of time. She did not cherish or desire the attachment, but it had been glued to her for as long as she could remember, so she had just come to accept it.

However, over the last few years her dark shadow had accompanied her less and less frequently, which had both surprised and pleased Jenny. She hadn't understood the reason, but she certainly wasn't going to complain about its increasing absence!

But, it always lurked.

And, now, Natasha had disappeared, again.

Gripped with fear and panic, and back in familiar territory, Jenny would, once again, spend this Christmas season with her uninvited and unwelcomed shadow.

CHAPTER 3

Would this ever end? This never-ending dread which Jenny felt in regards to Natasha's disappearances. The fear was eating up her stomach lining. Her helplessness triggered tears.

Cathey had been watching Jenny from the kitchen. Seeing Jenny's tears, she knew exactly what to do. Softly entering the living room, she sat next to Jenny and put her arm around her. Cathey's voice was normally silky smooth, but even more so when she spoke tenderly.

"The lights on the tree are beautiful, aren't they?" From experience, Cathey knew that Jenny needed some breathing room before transitioning into a discussion on feelings.

Placing a tissue in Jenny's left palm, Cathey continued.

"Such a dreary day, isn't it? Looks like more snow on the way."

Sniff. "Yeah, I guess so," was all Jenny could utter at the moment.

They sat for another few moments staring at the tree and presents. Jenny had already spotted which gifts were hers. They were the ones neatly wrapped in gold, red, and green shiny wrapping paper with snowmen and angels hanging from the bows. The boys' presents were wrapped differently —a tradition which began the second Christmas after coming to live with the Abbott's. Theirs were wrapped in newspapers because they didn't know how to save the beautiful wrapping paper like she did. Jenny had always been careful to cut through each taped piece while gingerly removing the bows so as not to disturb or destroy the paper. The boys always grew impatient with her as they endured her turn at unwrapping. Randy had said that ripping open packages was a "boy" thing and that each should respect the others' style of unwrapping.

Jenny sighed before asking a question. "Mom, why does life have to be so complicated? I mean, why can't things just go smoothly and stay going smoothly?"

Patiently, Cathey replied, "Honestly, I don't know. Why? What's going on? Why are you so sad on Christmas Eve?"

Jenny's sigh this time was ten times longer than her previous one. Sometimes, it was difficult to talk with her mom about things that her first mother had done or was currently doing. Jenny's personality was one which did not want to burden others with her problems. She had learned this bad habit early in life and had discovered that they were hard to break. Knowing that her burden would lighten after talking was, sometimes, not enough motivation to get her started. But, Jenny was about to explode. Or, implode. She knew she must share this heaviness.

"Why did Natasha have to disappear during my Christmas break? She's been gone for weeks now and nobody's heard from her. I just know that can't be good. I wanted my time off from school to be fun. I didn't want to have to worry about anything. Worry about . . . *her*. I mean, I don't mind if she disappears during the summers because, even if she's gone for a few weeks, then at least there are a lot of other weeks that are left to do fun stuff. But, Christmas break is only two weeks long. Why couldn't she have waited?"

The name which Jenny called Natasha changed depending on her mood. When Jenny was angry, she would call her *Natasha*. But, when she was happy and talking with her in person, she would call her *Mama Nat*. Cathey didn't mind. Jenny had given Cathey her own name—Mom—and she had beamed with that from the start. Whatever the children wanted to call Natasha was fine.

The boys had called Cathey *'Mom'* since the day they were adopted. It had seemed quite easy for them. They were young. Not like Jenny who had been an "older" six-year-old. It had taken Jenny longer to transition into using that term for Cathey. She didn't want to hurt Cathey or Natasha. *Divided loyalties.* That's what Cathey had called it. She had explained to Jenny that she didn't want there to be divided loyalties. Cathey wanted Jenny to love *both* of them, not to be placed in a situation where she felt it was an "either/or" situation. Cathey had always said that everybody needed as much love as they could possibly get.

Leaning back into the couch, but with her arm still on Jenny, Cathey spoke softly.

"Honey, I am so sorry that your vacation didn't turn out the way you wanted. I know how worried you are about Natasha. I'm worried, too. I thought we'd have heard something by now."

Sarcastically, Jenny replied, "No. We won't hear from her until I'm back in school and my break is over."

Cathey sat quietly.

"I'm sorry, Mom. That sounded hateful. I don't know what's wrong with me. I feel like I want to break something."

"Jenny, nothing's wrong with being angry at Natasha. You're disappointed, scared, hurt, and angry. It sounds like the thing that is breaking is your heart."

There it was! Cathey always knew just what to say. She had such a healing and soothing presence. Jenny melted into her arms like butter and sobbed.

Randy stood at the doorway. "Everything alright in here?" He looked at Cathey for direction. Should he join them or should it just be the two of them?

Cathey shook her head. "No. Jenny's just having a hard time. We're trying to work through it."

Randy came over, stood beside Jenny, and stroked her hair. "I'm sorry, princess. I hate to see my girl cry. Is there anything I can do?"

Reaching up and taking his hand, Jenny uncharacteristically sarcastic said, "Yeah, go find Natasha and bring her back. Bring her back so that I can slap her, just like she has slapped my heart."

The sound of screams from boys running through the kitchen captured Randy's attention. Cathey offered a pleading look as if to say, *please take care of the boys while I take care of Jenny.*

Taking his cue, Randy bent down, kissed his angel on top of her small head, and said, "Just let me know if you need me to go beat her up. Until then, I'll go round up the boys. I love you, Jenny."

She began to grin at her father's last comment. "Love you, too, Daddy."

Leaving the room, Randy pretended to run after the boys. "Boys, let's go shovel the sidewalk and get the ice off of the steps. Others will be getting here soon. Last one outside's a rotten egg!"

Jenny and her mom could hear the scramble of multiple pairs of feet scrambling for the door. After hearing the door slam, they heard nothing but silence.

"There, that's better," Cathey said turning back towards Jenny. "Now, what are we gonna do?"

"Well, that's just the thing. There's nothing we can do. Just wait until she decides to bless us with her presence, I guess."

"You sound really, really angry with her. And I don't blame you. You're scared for her and yet you can't do anything about it. Talk about frustration and helplessness! That's one tough combination."

Jenny inhaled deeply and then exhaled slowly. Her mom had understood her feelings towards Natasha, and it felt good. Relaxing a bit, Jenny looked at her mom and asked, "Then, is there anything we *can* do?"

"Yes," her mom said emphatically. "We can pray for her. Actually, we need to pray for both of you."

Knowing better than to question the importance of this option, Jenny asked it anyway. "Well, what will THAT do?"

Hearing Jenny's last comment indicated to Cathey just how hurt, angry, and scared she was this time. And, the intensity was certainly getting the best of her and stealing the better part of the Christmas season.

"Before we pray for Natasha, let's first pray for God to heal *your* broken heart." They sat, side by side and hand in hand while Cathey prayed for Jenny's heart to be free from the grips and imprisonment of fear and anger. From personal experience, Cathey knew that, before Jenny could rightly pray for Natasha, her heart needed to be right with God's. Otherwise, her prayer would come from a place of unforgiveness, which could render the prayer powerless.

Praying usually softened Jenny's heart. She found it very difficult, almost impossible, to simultaneously come before God *and* be angry. Somehow, being in the presence of God's holiness reminded her of just how big *God* was and how small *she* was. But, she just couldn't do it this time. Jenny quickly transitioned from feeling mostly scared to mostly enraged.

In a sudden outburst, Jenny jumped up from the couch, dropped her mom's hand, and stomped off, yelling, "I SHOULDN'T BE THE ONE WHO HAS TO PRAY FOR *HER* ALL THE TIME. I'M TIRED OF PRAYING! YOU PRAY IF YOU WANT TO, BUT I'M NOT GOING TO."

CHAPTER 4

"Jenny? What happened?" Her father was stunned as he opened the garage door.

But, it was no use. She blasted by all of them without hesitation and ran straight into her room, slamming the door shut.

"What happened in here, Cathey?" Randy entered the living room filled with agony at watching his daughter sob.

"She's really angry this time, honey. I don't know what to do. She can usually turn the corner on this and at least pray for Natasha. But she's having none of it this time. She is so mad at Natasha for disappearing again. And, I can't blame her. After all, this is her Christmas vacation and she was really looking forward to having some fun with friends and family. But, all she's done is worry. Jenny hasn't spent *any* time with friends. She said they just wouldn't understand what she was going through, and she didn't want to have to explain it again."

"Should I go in and talk with her?"

"No," Cathey said. "Just let her be alone for awhile. She's taking it pretty hard. Maybe after awhile you could go up and talk with her. I just wish Natasha would call and at least let us know that she's safe and alive."

"You know that I love Natasha, but I gotta tell you, I'm really frustrated with her right now. I hate that Jenny has been so hurt by this—all of the kids. But, there's nothing I can do to fix this. I just feel so . . . helpless."

"We all do, Randy. I don't know what to do either. I've called Kaylee, Cheryl. I've even tried calling Delores, and even her NA sponsor. Nobody's heard a word from her. This is the longest time she's gone without letting at least one of us know where she is."

These people have been a major part of Natasha's support system. Cheryl has been the director of Crisis Pregnancy Outreach, the Christian agency through which Natasha's children were adopted by the Abbott's, for almost thirty years. Miss Delores was the housemother at the group home where Natasha had stayed until she could get on her feet. Delores was like a second mom to Natasha. Whitney was her NA sponsor and had been for several years now. And, Kaylee, her mentor, had seen Natasha through the roller coaster ride of these past few years. But, none of them had heard from Natasha.

Over the past few years, Natasha had developed some friendships at the church she attended. After she had been sober for awhile, Natasha participated in the young adult's Bible study and other classes periodically presented. Initially, she was withdrawn, shy, and rarely wanted to be involved in any activities. But, with time and familiarity with others, she had made significant efforts in forging new friendships and had been met with a fair amount of success.

Relationships had always been difficult for Natasha. She had rarely trusted anyone, which made it difficult to have any long-term friendships. Natasha's parents had not won any awards for "parents of the year." Her father had been in and out of prison for drugs while her mother had been in and out of relationships with men and her addictions, all of which had stolen precious years from the family. Her sisters had been involved with their own lives, their own men, and their own means of survival. Being the youngest, Natasha had but two champions for her: her grandmother and her eldest sister, LaVerne.

Gramma had not been well enough to step in to care for all of the children when their father had gone to prison and their mother had run off with another man. She had tried, but there was only one of her and so many children. They had all lived with her for a bit, but it had become crystal clear that other plans needed to be made. The older children had moved out shortly thereafter, to live on their own, but there was still the matter of the youngest child.

So, by default and by reasoning that she was the eldest, LaVerne had taken on the responsibility – sometimes from joy, but mostly out of burden – of caring for Natasha. Though LaVerne had been relieved that Natasha had not caused many problems initially, her patience was challeneged when Natasha turned up pregnant at sixteen, the first time. But, when she had become pregnant a second time, LaVerne had washed her hands clean of the role of trying to parent someone who didn't want to be parented.

Natasha hadn't cared. She had made plans of her own. Well, not really plans; more like romantic dreams about living with Juan, her second baby's father. He had come from nowhere, really, just out of the blue. They had met at a park while Natasha was taking Jenny for a walk in the stroller. He had been there, too. Said he was out for a walk and just wanted to enjoy God's creation.

Juan had been a real charmer. He was good-looking and knew all the right words to say to a lonely, young girl, who needed a knight in shining armor to whisk her away and live happily ever after.

But, that dream died.

It hadn't taken her long to become convinced that he was no knight—at least not in shining armor, but of filthy armor. Their love had bloomed, or so she believed, and produced a child. He had suddenly disappeared the same day she told him that she was pregnant with his child. Just as suddenly as love had hit, it was stolen.

How had that happened? She had thought he was excited, though she remembered that, on that day, he had become rather quiet as hours ticked away. But, by the moon's rising that night, Natasha had realized that there would be no fantasy family. No whisking away. No living together. No wonderful marriage. And, no happily ever after.

Once again, her dreams had been destroyed.

She had been lied to again. Just like before. Jenny's birth father had been much older, though she had never been sure of just exactly how *much* older. Figuring that he had been in his thirties, okay maybe late thirties or so, he would be ready for a permanent relationship. And, he must have wanted a family because why else would he have treated her like a queen and want nothing else to do but be in bed with her? He had heaped attention and affection on her. At first! But, as in the case of Juan, as soon as he heard about Natasha's pregnancy, he had disappeared.

To say the least, life had been decidedly difficult for Natasha. These two men, boys really, had taught her some hard lessons about life and love, and life *after* the consequences of love.

In early childhood, her parents had taught her about life when the addictions were the love, and how to survive life without them. Her sisters, too, had taught her about life when bitterness and unforgiveness had been the drug, squeezing every last drop of joy out of life's equation. Natasha's children had also taught her about life and love, when love had not been enough to parent. She had been just a child raising her own children.

Yes, Natasha had experienced the betrayal bonds of love, but not the healing hands of it. Natasha's own addictions certainly had not helped develop strong bonds with others either, and had actually played a strong role in keeping her relationships nothing but dysfunctional. Which, in turn, caused her to trust others even less so. It had been a chaotic, selfish, circular pattern for years, creating a monster which had just continued to gorge itself.

However, there had been one who had shown her a different facet of love. That love could be good, nurturing, healing, and strengthening.

Her grandmother had been the one to point them in the direction of true Love. Jesus. She had read the Bible every single day of her life. Tried to get them to read with her, but they didn't really understand anything she read. It's not like she hadn't *wanted* to *get it,* but she just couldn't get her head around the Bible and that Salvation stuff.

Church attendance had been required anytime they were with their Gramma. *No ifs, ands, or buts,* as she used to put it. If Natasha and her siblings hadn't been so hard-hearted about religion, it might have been their saving grace. The people had been good; music, too; and, even a sermon or two had caught Natasha's attention. She'd just not wanted to accept anybody else's love if she couldn't have her parents' love. Somehow, her twisted thinking at that time had made sense to her.

The more her grandmother pushed it on them, the more they pulled away from it. Natasha had known she wasn't right to be so hard-headed, but somehow the rebellious monster just wouldn't leave. Religion hadn't stuck to her sisters either. Made their grandmother madder than a stirred-up hornet's nest. She'd just throw up her hands and walk off muttering something *about one of these days . . .* whatever that meant.

Eventually, Natasha found out what that had meant. All of her prayers had paid off because Natasha got baptized while living at the Transitional House. And, not just by water, but by the Holy Spirit, too. Came upon her all at once when she came up out of the water. Not only had her spirit been cleansed and renewed, but it had been mightily strengthened and strangely warmed. It had even made her lightheaded.

In the years after that monumental moment, Natasha would come to rely on that guidance and strength, especially in tough times. *Walking the talk* as a new Christian had proved to be quite an uphill battle. But, she had more successes than relapses.

Jenny had been proud of Natasha's hard work during those years. She still loved her first mother. There was no question about that. But, love wasn't helping much at all this Christmas Eve. In fact, tonight, she almost wished she didn't love her quite so much. Maybe then it wouldn't be so painful for Jenny when Natasha disappeared like this.

Deep in thought, Jenny was unaware of the soft knocking on her bedroom door.

"Jenny, can I come in?" The familiarity of her father's voice comforted her.

"Sure, Dad. Come on in." Sitting cross-legged on her bed, she fiddled with the tissues in her hands.

"How's my princess?"

Shrugging her shoulders was as much as she could muster for the moment.

"You've had a couple of tough weeks, haven't you?"

Starting to shred her tissue, Jenny nodded her head.

"Not exactly how you thought this vacation was gonna go, huh?"

"Why does she always do this to me, Daddy?" She was still crying, but her anger rumbled like the stage immediately preceeding a volcanic eruption.

"I don't know," he said as he went over and sat next to her.

Frustration popped her cork. "I JUST HATE IT WHEN SHE DOES THIS! Natasha's not thinking about anybody but herself. She's not thinking of me or Nathaniel or the twins. She's not thinking about David. She's only thinking 'bout herself and what *s-h-e* wants."

Randy was a patient, sensitive, and compassionate man. A good man. It drove him crazy when one of the children hurt like this. He wanted to make it all go away. But, this was not the kind of pain that he could fix. He couldn't put a bandage or a sling on it. He couldn't drive her to the doctor's office and have him prescribe an anti-hurt pill. He couldn't make her pain vanish, but he did know how to do one thing!

He knew how to listen. At least he could do that much. He had learned this valuable lesson from Cathey. Years ago, when she came to him with a problem or concern, she would sometimes become frustrated with him because he always tried to fix it. Find a solution, that's what needed to be done! It's what men do, right?

Right? He had asked.

Wrong! Cathey had told him.

She just needed him to listen. He didn't need to provide a solution or try to fix it himself. She did not need options or suggestions, and she certainly did NOT need any criticisms or judgment. She needed his ears.

Period. Not his mouth. It had been a steep learning curve for him, but, with years of opportunities to practice, he had conquered it. Mostly!

Randy figured that these newly acquired skills would come in handy right about now. So, he lent her his ears and shut his mouth.

"Ya know what I mean, Daddy?" she asked rhetorically. "She has SUCH bad timing. I just hate her." Jenny continued on her tirade for a bit longer before the wind in her sail died down. *Angering* is a very tiring thing and, after about thirty minutes, Jenny had become exhausted and plopped in her father's lap.

As Randy stroked her hair, he kept repeating, "I am so sorry, sweetheart. I am just so very, very sorry."

They sat in silence for a few more minutes before Jenny sat up, mopping up the last of her tears. Hearing the boys' voices in the kitchen or running around the living room, she recognized that they may need lassoing or coralling, but her father said nothing. His place was with his hurting child, and the rest of the world could go on without them. Randy would not leave a hurting child. He would wait until Jenny felt better and not one second sooner.

Eventually, Jenny announced the transition of moods with the final blowing of her nose and the straightening up her spine. Inhaling deeply, she said, "Guess there's nothin' we can do about it now, is there?"

"No, I guess not," he responded.

"So, I guess we're just supposed to wait, huh?"

"Yes, I guess so."

"Well, then, that's that! She's not gonna take up any more of my Christmas Eve. She's already had too much of it," Jenny resolved.

"There's my princess," a comment which brought a smile to Jenny's face.

"Daddy, I don't want to grow up," she said with a stronger voice.

"Well, the good thing is, you don't have to do it all at once, and you certainly don't have to do it tonight!"

Though Jenny did not want to grow up, Randy thought it ironic that her words indicated that she was, indeed, maturing. That she turned herself around so quickly, from a place of such devastation, testified to that fact.

The boys' increasing decibel level prompted Jenny to stand. She had learned much too early in life to be too attuned to the needs of her younger brothers.

"Well, Dad, should we go face the monsters?"

Randy laughed. "I'll take care of them. But, I know what you can do for me."

"What," Jenny asked in excitement.

"Well, I happen to know that there are some presents under the tree with your name on them. What d' ya say we gather up everyone and see how much of a dent we can make?"

Squealing, Jenny said, "Well, what are we waitin' for?"

Randy loved that grin of hers. And, he was pleased to see it again.

But, how long would it last? How long would it before they would hear from Natasha? With each day, his fear grew, but he wasn't about to indulge it now. Not tonight. For the sake of the children, not tonight.

"WHAT ARE WE DOING HERE, 'Tash? And, pass the joint, will ya? Quit being such a joint hog."

"Hush! I'm just lookin' at somethin'," Natasha said with striking irritation.

"You pot pig, you!"

"Jus' hold on, bonehead. I'm jus' wantin' to see something, that's all. Jus' cool your jets. Here take this thing, I don't want anymore of it." As Natasha passed the joint to Dyno, some ashes flicked onto the seat, burning a hole in the upholstery. Both began to laugh hysterically at the incident.

"Glad it ain't my car," Dyno choked out after taking a hit off the joint.

"I been meanin' to ask you, whose car is this anyway? I ain't seen you in this one before. What'd you do, steal it?"

"Oh-h, c'mon, 'Tash. Now, you know that I don't go 'round stealin' things." Pretending to be offended, Dyno continued. "Me steal? Ouch. I'm deeply hurt that you would even think that. Nah, there's no need to steal, girl. They're always somebody willing to, umm . . . how shall I say . . . let you . . . *borrow* things. But, I always return them."

"Actually, you mean that you return things *before* they *report* your hiney," Natasha said with sarcasm.

"It's all about timing, 'Tash. Just all about the timing, my friend. If I can get the *borrowed* things back to the owner in a timely fashion, then why would they be upset? I'm not gonna keep nothin'—well, not for long anyway." Natasha wondered if he knew how stupid he sounded. And wondered why she was stupid enough to agree to drive a car that she was now sure was stolen.

But, Dyno seemed to pay no attention to the skewed look on Natasha's face. "Now, what are we doin' here in this neighborhood? You gonna tell me or not?" Cough, cough. "They got nice cars around here. You thinkin' of . . . borrowing a car of your own?"

Natasha was getting increasingly frustrated with her old friend with each passing moment. "No, deerbrain, I'm not. Now shut up!"

"Why are you slowin' down?"

Thinking that this question was not worthy of an answer, Natasha sat silently, having stopped in front of a particular house. Though her brain was a bit foggy tonight after a fair amount of partying, she was sure that this was their house. Over the course of the past few years, Natasha had been there countless times, as recently as about a month ago, from what she could remember. But, in such a drug-altered state and in the dark of the night, she couldn't recognize it as readily.

Inching her way over towards the mailbox and trying to focus her eyes on the address, Natasha was assured.

She slowly read aloud the address. "Hmmm . . . 9816 West Barbour Street . . . yup, this is the place. I was right after all. I recognize it now." Her knowledge was confirmed by the name which sat atop the mailbox: *The Abbott Family*.

They sat in front of a one-story, white stoned house with a three-car garage that wrapped around the back. The curtains in the front room were still open and they could see people standing in front of the Christmas tree. She couldn't see exactly what they were doing, but she was sure that the plates held in their hands cradled an array of food. Natasha knew that Cathey loved cooking, and she was great at it. She, also, knew that her little Jenny loved to help Cathey in the kitchen. Tonight, on Christmas Eve, they would have prepared a feast fit for royalty. Envious of their eating, Natasha's mouth began to salivate. It did not go unnoticed by Dyno either.

"Man, oh man, looks like some wicked stuff they're eatin'. Wonder if they'd have a little somethin' extra leftover for us? Lookin' at this is givin' me the munchies. C'mon, let's get outta here. Take me to the nearest store. We'll get us some chips 'n stuff. Well, you can get it, I mean. I lef' my wallet at the party. C'mon, 'Tash. I'm gettin' bored just sittin' here. Let's either go in or move on."

Straining to see them in greater detail, Natasha rubbed her eyes which had been irritated by the smoke swirling, yet stagnant, around her face.

Dyno kept harping on her. "We were having us some fun awhile ago, 'Tash, and now you got all serious on me. What is *up* with you?"

"If you'd stop blabbing on and on, I'd tell you."

Dyno pulled out the bottle from under the seat and took a long, wet swig of cheap wine. "Fine, FINE. I'm quiet now, so tell me what's goin' on with you, and why are we still at this house?"

With tears beginning to form pools of sad tears in her eyes, she spat, "It's my kids. Okay? My kids are here. This is where they live, dimwit. You happy now?"

"Oh, um, yeah . . . sorry." She thought he was going to say something compassionate, but she should have known better.

"Okay. Your kids are here. So, while they're in there, you're here with me and we got us some partying to do. So, let's get on wit' it."

If looks could kill, Dyno would have been dead before he finished the last word.

"What?" he said dumbfoundedly. "Why're you lookin' at me like that? You know I can't stand it when you start to whine 'bout your kids. Look, you gave 'em up. That was years ago. So, just get over it so that we can get on with it."

He never even saw it coming. She clocked him on the back of the head, good and hard. Now, she was angry. "OH, I *KNOW* YOU DIDN'T JUST SAY THAT!"

"OUCH! That hurt, 'Tash. What did I do?"

"Well, you can just get over *THAT*, can't you, wuss?"

Natasha threw the gear into "Drive" and tried to speed off, but the tire spun because of the black ice on the road. The weather had turned ugly late that afternoon and all the roads were now icy.

The back end of the car slid right into their neighbor's brick mailbox, hitting it with enough force that it made a loud noise as it ripped off a few bricks. Loud enough for everyone to hear! Including the Abbott's.

Glancing out the car window and into their living room, Natasha saw everyone rush over to peer outside. It was too late. They all saw her. At least, the family saw the stranger's car, but the windows were too fogged up for them to recognize that Natasha was at the wheel of a car that was quickly going nowhere.

While Dyno was laughing his head off, Natasha began to panic. "What if they all come outside and see that it's me? What if they get the license plate number? Oh, Lord, why did I ever let you talk me into driving around?"

Dyno couldn't answer because he was rolling on the floor laughing. What in the world was so funny to him? Then again, what did he care? This wasn't *his* car, nor was *he* the one who was driving. He didn't know the people who had Natasha's kids, and couldn't really care less.

Dyno found everything funny, which was irritating her tonight.

"Ohhhhhh, dang, girl! You hit that little brick tower thingy. You got this big ole' car and you let a thing like that beat you up!" His screeching laughter got on her last nerve.

"Just SHUT UP AND HELP ME GET OUTTA HERE!"

Barely able to stifle his snickering, he threw up his arms saying, "What do you want ME to do?"

"Get outta the car and push it or something." Natasha seemed to be sobering up more quickly than she had intended. She glanced back toward the house just in time to see the entire Abbott family coming outside to watch the car from their front porch. She saw Randy come down the steps to make his way over toward them.

Simultaneously, Dyno had opened the passenger side car door and had one foot semi-firmly placed on the curb—as firmly as he could place anything in his presently plastered state. He was going to help get the car back on track so that they could leave the neighborhood, but he wasn't nearly fast enough.

In her alarm, she yelled, "NEVERMIND, YOU IDIOT. CLOSE THE DOOR. SHUT THE DOOR! I'm locking it so they can't open 'em. Here they come!"

"Here *who* comes?" Dyno asked with a puzzled face, having already forgotten.

While poking his temple with her finger, Natasha glanced over at him and impatiently said, "Here is your brain, numnuts, and here is your brain on drugs."

She made a mental note to self: *He's been smoking far too much weed for far too long.*

Still yelling, Natasha continued. "THE ABBOTT'S, YOU IDIOT. HERE HE COMES! WE GOTTA GET OUTTA HERE. NOW!"

With Dyno's right leg still flailing out the door, he shoved the other leg inside as the tires caught traction, and off they sped around the corner and away from those who, unfortunately, knew her best and loved her most.

After they had left the neighborhood's entrance, Natasha began to breathe again. "I hope my kids didn't see me. That's all I'd need. First, I disappear on them; then, I ruin their Christmas Eve; now, I've destroyed their neighbor's mailbox. I just hope they didn't figure out that it was me."

Dimwitted and dumb, Dyno's response was less than empathetic. "You have gotten FAR too serious, girl. Lighten up. Nobody saw us. They might'a seen the car, but they didn't know it was you."

"Yeah, well I hope not," Natasha said shaking her head at her own destructive antics.

"I thought it was f-u-n-n-y. You should be on that show. You know the one I'm talking about? That Cop show. You were just like one of those people, girl."

Neither said a word for a bit. Natasha didn't know if it was safe or not and her heart was having difficulty calming down.

"Well," Dyno said while taking a hit off of another blunt, "I guess we oughta go back to the party and give that dude back his car. He's probably missin' it right about now. He said somethin' about having to go somewhere tonight. Unless he's too stoned!" Laughter spewed out the side of his mouth. "What was that guy's name anyway? I've seen him at several parties, but I just can't remember."

As he was trying his best to make his mind think and recall, in the meantime, Natasha's anxiety was escalating. "But, the car's probably all smashed in where we hit the mailbox. What about that, you idiot? Who's gonna pay for that?"

With a sarcastic smirk, Dyno said, "Who said anything about needing to pay for it? The guy'll never know. We'll just put the keys right back on the counter where we got 'em and he'll never be the wiser. Then, he can find out on his own about the bashed in side when he gets up in the morning. He won't remember anything."

Slapping him again on the back of the head, Natasha became exasperated. "You are twisted, Dyno. You know that? Just twisted. We can't do that."

Slightly agitated, he said, "Don't down *me*, girl. You got a better idea?"

After taking a moment to consider her alternatives, she answered, "Um, no, not right now, but unlike *you*, I'm not done thinkin' yet!"

They hadn't driven very far when, suddenly, Natasha looked in her rearview mirror. Her stomach clenched tightly.

"Oh, God! Oh, great! That's just great!"

"What?" Dyno asked while putting his feet up on the dashboard.

"It's the cops!"

CHAPTER 5

Officer Slater slowly approached the rear of their vehicle. Noting that the driver was not rolling down the window, he cautiously knocked on the driver's side with the back of his knuckles. "Ma'am, roll down your window please." Never before had Natasha heard of anyone sweating blood, but if it were possible, she would be covering the seat with hers. And, while she was trying not to have a nervous breakdown, Dyno was trying, not so successfully, to refrain from laughing his head off. For some particular reason, he seemed to find this funny. He found everything funny when he was high. But, she knew it was only a matter of minutes before he was going to get that smile wiped off his dark, black, twisted face.

Natasha shot him a quick but deadly look, but he wouldn't be robbed of an opportunity to display his stupidity.

"Jus' chill, girl," he whispered. "Cops get more suspicious if you're all whacked out and jacked up."

Officer Slater knocked again on the window, only this time much more assertively and slowly. "MA'AM! I need you to roll down your window right now!"

Keep your cool, just keep your cool, Natasha kept repeating to herself.

Natasha rolled down the window about two inches. "Um, yes, Officer. W-what's the problem?"

"Ma'am, I've stopped you because you have a busted back tail light. Did you know that?"

"Huh?" Natasha said disbelievingly. In worrying about the illegal substances in the car (and inside her), she had nearly forgotten about the accident which must have broken the tail light. Grateful that this was the only reason for being stopped, she still had not rolled down her window. Didn't want to give the officer any other reason to continue on his mission.

However, Officer Slater was just getting started. Now additionally guarded due to the driver's non-compliance, Slater insisted that she roll the window A-L-L the way down. NOW.

As Natasha did so, the officer turned his flashlight on their faces, illuminating the smokey inside. Catching the sweet, particularly recognizable odor of pot as it wafted out the window, Slater stepped back and said the inevitable.

"Ma'am, I'm need you to step out of the vehicle, but first I need to see your driver's license and proof of insurance."

Out of the corner of her eye, Officer Slater noticed a fellow officer's police car cautiously approaching. Parking his vehicle, Officer Tate stepped out and walked over to his partner.

Natasha nervously reached for her purse, but knocked it off the seat spilling the contents on the floor of the car. "Oh, shoot. Um, hang on a minute. I know it's here; uh, I just gotta find it."

Dyno placed his hand over his mouth to squash the sound of his sloppy laughter.

"Oh, yeah, I mean, yes, here it is," she said as she retrieved her license from her overly stuffed, faded brown wallet.

Picking up her purse and throwing it at Dyno, she whispered impatiently, "Make yourself useful for once and pick up all my stuff and stick it in my purse. Can ya at least do that?" Then, Natasha opened the car door and slowly stepped out.

"Uh, yes sir. What's the problem, officer?"

Officer Slater took the license. "Just step over here so that we can close your door. We don't want to be a hazard to other vehicles on the road, especially on an icy night like tonight."

"Yes, officer, sir. Okay." She and Dyno must have been inside the car for too long because her legs shook a bit while urging them to move.

Focusing on the tasks at hand, Officer Slater motioned for the back-up officer to come over. "Yeah, Steve, could you take care of the passenger? I think we need to check both of them, if you know what I mean."

"Sure. Be happy to," Officer Tate said as he took his stance over by the passenger's door.

Not wanting to draw any attention, Dyno faced forward, trying to stay perfectly still as he awkwardly pushed the bag of pot and pipe under the seat. The pipe was still hot and he knew he was taking a risk by shoving it under the seat next to the trashy papers, but he had no other choice. He had to get it out of the cop's eyesight.

As he threw the pipe underneath, it hit the wine bottle, making a loud *thunking* noise, gaining the attention of both officers. Wincing at the loud noise and his obvious mistake, Dyno glanced slowly toward his audience. The thought crossed his mind that this situation might not turn out as well as expected for either of them. Suddenly, he didn't feel like laughing anymore.

Officer Slater studied her license. "Your name Natasha?"

Natasha wanted to say something sarcastic like, *Well, duh, that's what it says, doesn't it?* But, she wisely refrained.

"Yes, officer. That's me."

Ma'am, have you had anything to drink tonight?"

"Uh, no, not really," Natasha replied carefully enunciating her words so as to cause no suspicion. But, she wasn't fooling anybody.

"Let me ask you this. Have you consumed *any* alcohol tonight or any other substance?"

Glancing at her partner in crime, Natasha saw that Dyno was about to get grilled for the same thing. The first clue was when she saw Officer Tate holding the mostly empty bottle of wine in one hand and the still-warmed pipe in the other.

Shoot, Natasha thought. *Here we go.*

YES, YOU CAN CALL SOMEONE," said the clerk at the precinct.

"Well, thanks, but I can't use the phone while I'm handcuffed," Natasha offered sarcastically. "And, what happened to the guy I was with?"

"He's being booked in another area. You can use the phone over there."

Making her way towards the phone, Natasha rubbed her wrists. Handcuffs were not all that comfortable, she decided.

Natasha decided to call Cheryl, the director of Crisis Pregnancy Outreach. *She'll understand,* she thought. The phone rang several times. Natasha wondered what time it was.

"Hello?" Cheryl said.

"Hi, um, Miss Cheryl, it's me, Natasha," she confessed with shame.

"I wondered who would be calling me from jail."

"Huh? Oh, yeah," she replied remembering that Cheryl had caller I.D.

"Well, uh, I got me into a little bit of trouble and I was wonderin', um, if you could, I mean, if you would help me."

The voice from one who was always perky asked, "Well, Natasha, what have you gotten yourself into this time?"

Natasha suddenly became very nervous and began talking very rapidly.

"Well, it's pretty big this time. See, I was with this friend of mine and we thought it'd be a good idea to jus' go drivin' around and then . . . and then . . . . I don't know what happened. First, there was ice and then we hit the mailbox and then there were police lights and I had to stop and . . ."

"You're going to have to slow down, Natasha. I can't understand what in the world you're saying."

"Okay, okay. What I'm tryin' to say is that things are not good here."

"I can't imagine they would be since you're calling from the jail. What did they charge you with?" Cheryl was relieved to hear from her, but couldn't help but be somewhat disappointed that she had obviously relapsed into old patterns of behavior. But, at least she was alive and she could let the Abbott's know that she was now safe, especially now that she was locked up.

She took a deep breath before confessing. "They charged me with DUI, possession of paraphenalia, possession of pot, stolen vehicle, broken tail . . ."

"Natasha, what in the world! You said you were with a friend. Who was it?"

"Well, I don't know if I ever told you 'bout him before or not. His name is Dyno and we were just . . ."

"Oh, my gosh, Natasha! No! You were with *that* low life? Are you back with him again?" Cheryl said, remembering that he was one who kept appearing out of nowhere and interrupting her life. "Wasn't he the one who kept calling when you lived at the Transitional Home?"

"Oh, um, yeah. I guess you do remember him."

"Natasha, why would you hook back up with that slug? I thought you were rid of him and all of his *ways*. I can't believe you would do that. You were doing so well. Oh, how sad. I'm just sick for you."

"I know, I know, Miss Cheryl. I shouldn't have been with him. But, well, it's a long story. Anyway, I was wonderin' if you would, uh could, loan me some money to get out."

"Oh, Natasha, you know I hate to see you in there, but I don't think it's what the Lord would have me do this time. I have no idea how much money that would cost, but I certainly don't have it."

Stunned, Natasha answered, "You mean you won't get me out?"

"Well, actually, it sounds like you need to stay in there and detox anyway for a few hours. You're still slurring your words!"

"You won't come get me?" she asked, now almost incensed.

"Why are you so surprised? Why in the world would you think that I would just immediately plunk down some money to get you out of a situation that you clearly got yourself into? That just doesn't make any sense to me. It's probably going to be at least $1,500 to $2,000! Maybe even more."

She had a point, but Natasha did not want to admit it. She figured that Cheryl would loan her the money due to their long history together. She had first met Cheryl in the hospital five years ago after having given birth to David. Cheryl had been so kind and so sensitive to her feelings, and seemed to really understand her needs.

Yes, she reminded herself, Cheryl was, and continues to be, kind and generous. That was a fact. So, maybe Cheryl was right in her thinking. Maybe she shouldn't be bailed out. Maybe she should just spend some hours—or, however long—then, get a bondsman to put up bail, and then she'd be done with it.

Feeling a bit stronger, Natasha thanked Cheryl for listening and apologized for asking her for the loan. "You're right, Miss Cheryl, you shouldn't give me money, but, um, if you're downtown by the jail, would you come and visit me?"

"I surely would, Natasha. But, you need to get sober first. I'm not gonna talk to anyone who's clearly so under the influence. Let's just see what the Lord has in mind for you. Let me know when visiting hours are. Now get some sleep!"

"I should know somethin' soon. I'll call you when I hear."

By the end of their brief conversation, the police station had become extremely busy and difficult to hear the voice over the phone. Natasha wondered, *What was it about Christmas Eve that seemed to bring out all the crazies?* Then, she reminded herself that she was now one of them.

Cheryl wanted to end the conversation on a positive note, so she reminded Natasha that she was strong, and had survived many difficult situations over the course of her life. The past had been painful, she told Natasha, but it had also strengthened her. And, she had enough fortitude and friends to face this.

"Oh, one more thing, Natasha. Do you want me to call the Abbotts and tell them that you're safe, or do you want to do that?"

"NO! I don't wanna do that. I don't want 'em to know what happened. What am I gonna do? What are they gonna think of me?"

"You don't trust them? They've been through this with you before, Natasha. Your addiction is no surprise to them."

"I don't mind you telling Randy and Cathey. But, do you have to tell Jenny? She's the one I'm worried about. She's called me so many times that I've lost count. I quit answering 'em weeks ago. I jus' got so tired of feeling . . . . I don't know what."

"Guilty?" Cheryl asked.

"Yeah, guilty, I guess." She sighed long and hard. I know, I know. I deserve what I get. I'm just tired of letting her down. Seems like I'm always disappointing her."

"Well, yes, you have hurt her, but to keep this information from her would be cruel. She's been worried sick about you. Don't you think she's suffered enough?"

It shouldn't have taken Natasha long to answer, but it did. Finally, she conceded.

"You're right, Miss Cheryl," she replied in shame. "Well, would you call them for me, then? I can't call out again until . . . until I don't know when. So, would you be okay with calling them?"

"Sure. I'll call just as soon as we hang up. They will all be so relieved to hear the good news."

"Yeah, right."

"Remember, they all love you, Natasha. That won't ever go away. They'll just be glad that you're safe. I'll call you in a day or two and we'll see where things are, okay?"

"Thanks, Miss Cheryl. I appreciate it. Thanks for talking with me and not hanging up. Oh, and um, Merry Christmas."

Natasha knew she was loved by the Abbotts and her children, but she also knew that Jenny was going to be mad at her—if she wasn't already. Since Natasha had decided to get sober—and take it seriously this time—she had really been upset each time she had disappointed Jenny, and the feelings worsened with each relapse.

After hanging up from Cheryl, she continued to feel the impact of the consequences of their evening. It was late and she was tired. Coming down off her high was more depressing this time. Time to go to her cell and sleep it off. For a moment, she wondered where Dyno was, but her concern didn't last long. This was all mostly his fault anyway. It was *his* idea to "borrow" that car in the first place. It was *his* wine and *his* weed. They wouldn't be in this mess if he hadn't brought her along in all of this.

She was alone and it was Christmas Eve.

Merry Christmas!

CHAPTER 6

With a foreboding mixture of feelings, Cheryl made the phone call to the Abbott family. She suspected that they would be simultaneously relieved and angry at Natasha's latest antics, and their response only confirmed it.

It was Christmas Eve and neither Randy nor Cathey wanted to disrupt their family time with a possibility of having it spiral downward by hearing the news about Natasha. They discussed it between themselves, reviewing the pros and cons.

Finally, Jenny became apprehensive about the phone call and the subsequent absence of her parents. She could see them in the kitchen discussing something which appeared to be serious. They whispered so softly that Jenny was unable to determine their words or even the topic of discussion.

With anxiety peaking, Jenny could stand it no longer. She had to say something.

"Hey, Mom, Dad? You gonna come back in? It's your turn to open a present. What are you guys talking about?" Suddenly, her brothers noticed what Jenny had been aware of since the phone call and joined in with their sister in requesting their parents' presence.

"Yeah, Mama, come on, come on. Your turn, your turn," David said running off to drag them back.

"Honey, we'll be right there. Your dad and I just have to talk a minute about something that's come up. Why don't we take a break and get some dessert. Here, come get a plate. We have two kinds of pie, so you can decide which you'd like. Here are some forks, and the whipped cream is in the refrigerator."

All except Jenny came running into the kitchen, practically climbing over each other trying to get to their delicious destination. Jenny held back as her eyes telescoped and fixed on the eyes of her parents. Both were looking at her, but wore different expressions. She couldn't tell exactly what they conveyed, but neither indicated that they had just won the million dollar sweepstakes.

Gradually, her father approached her while her mom dished up sections of pie to her brothers.

"What is it? Did something happen? Was it Natasha? It was, wasn't it? Is she okay?" So many questions!

"Slow down, princess, and let me tell you."

"Oh, God! I knew it, I knew it. She's dead," Jenny whispered with hands covering her eyes.

"No, no, no. She's fine. That was Cheryl on the phone. She called to let us know that she had just talked with Natasha."

"W-where is she?" she asked cautiously.

"Sit down, Jenny."

"I don't wanna sit down. Just tell me. Where is she?" Jenny was becoming increasingly anxious, but it oozed out as frustration towards her father.

Her dad looked at her with one raised eyebrow.

"Sorry, Dad."

"It's okay, honey. Natasha's in jail. She was picked up tonight—she and a friend were both picked up."

Scared and wide-eyed, Jenny asked the inevitable. "What did she do?"

"Cheryl didn't know all the details, but evidently, there were a few charges," he said hoping that she would not ask for the details.

But, Jenny waited silently for more information.

"The police charged her with driving under the influence of something, possession of drugs and alcohol, driving a stolen vehicle, and driving without insurance. I guess that's all, I can't remember what else she said. I mean, that's enough, but those are serious charges, Jenny. I don't know what's going to happen to her. We'll just have to wait and see."

Randy was not prepared for what came next. He anticipated that Jenny would be either tearful or angry, so braced for whatever would come. But she showed neither.

Jenny's face turned blank and her emotions numb, at least as far as he could tell. With tears dried, she stood up, face lifted high, and glided into the kitchen without a word.

"Mom, can I have a piece of pie?" Jenny's voice was monotone.

Glancing at Randy before looking back at Jenny, Cathey said, "Of course, sweetie. Um, what kind would you like? Pumpkin or apple?"

The rest of the evening went surprisingly and unusually well. They continued to open what was left of their gifts after everyone had finished their desserts. After spending a moment or two in her room, Jenny returned to help her brothers finish passing out the last presents. Everybody seemed pleased with their gifts, mostly toys for the boys and clothes for Jenny. Oh, how she loved her cute clothes. Pink and purple were her favorite colors, and they looked gorgeous on her silky smooth, milk chocolatey-colored skin. It was the perfect combination for her skin tone.

Cathey thought that Jenny had seemed rather quiet, but Randy didn't see much difference in her. After they had picked up the living room a bit, they all prepared to go to the midnight church service which was always so incredibly special.

Maybe the late hour helped create the warm, intimate ambiance in the church, or maybe it was the multitude of poinsettias gathered around the altar. The tall, white candles in their tiered, golden stands added a glowing effect which softened people's worshipful faces.

The oldest two children, Jenny and Jeremiah, were allowed to attend the late night service, but Nehemiah, Nathaniel, and David had to stay home with Randy because they were too young to stay awake through the service. Actually, this was Jeremiah's first year to attend, and Jenny's second. In previous years, they had attended the family service which was usually held in the late afternoon.

A year ago, Jenny had joined the youth's choir and had loved every second of it—except the part about having to sit next to big 'ole pesky Bobby. He always sat near her, sang just short of on-key, and couldn't seem to remember or pronounce the words to the songs. She recognized that poor Bobby was a much-needed work in progress, but, honestly, did God have to do this work on him around her?

Other than Bobby though, music had become a special and integral part of her life. Worship and praise music was her favorite genre. She had been able to take piano lessons from one of Cathey's friends and had learned much over the past few years.

Actually, one of Jenny's earliest and fondest memories, after having been adopted by the Abbott's, was one in which she and Cathey were sitting on the piano bench together. At six years of age, Jenny was utterly amazed at Cathey's ability to play the piano while simultaneously singing.

Jenny knew then that she wanted to follow in her footsteps. And, for the most part, she has, although her voice sounded more like a meek than a mighty mouse. *It'll come one day*, Cathey kept telling her. *Give it time.*

Jenny came to love piano partly because of the love Cathey had for it and for her, but mainly because she could feel a tingling sensation each time she played. Music, Jenny felt, was one of God's special gifts to His people, and playing each piece was like hugging Him back in gratitude. She had been strangely warmed by music—as though she was on the receiving end of a telephone conversation directly linked to God. There was something very intimate about it. A kind of shorthand way of communicating. Jenny believed that what could not be expressed in words could more fully be conveyed with notes on a staff and a song sung from the heart.

But, playing the piano was not the only thing she had developed a love for. Though usually shy in nature, singing words seemed to calm Jenny's spirits—or lift them up, as with praise songs. Some of the hymns played in church felt more dirge-like, as though they should only be sung at the saddest of funerals. But, others made her soul instantly develop broad wings with which to soar.

Cathey said she could take voice lessons, too, someday. But, not just yet. In the meantime, she would sing in the church's children's choir, at school, with friends, in the car, in the shower, and in the privacy of her room. And, of course, she would continue to sing with Cathey, her mama.

After they had opened all the presents, it was time for the family to go to the midnight service. Though Jenny loved the yearly Christmas Eve midnight service, she knew that this year would be different without Natasha with them. In previous years, Natasha had joined them for this special service. But, not tonight. Despite Jenny's attempts to cover her disappointment, she found it extremely challenging to halt its downward, dragging effects on her spirit.

Silence erupted into praise when the congregation sang, denoting the start of the service. Jenny was touched by the joyful faces of worshiping people. With faces tilted towards Heaven and eyes closed, they seemed to glow with gladness and gratitude. The mood was infectious, and the traditional carols uplifting.

After the Scripture readings, Pastor Dave began the sermon time with a sweet prayer. "Father God, our eyes are on You tonight. You sent your son into the world as a baby, born of a virgin, and conceived by the Holy Spirit. We give thanks for Mary, God's willing servant, who bore the babe. And, we give You our gratitude and praise that You would go to such lengths to be with us. Tonight, let us be restored by hearing your Word. Open our spiritual ears and eyes so that we may hear the message You would have for us. In His precious Name we pray. Amen."

Pastor Dave, middle-aged man and well-loved by the congregation, began the sermon in his usual way. Slowly, contemplative, and softly.

"The readings for this wintry Christmas Eve are from Isaiah and Luke. One from the Old Testament and one from the New Testament. The prophet, Isaiah, is trying to reveal to us a message of hope. And, of course, Luke confirms what we have already learned: God sent a Savior for us. He's sent us a Savior because He loves us and because we need it, even though we often forget. God is trying to give us a sign that His Kingdom will come. The prophet wrote, 'Therefore the Lord himself will give you a sign: The virgin will be with child and will give birth to a son, and will call him Immanuel—which means God with us.'"

Jenny's attention began to wander elsewhere. In thinking about Jesus' mother, she began to think of Natasha. It's not that she wasn't interested in the sermon; she just couldn't stop thinking about her birth mother's circumstances. Natasha was actually in jail! What a mess.

Jenny, her brothers, and her adoptive parents were sitting in their usual places, third row from the front on the left side. They had been present in that pew almost every Sunday for the past five years and had enjoyed as many Christmas Eve services—four of them with Natasha present with the family. But, not this year. She was gone again. "Children should never have to get used to the absence of a parent," Jenny thought. But, Jenny's memories mostly involved around her birth mother's absences from their dreary apartment, leaving a six-year-old in charge of her siblings. The year before they were adopted by the Abbotts had been the worst. Natasha was either preparing to go "out" for the night, was already "out," or returning from being "out."

Addictions had stolen her mother. Jenny now knew that her "going out" times usually involved men or drugs, and usually both. Jesus had his mother with him all the time. She was never taken away by drugs or such things. Jenny wondered why Natasha couldn't have been like that. But, Jenny never allowed herself to go very far with this thinking before remembering that she now had a mother—Cathey—who exuded the very essence of a great mother. Not just a mother, but a mom. And, she got a dad out of the adoption, too. She couldn't have asked for anything more—except to have Natasha safe, and to be rid of ever-present guilt.

Jenny's attention was suddenly drawn back to the pastor and his sermon.

"Now, the Lord goes by many, many names. In the Old Testament, He was known, among other names, as Yahweh, Creator, and the Almighty. In the New Testament, He was called Savior, Wonderful Counselor, Mighty God, Prince of Peace, and Immanuel—God with us. Why are these names so important? Why didn't God just call himself Sam or Harry? Maybe even Fred?"

Laughter erupted from the congregation.

"Why not be a little more casual about the name? You know, a little more laid back? Well, to the Israelites of old, names were very, very important. In addition to identifying a person, names were used to reveal something about the person's characteristics or circumstances in their lives. Some were even prophetic names—of an event to come. Like the name, Obadiah. Obadiah was a relatively unknown prophet in the Old Testament, but his name meant *servant of the Lord*. Or, Nahum, which was another prophet whose name meant *comfort*. Zechariah was another prophet whose name meant *Yahweh remembers*. Zechariah told his people that God worked in their lives even when they couldn't see it. He wanted them to know that God remembered them and would never forget. Yes, names were very important in the Old Testament."

The pastor paused before continuing. "Knowing this, then, we can see why it was critical to God that His Son be named Immanuel, God **with us**—and Messiah, which means Savior. God saved us and wants us *with* Him, always. He would **never** leave us."

What did he say? Jenny wondered, noticing the increase in Pastor Dave's passion.

"What an incredible gift our Heavenly Father gave to us that night over two thousand years ago. And He's been planning Jesus' birth since before Creation. Immanuel! God *with* us! Do you understand how important this is to all of us? It means we never have to *feel* alone. God as Creator and Father has been with us since before the Beginning, but He gave us Someone *with skin on*. Jesus! Your Heavenly Father knew that there would be times in your lives when you would feel alone, or maybe people would turn against you. You might have wondered if He ever existed or cared about you or the world. I know I've wondered that myself when times are dark, when I'm emotionally distraught. I want you to do something right now. Now, bear with me in this. I'd like you to think of a time in your life when you have felt all alone. Not just lonely, but *really* abandoned. Maybe a time years ago or maybe as recently as this week. Sometimes, the holidays don't bring out the best in our families. They hurt us or we hurt them." He paused long enough to allow thought about this point before continuing.

"Okay, so do you have a time in mind now? Don't answer this aloud, but I want you to visualize the circumstances. When was this time? By whom did you feel abandoned? How old were you? Where were you? Maybe you were even in a room filled with people but yet felt totally separated."

Jenny found herself answering these questions, though it was painful. *Well, I'm feeling abandoned right about NOW. By Natasha. I'm eleven years old, and I'm in church and she can't be with me because she's in jail.* At this point, she couldn't silence her mind. Jenny began to think of the multitude of times, years ago, when she was left alone to care for her younger siblings.

She didn't want to cry this Christmas Eve, but her tall, impenetrable, Jericho-high emotional wall began to collapse, brick by brick. *Oh, God. Not in church. Not now. And not for Natasha. No more!*

Her nose stung as tears filled her eyes. *Stop it! Quit it. I am NOT going to let myself do this. She's taken enough of my life, and she's not going to get my Christmas Eve.* Jenny tried to fight back the tears as she continued to listen, but they felt like huge, heavy canon balls exploding from her tiny tear ducts.

Pastor Dave paused for what seemed like two lifetimes. "Now, I want you to ask yourself the most important question of all." With closed eyes and suspended breathing, the congregation fell silent.

"In the midst of your circumstances and in the midst of your pain, where was Jesus? I don't mean this in a general, vague, intellectual way. I want you to return to your situation—the one you thought of a few moments ago. Visualize it again in your mind. Purposefully set the stage of where you were and who it involved." He waited so that his sheep, the people with whom God has entrusted to him, could gain back that scenario.

"Look around the room—or wherever you are. Whether your situation is indoors, outdoors, alone, amongst many, or even in a swimming pool, Jesus is there. I promise you. He is there with you, right beside you. Whether you are thinking of an event which happened ten, forty, sixty years ago, or just yesterday, He was with you—then and He's with you now."

The pastor looked out over his flock of about two hundred and saw that tears were flowing down the faces of many as they visualized Jesus with them in their pain. He heard several gasps from those who, with closed eyes were becoming fully aware of His holy presence in their lives, both past and present. Others began to whisper prayers of thanksgiving and praise, while still others nodded their heads in agreement.

"We have such an incredibly loving Father. Not only did He send His Son for our salvation, He sent Him so that we would never have to feel alone—ever again, in any situation—past, present, or future."

"Don't you see?" Pastor Dave implored his flock. "God knew there would be many difficult and fully challenging times which would be incredibly painful. And, He knew there would be times when we would disappoint or hurt each other—not because we wake up one morning and say to ourselves, '*Well, who's going to be my target today?*' No, most of us don't want to intentionally hurt anybody. We just can't help it sometimes because of our sinful nature—the very reason why Jesus came to earth. Hurting people hurt others. Wounded people wound others. Church, we must stop this cycle. We must have the Lord heal us so that we can offer the Healing Agent to others. We must tell others about this Mighty God who can save and heal."

"Our Heavenly Father is the God of opposites. Because we are sinful, God sent a sinless One; because we hurt each other, God sent One Who would heal; because we refuse to forgive, God sent One Who would show us how to forgive; and, just when we think God is absent or distant, God reminds us that He sent us a baby—a real human being, an innocent lamb—to be in the world *with* us, who would experience every kind of pain, suffering, humiliation, and temptation that we would ever encounter or imagine. And then, to put the icing on the cake, He sent us the Holy Sprit, Who is always just one whisper away. He surrounds and fills us with love—not the human kind of love, but a love and peace that defies understanding."

Cathey had been watching Jenny throughout the service, and her heart broke to see her in such pain. She reminded herself—yet again—that she could not be the one who could fix Jenny's broken heart, but it didn't stop her from longing to try. She knew that one of the traits of being a good mother was to be there for her children, when *they* needed her, not just when it was convenient. And, she reminded herself that the best thing she could do for Jenny—or any of her children—was to be there to help turn their hearts towards Jesus, which is what God wants most from us. She reminded herself what God had said about Jonathan in the Old Testament. He defined Jonathan as the best and truest kind of friend to King David because he was always there to help turn his heart towards God. Turning to Jesus does not mean that life would be pain-free. Cathey knew that pain is a natural part of life and for some, it's the perfect trigger which drives us to our knees.

Jenny became aware that Pastor Dave was winding down his sermon. He concluded by reminding the congregation to focus on the Perfect Son, not on the person in our current lives who we wish would be perfect. "There is room for only one Savior. The Son of God has come and has given us an understanding, that we may know Him who is true. He has a name—and it is Jesus, the Messiah. Immanuel—God with us. Amen."

As the service continued, Jenny and Cathey realized that communion held a special meaning for them that night. Both needed healing for their broken hearts. God touched the depths of them in a gripping, yet soothing, fashion when partaking of the Bread and Blood of Jesus. As they remembered the Last Supper, they had a renewed sense of Jesus within them—Immanuel—the One who would be, forever and always, with them and in them, regardless of circumstances.

While wiping away her tears, Jenny remembered that her favorite part of the service was coming—when they all sang "Silent Night". She thought it was an utterly amazing feat that such a hymn, which began as a poem written in the year 1816, could still move even the most hardened-of-hearts to tears. With dimmed church lights and soul-feeding lyrics, the congregation worshiped the Lord with reverent voices, no doubt making all of Heaven smile, singing, "Silent night, Holy night, all is calm, all is bright. Round yon Virgin mother and child, Holy infant so tender and mild. Sleep in Heavenly peace, sleep in Heavenly peace . . . ."

Oh, if only there were more verses! Jenny could have sung this hymn all night. Sleep in Heavenly peace.

If only I could.

CHAPTER 7

"Why won't Jenny even talk to me?" Natasha asked Cathey as they walked down the tiled hall of the Courthouse. The red-bricked building held decades of memories for this Oklahoma town. If the walls could talk, they would spew stories of violence, crime, and families torn apart by the behavior of its inmates.

Randy and Cathey had discussed Natasha's situation at length and had finally decided to put up the bail money, not for Natasha's sake but for the children's sake, especially Jenny's. There was no question that the Abbott's loved Natasha and were pained to see her relapse again, but they did not want Jenny and the others to see her in jail. Jenny had simply been put through too much and this was certainly not the season they wanted her to see Natasha's accrued consequences.

Cathey and Randy prayed that Natasha would not be a flight risk as they offered bail even though finances were tight with five children at home. They considered it a loan which Natasha would have to repay over years upon getting, *and maintaining*, employment.

Slowly, and with shame and embarrassment, Natasha walked out of the six-story building and down the crackly concrete steps with Cathey. It was cloudy and quite cold, and the glare made both squint.

"Thanks for puttin' up the money," Natasha said softly and sparingly. "Appreciate it."

"I know," Cathey replied politely and compassionately. "You're welcome."

"Where are the kids?"

"Randy is home with them. Good thing he's on vacation."

They walked to the parking lot in silence. Natasha knew how disappointed and angry Cathey must be. They all must be. And it prickled the top of Natasha's head to know it.

After entering the car and fastening her seat belt, Natasha sheepishly said, "I'm sorry, Cathey. I'm sorry for puttin' ya out like this. You mad at me?"

"Natasha," Cathey began after pausing. "You know we love you. Nothing's going to change that. I'm not mad. Frustrated, maybe, but not mad. Randy and I have been very concerned about you, and have been for quite awhile. We knew something was wrong because you haven't been calling or coming over. Jenny is tired of waiting for you to call back, too."

"Is she mad, too?"

"Natasha," Cathey said more emphatically. "I am *not* mad. I'm scared for you. This addiction thing is really strong and seems to really take you away from us, from the children, from yourself, and most importantly, from God."

"I know. Okay, you're not mad. But, you didn't answer about Jenny."

"Well, I must be honest with you about her. Yes, Jenny is very angry at you. She is tired of being disappointed and having to worry about you so much."

Natasha became defensive. "Well, she don't *have* to worry 'bout me. I take care of myself just fine. She has *you* as her mama now. She should just worry 'bout you."

Cathey had seen Natasha's defensiveness many times before and knew better than to try to interject logic into the conversation. When she was in this mood, there was not much to do than to allow her to vent.

Liz, the therapist whom they had seen on occasion through Crisis Pregnancy Outreach, had taught them much about addiction and how deeply it affected all members of the family. Randy and Cathey had attended many sessions during the times when Natasha disappeared. Neither had grown up around addiction, so many of Natasha's behaviors had come as a shock. When they told the therapist the types of things which Natasha had done and said, Liz would nod her head and say, "That's the addiction talking, not Natasha."

Natasha's sarcasm and immaturity had provided the perfect example of what the therapist had told them. Natasha's overreactive and immediate defensiveness was the voice of addiction.

While briefly remaining silent, Cathey further remembered that the effects of the "stinking thinking" (as they call it in NA and Alanon) stayed with her for weeks *before* a relapse and for weeks *afterwards*.

Natasha shook her head as if to throw out the cotton in her head. "Just forget I said that, okay? I don't know what's wrong with me. I'm just actin' stupid. Jenny's got every reason in the world to be mad at me. I get that. Just don't pay any attention to what I say right now."

"Natasha, do you want to talk about what happened? Maybe this has been too much for you lately. I'll gladly listen if you need a friend."

"Nah. Not right now," Natasha replied feeling especially embarrassed.

Cathey was pleased to hear that Natasha seemed to really feel the consequences of her actions. She seemed to understand that she can't play around with her addiction or anyone associated with her past. But, unfortunately, Cathey spoke too soon.

"I don't wanna talk about anything, but can I ask you something, Cathey?"

"Of course you can. Ask away," she answered as she flipped on the left-hand blinker, looked over her shoulder, and prepared to turn.

"Do you happen to know what happened to the guy who was with me? Nobody at the courthouse would tell me anything about him. I'm just worried 'bout him. Did he get bailed out by anyone or is he still in there?"

At certain times, Cathey felt like she was addressing the adult side of Natasha. At other times, like now, she was peering into a child who hadn't grown up yet. And, it angered her. Cathey's adrenaline was released upon hearing these ridiculous questions. She had been fearful for Natasha a moment ago. Now, she was enraged.

"I can't believe you are thinking about him at all right now. He's the last person you need to be concerned about, Natasha. Do you not g-e-t that? Don't you understand that you two created this huge mess together? I don't know all the details, but I know enough to understand that he should be the last person on this planet you should want to talk with at this point. And, just let me say this," Cathey said while pulling the car over into the nearest business parking lot. Gathering a big breath to calm her voice and nerves, Cathey turned to face Natasha whose eyes had widened at Cathey's angry response.

"I did not come all the way downtown and plunk down big money we don't have just to have you think that this is some kind of a joke. You should not be taking this so lightly. This is serious, Natasha! And, if you're going to continue this downward spiral, then tell me now. I don't want to watch you do this and I *know* for a fact that the rest of the family doesn't either. So, which is it, Natasha? You decide this, right here, right now."

Gulping before answering, Natasha blurted out, "No, no, you don't understand. I wasn't asking about Dyno for *me*. I was, um, just wonderin' if he, uh, had to go through all of this, too. I want to make sure that he's payin' for this as much as me." Natasha switched gears suddenly and grew intolerant. "Actually, *he's* the one who got *me* into this mess, so he should get way more jail time than me. Boy, I am SO mad at Mr. Stupidity."

Cathey just stared at Natasha to see if she could read her face. Was she lying or was she being straight with her? They've been through this with Natasha so many times in the past. Cathey desperately wanted to believe her, but the niggling in her spirit wouldn't be silenced. Natasha had never before been in this much trouble. Was this enough consequence to get her attention once and for all? As sad as the truth was, Cathey simply did not trust her.

Sensing that Cathey was still wavering, Natasha further tried to convince her that she was not going back to her old lifestyle. Cathey saw her lips move, but heard only empty words and false promises, especially since asking about Dyno. *What a stupid name anyway. Who would want to be called by that name?* Cathey couldn't imagine.

Cathey's car was still in "park" position when she looked up at Natasha who was still talking. *That girl could sell a block of ice to an Alaskan if she wanted to.* The time passed slowly though they had been stopped for only ten minutes. Cars zoomed passed them, one right after the other, even though it was mid-morning. She guessed that the traffic had increased because of the holidays.

Tears fell down Cathey's soft, round face. She couldn't listen to any more of Natasha's words. All of this pained her so! And, it was such a waste of time.

Cathey's shoulder-length, dark blonde hair covered half her face. Sadness enveloped her heart about the situation, but particularly with how she had blown up at Natasha. Taking a brief moment to silently pray, Cathey retrieved a tissue from her purse and wiped away the tears which had escaped her almond-shaped eyes, parting her make-up like the Red Sea.

Having gathered her wits, Cathey made a second attempt at communicating her feelings in a more positive way.

"Natasha, I am sorry for raising my voice at you. I shouldn't have handled it like I did. What I want you to remember in all this is that we love you and, more importantly, Jesus loves and adores you. Please remember all the grace which He has shown you in past times. And, please don't take that for granted. Jesus has rescued you so many times, and for you to continue in this relapse would be like slapping His battered face on the Cross. There's always a way back, Natasha. God has always provided a way back since before time began. And, its name is *repentence*. Please turn back to Him. Just remember that. Now, what do you want to do? Do you want to come home with me? Do you want to go to your mentor's house? Go to an NA meeting? Or just go home?"

Natasha was taken aback by the sudden and softening change in attitude from Cathey. It caught her offguard. It had always been easier to continue drinking and smoking pot when people were mad at her. As unreasonable as it sounded to others, she could justify her use more easily when she was mad at those who were mad or disappointed at her. The anger was a way of distancing herself from the reality that she had disappointed those she loved most. It never worked well beyond the reach of a good alcohol buzz, but she didn't know how else to manage those feelings—actually, *any* feelings.

Natasha wasn't sure what she wanted to do now, especially after seeing Cathey's tears and hearing healing words from a softened heart. Shaking her head more from confusion than anything else, Natasha quickly replied, "Just take me to my apartment. I need a shower."

Cautiously, Cathey complied, knowing there was not much support for Natasha at her apartment complex. In fact, this was the exact apartment complex in which she lived immediately before she had to relinquish her children because of neglect. No, not much good support at all. Cathey did not want to take her there, but knew this was not a battle she could fight for her. Natasha had to battle this one out with God, but Cathey could certainly pray for God to keep her safe, which is exactly what she did upon dropping Natasha off, and would continue to do so in the weeks—or months—ahead.

As Natasha closed the car door and began to walk away, Cathey rolled down the window. Despite the bitter cold air pouring in, she couldn't let her walk away without saying something else.

"Natasha!" she yelled and motioned for her to come back. As Cathey watched her return to the car, she tried to think of something helpful, something encouraging, something so that she didn't have to see her walk away and wonder if it was the last time she would ever see Natasha. She had come to learn that addictions steal everything. E-v-e-r-y-t-h-i-n-g! Not just a good friendship, money, a sustaining job, a functioning car, but one's life.

Overwhelmed with guilt and anger, Natasha slowly approached the car and began babbling defensively without thinking.

"I know, I know. You wanna know when I'm gonna get around to gettin' you your money. I'll pay you back for bailing me out. Just gimme a little time to get a job. I just don't have it right now. You can't expect me to have it right now, can you? If you have to have it right now, then I guess I could sell something and . . . ."

Shaking her head, Cathey interrupted.

"NATASHA! I was just going to ask you if you'd like to come over to the house for dinner in the next few days. The kids are still on Christmas vacation, so we can do it most anytime—just whatever works with your schedule." When she saw Natasha hesitate, she offered another suggestion which might be a little less overwhelming.

"Or we could have lunch—the two of us, if you'd rather not see the children just yet."

Natasha was shocked and torn. She certainly did not expect such an act of kindness from Cathey, especially on the heels of Natasha's latest stunt. On the other hand, of course she'd like to see her children! Just because she allowed them to be adopted didn't meant that she would ever stop loving them with her whole heart. She just wasn't ready to see them *yet*. How could she face them—mostly Jenny—when she knew that they were mad at her? The thought of isolating in her apartment sounded sweet. Not answering the phone. Not answering the door. Just keeping away from everyone for awhile.

Natasha just wanted to be left alone. But, she knew she wouldn't really be left all by herself. Her friend, *misery*, would always be with her. Her grandmother had another name for it, though. Whenever Natasha had been in one of her *p-r-o-l-o-n-g-e-d* bad moods, her grandmother would always say, *If you're gonna be dancin' with Satan, you might as well start diggin' your own grave.*

For the longest time, Natasha hadn't a clue as to the meaning of that phrase. *Dance with Satan? What in the world is that supposed to mean?* Well, she found out long ago when her father had been imprisoned and her mother had run off with an abusive alcoholic. Natasha and her siblings had to stay with their grandmother for awhile. But, as it turned out, the children were just too much for her to handle. So, the older siblings moved out on their own and Natasha lived with her older sister, LaVerne, who really did not want her, but found her cooking and cleaning services pleasing.

Often feeling rejected and unwanted, Natasha would go into self-pity mode for lengths of time, which always seemed to push others away further.

So, the Satan dance would go something like this: he (the worm) would take the first "step" by whispering a lie into her mind like, *Nobody wants you.* But, rather than responding with a firm yet polite reply like, *I do so appreciate the offer, Worm, but no thanks,* she'd gladly take his hand and "dance." She would acknowledge his first step only to match his with a step of her own—she would enthusiastically agree with him. She would say to herself, *You're right, you petulent pod, nobody wants me.* He would, then, follow it up with the second "step," another murmur like, *There must be something wrong with you or they would love you.* Again, she would follow Satan's lead and offer up another untruth of her own; *I am such a burden to people.* Let the dance begin!

The Satan Samba was engulfing and entangling. It was nearly impossible to get out of his trap by her own strength or wisdom. Grandma said that Satan's desire is to keep people so engrossed in him that we never pay attention to what God has in store for us. And, during this dance, we often talk right over God's voice, missing all signs of assistance He offers. When we are drowning in Satan's revelry, we literally miss the multitudes of "life-saving rings" God throws us. Grandma always said that Satan's goal is to spiral us downward so fast and far that we quickly reach a state of hopelessness and unbelief in God. When we get to this point, the dance is over and Satan wins another soul.

Though her Grandmother's words were wise, they were very difficult to grasp. They always seemed to slip out of her hands so easily, like trying to grab a rope soaked in cooking oil.

"Natasha?" Cathey said while looking at her blank stare. "Are you still here?"

Suddenly brought back into the conversation, Natasha tried to remember what they were talking about.

"What'd you say?"

"I asked you if you would like to have lunch with me or dinner with the family sometime over the next few days."

"I-I dunno. I j-just can't right now. I just have to go now. I'll call you in a few days," Natasha stuttered before escaping to the safe isolation of her apartment.

Cathey encountered powerlessness again.

Cathey prayed for a God-sized intervention.

She's going to need big help this time.

CHAPTER 8

Ah! The sweet sound of silence, Natasha thought, as she lay in bed. The apartment was darker than usual due to the closed, torn curtains and the cloudy sky. She stretched and gradually rolled over to glance at the clock. Her old, black sweatshirt had twisted around her, and the matching, faded sweatpants gathered up above her ankles, irritating her. Preparing to do battle with the sheets and blankets which held her hostage, Natasha gathered a minimal amount of strength and yanked them off with a grunt.

How long have I been sleeping? she wondered. The little, white clock said ten o'clock, but she couldn't figure out if it was morning or night. Rubbing her eyes and placing her right hand on her tossled, tangled, black hair, Natasha tried to shake off the groggies. Her left hand fell outstretched onto the bed, hitting something which crackled. Glancing at the variety of items next to her, she remembered bringing some munchies to bed with her last night, or was it the night before? *How long had it been?*

Looking over the battle ground, she discovered a half-eaten bag of cheap potato chips, several opened packages of cheese and crackers, and several cola cans. It was all store brand names and she hated it. She wanted to buy something with a brand name, like Pringles, but having little money, she had to settle for the cheap stuff. None of it was particularly cheap, though, or maybe she just didn't have enough money.

There was a noise coming from under the pillow. "What is that?" Reaching underneath the flat pillow, she discovered the source—her cell phone. Natasha had forgotten that she had shoved it under the pillow one time to keep it silent, but had been too tired to put it on silent mode. In reaching to grab it, she pushed it onto the floor behind the bed, so it continued to sing until it went to voicemail. "Scared me to death," she said aloud. Waking up a bit more, Natasha remembered that the phone had rung several times, but she had ignored it. "I can only imagine how many messages I have and who they're from," she grumbled.

Climbing out of bed seemed to be quite an accomplishment for Natasha. Opening the dingy green curtains, she now understood that it was ten o'clock in the morning. The glare blinded her, making it more difficult to find the phone. Flopping onto the unswept floor, she waved her hand under the bed searching for the lost phone. As she pulled her hand back, she discovered that several dust bunnies had become stowaways on her sleeve. But, she didn't care. She just brushed them off back onto the floor and searched a second time for the elusive phone.

Finally grasping the little bugger, she glanced at the screen and noticed that she had ten missed calls and three voice messages. Two were from Cathey saying that she had not heard from her and wanted to know if they could get together. The last one was from her mentor, Kayleen. Somehow, she had been notified by someone of Natasha's latest illegal antics and wanted to "speak with her."

An attractive, tall, slender woman in her thirties, Kayleen had been a monumental influence in her sobriety and healing. They had some difficulties at first when they were introduced, but only because Natasha was in her phase of rebellion and denial. She didn't like the way that Kayleen had approached her and, basically, had known how Natasha was going to respond. Come to find out, Kayleen had had her share of "antics" in her own teenage years. Knew all about rebellion, addiction, hopelessness, suicide attempts, and eventually forgiveness. She had been the perfect teacher and mentor for Natasha.

Wondering if she should return Kayleen's call, Natasha reminded herself of all the good things that she had taught her, and began to feel guilty for not staying in touch with her over the last few months. Kayleen had warned her that this might happen. Disappearing off the face of the earth seemed to be a function of addicts when they didn't want to be caught doing something they shouldn't be doing. Avoidance was one of Natasha's specialties, as far as bad habits go.

Disgusted at herself and angry that she had been so predictable, Natasha studied the phone as if it were a foreign object, while multitudes of questions clawed at her sanity. *Should I call or should I wait? Kayleen's probably not home anyway right now. She'd be at work and I wouldn't wanna interrupt her there. But, this was kind of an emergency, wasn't it? Oh, wait, this is the Christmas season. Would she be at work or would she be at home with her family? I really shouldn't bother her at home, especially since it is family time.*

However, Natasha knew that, at this point, she would need a swift kick on her backside to stop the harrowing downward spiral of this relapse, but she seemed to be so double-minded about this.

Throwing the phone into the pillow, she walked away from it. For now. She'd go get something to eat first, though she had been eating junk food all night. She needed something of sustenance. The refrigerator seemed like an old friend whom she hadn't seen in awhile. She hadn't had "real food" since . . . she couldn't remember. The old, white, paint-chipped cupboards held more interesting and enjoyable things for her. Pilfering through the potato chips, candy, empty wrappers, and . . . *what's this?*

Staring back at her was a baggy filled with seeds, leftovers from a nickel bag of pot. *Where did this come from?* Moving aside the only can of tomato soup, she pulled out the scraps of past parties, all contained within the bag.

With pot in hand, Natasha discovered an entirely new level of double-mindedness. Her head began tornadoing into a full-blown deadly storm. *Should I? Shouldn't I?* She hated this war. The battle was constant. This endless, time-consuming, self-destructive war! Natasha was tired of it. She wanted it ended, once and for all. So, what did she mean by that? Once and for all? She didn't really mean *for good*, did she?

What would Liz, her therapist, have to say about this? Would she say that these were actual suicidal thoughts? Did she really want to kill herself? Make herself go away forever? Natasha began to perspire, and her heart began to beat rapidly, as though it were going to explode in her chest cavity. Had she ever heard of anyone whose heart literally exploded inside of them? Was that possible? These thoughts were not helping her pulse, but she couldn't help thinking them. The beautiful, dark color of her face began to fade into ashen white. Her entire body began to burn hot and cold simultaneously.

Where are the keys to my car? I have to get out of here.

But, she wasn't going anywhere. Not for awhile, anyway. Her knees began to get weak and she felt her hands reaching for the kitchen chair. The room began to spin out of control. *What's happening?*

Off in the distance, she heard the phone ring. This time it was a familiar sound—an unwelcome friend. The ring of help, possibly. Struggling to remember where she had placed it, Natasha pushed herself up and followed the sound to the bedroom. Her arm acted alone, as if it was a separate entity from her body, but she was thankful for its independent motion. Grabbing the phone while collapsing on the bed, she answered it.

"H-hello?" Natasha sounded weak.

"Hello? Natasha? Are you there? It's me, Kayleen. Can you hear me?"

"I c-can't . . . no . . . somethin's wrong . . . ."

"Natasha! This is really important. Listen, honey, did you take something? Are you on something?" Kayleen was fearful that she had overdosed on something. Why did she always think of the worst-case scenario? She hated that about herself, but she figured that it had to do with her own horrible past experience with it. Kayleen's stomach clenched.

"Natasha! Answer me. Did you take anything?"

"N-no. I jus' don' feel so good, like I'm gonna pass out."

"Do you want me to call 9-1-1? Do you want me to call an ambulance?"

"N-no, I . . . you . . . can, or I m-mean, would you . . . ."

"I'm coming over, okay? I'll be there within about fifteen minutes," though it was normally a twenty-five minute drive. "You'll be okay until then?"

"Yeah," Natasha answered briefly.

"Okay, just stay on the phone with me. I've got my keys and I'm on way now," she said as she called out to her husband to watch the kids. Trying not to panic, Kayleen drove faster than she should have on the side streets. Time moved so slowly, though. She felt as though she was in slow motion and hated the feelings of fear and helplessness. *Come on, come on, come on,* was all she kept saying.

Finally, she arrived at Natasha's apartment. Not knowing what she would find, she knocked feverishly on her door.

"Natasha, it's me, Kayleen. Open the door." Kayleen was glad that Natasha had finally gotten back into the habit of locking her door, but why did she have to start at this crucial time?

Hearing a soft shuffle, Kayleen began to calm down. *At least she was up and walking around,* Kayleen thought. After what felt like years at the front door, Natasha unlocked and opened it.

Kayleen rushed in and immediately assessed the situation. Seeing that the situation was not urgent, she urged Natasha to sit down on the once familiar couch—the one she had given Natasha when Kayleen bought her new set.

"Now, tell me what's going on, Natasha," Kayleen said relieved. "Do you have the flu or something? You don't look well at all. And, you certainly didn't sound good on the phone."

"I don't know what happened. I got up and came into the kitchen to find me something to eat. And, all of a sudden, I started feeling awful. Like I was gonna faint or somethin'. The room was spinnin' and I got hot and kinda cold. I don't know, it was all kind of weird." Natasha was torn about telling Kayleen everything that had happened recently. She knew she should. It would help get her going in the right direction, but the words just weren't forthcoming.

"When was the last time you ate something?"

"It's been awhile. I mean, I've had some chips and stuff, but nothing like a real meal for a few days I think."

"Well, we need to take care of that right away. Do you have anything here I can get you, besides those nasty chips and candy?"

"Um, some tomato soup."

"Nah, that's not gonna do, girl. Do you feel good enough to get out? I'll take you somewhere to get you a sandwich or something good for you, or I can bring something back here for you if you don't feel like going out. But, you need to get something in your stomach pretty quickly."

At that moment off in the distant, Natasha's cell phone rang. Placing her hand on Natasha's shoulder, Kayleen got up, gently pushing her back down to the couch.

"I'll get it. You just sit there for a minute." The phone kept ringing and Natasha wondered why she wasn't answering it or calling out the name of the person who was calling.

"Did you find it?" Natasha asked.

It took a few minutes for Kayleen to come back into the room, but when she did, she was loaded for bear.

"Yes, I found your phone—and a whole lot more," she said accusingly while dangling the empty bag of pot back from her long, slender fingers.

Natasha's face dropped.

Firmly, yet not angrily, Kayleen spoke. "Girl, you got some explaining to do. What happened and what is THIS doing on your bed?"

Natasha let out a long sigh. "It's a long story, Kayleen."

"Well, good, I'm in the mood for a good, long story. I'm beginning to understand a whole lot more, now, about why you're not feeling so well. So, do you feel well enough to get something to eat?" Without waiting for an answer, she said, "Get some decent clothes on. I'm going to take you to lunch and, while we're eating, you can spill the whole thing."

"Okay, but it's gonna take some time to tell it all."

"That's fine with me. Time is something I've got a lot of right now. Now, go on and get you on some better clothes."

Natasha got up, turned around, and went back into the bedroom. Though she was hanging her head, Natasha knew that this was the best thing that could have happened. Kayleen's timing was impeccable. Or was it God's timing?

One thing was true. She had a lot of explaining to do.

CHAPTER 9

After Natasha had finished telling about the entire ordeal of late, Kayleen asked about the previous few months when she had not heard a thing from Natasha.

"There has to be more to the story than just this, girl."

"Uh, no, not much more," Natasha sheepishly replied.

"Need I remind you who you're talkin' to? You can't pull anything over on a recovering addict. Oh, uh-huh. Now, let's try that again. Let's have the rest of the story covering anything and everything over the last few months."

Kayleen was cool as a cucumber. She had always known just how to get through to Natasha. She didn't put up with anything. Over her years of sobriety, Kayleen has sponsored many young women who thought they could *impress* the highly-acclaimed recovering role model with their obvious lack of insight, but it never worked.

Kayleen had a reputation in the recovering world of knowing how to worm her way through the young women's dark denial of their addictions. She had always forewarned every mentoree and sponsoree that she cared too much about them to allow them to stay in a lazy, dysfunctional state of mind. And, she had the experience to know every favorite trick in the book that addicts loved to use. She knew it because she, herself, had tried them all and it had done nothing except promote her to a near-death experience.

Having been a wild child for most of her teenage years, Kayleen had known the stark terror of one particular dark night ending in hopelessness and despair. She had been all too familiar with loneliness, rage, violence, rejection, and confusion—profound wounds which had pierced her heart and slashed her wrist. The deep wound from that broken wine bottle had partly been a frantic attempt at regaining control over her life, partly rage at her father, and partly the extreme isolation, all suffocating her like being tightly wound up in plastic wrap.

That night would never leave Kayleen's consciousness, though it held less power for her at present. It had been a violent night. She would never forget how the disastrous formula of alcohol, a bad family fight, rage, and rebellion could add up to such fierce finality.

The end of life. The end of *lives*.

Hers, almost. But the reality was that it had been the end of her parents' lives that night. Her father had been drinking, had started an argument—again—with Kayleen, the scapegoat as her father saw her, after she had returned home in a drunken state. She had been with some guy who had picked her up and taken her driving around. Over the course of the evening, they had consumed several bottles of cheap wine and had still been quite loopy when she returned home.

Her father had been enraged at her profound disrespect and rebellion, though he, himself, had consumed more than his fair share of a Jack Daniel's bottle that evening. Bad combination. Fatal combination.

Her father had hit her, backhanded her face, hard enough that she had fallen, hitting the edge of the wall. She had blacked out for only a few seconds, but long enough to have missed the hit which landed her mother on the floor, too. The fight was on.

They all had known how this would end. Someone would get hurt, maybe there would be a hospital emergency run, a lie about the injury would be told (and believed), nobody would speak for weeks, and then Kayleen's mother would end the silence by apologizing. Things would go well for awhile and then the sequence would begin again.

That night, in the midst of the yelling, Kayleen's mother had told her to run, because nothing good was going to happen if she had stayed. But, her full-of-pride father wouldn't have it that way. No, he had screamed at Kayleen, "*Leave and never come back.*" Awful words which could still prick her heart to this day when she recalled them.

Kayleen did leave, but her mother couldn't stand not knowing where she was going to go, especially since the back of her head had been cut and blood had been splattered. Her father had hated listening to his wife whining, whimpering, and droning on about Kayleen, so he gave in and said that they could go looking for her.

Her mother should have driven, not her father. Not the one whose blood alcohol level had registered three times the legal limit that night. Nevertheless, her father had insisted on getting behind the wheel of their family car-turned-weapon. Her mother was so frantic to find Kayleen that she had just caved in to her husband's demand to drive, though she had known that he was drunk.

If only . . . .
If only Kayleen hadn't gone out that night . . . .
If only she hadn't been drinking . . . .
If only she had not fought with her father . . . .
If only her father hadn't hit her . . . .
If only her father hadn't been drinking . . . .
If only she hadn't run away . . . .
If only he had not driven off the road and hit the tree . . . .

Oh, one could spend an entire life stuck in *if only . . . .*
The *if onlys* of life . . . .
Regret after regret had recycled in her mind over the course of those three months spent in the psych ward of the hospital.

Kayleen had been intimately familiar with dark, red blood dripping from her coursing veins that one evening so many years ago! And, she had the scars to constantly remind her of how quickly life can spin out of control.

Life was ironic. Simultaneous fatal moments. Her parents had died at the exact moment that Kayleen slit her wrist. While Kayleen had watched the blood drain from her vein, her mother had watched the last moments of life fade away from her alcoholic, abusive husband's grey eyes. He had never even seen it coming. But, she had. He had been driving too fast and she had tried telling him to slow down, but he wouldn't listen. He had been bent on a mission, but it hasn't been necessarily to find their daughter. The mission HE had tried to achieve was one where his pride would have remained intact assuring him that he had been the one *in the right.*

All of them had played a part in that night's horrible series of fatal events. And, during her stay at the hospital, Kayleen had been able to finally come to terms with that fact. She had been able to forgive them and, eventually, forgive herself.

The only thing that had haunted her all these years was the fact that her mother had taken her last breath, never knowing the fate of her daughter.

That had been the night Kayleen almost died, but it had also been the night of her rebirth. A new creation.

Kayleen had been very open with Natasha about all the gruesome details of that night and her three-month stay in the hospital afterwards. It had been a tumultuous time for her, but eventually a healing and sustaining Spring. All thanks to one person.

Though Kayleen had aliented many people in her teenage years due to her anger, there had been one person who had endured it with her. Sometimes in life, it only takes one person to change another one's world. One willing person, one desperate prayer, and one enormous God.

With one beautiful, colorful stroke of His brush, God had moved His hand mightily on her hideous canvass of life while she had been hospitalized.

It had begun the day Kayleen decided to kill herself. Darkness had engulfed her, shredding every last tidbit of hope. Nothing left in her—no family, no job, no laughter, no hope, and surprisingly, no more grief. She had shed her last tear and felt her last pain. Kayleen had just flat run out of everything, except for one final dust particle-sized prayer. Though she had doubted God's existence, she had nonetheless offered it up anyway, knowing that she had nothing left to lose. The prayer was brief, yet God's ears were poised . . . waiting.

Lord, if you're real and You don't want me to do this, then find a way to stop me.

He heard, then moved.

Help had come in the form of one willing, obedient servant. Mrs. Hardwick, Kayleen's high school English teacher, had decided to visit Kayleen that very day!

This woman's visit had been a changing moment in Kayleen's life, with regards to forgiveness of others and, especially, of herself. That visit had breathed life into her young, brittle, spiritually-starved bones.

Mrs. Hardwick had been keeping Kayleen in her thoughts and prayers in the months following the fatal car crash which killed her parents. That semester, she had seen such emotional pain in Kayleen's eyes. Others may have only seen the outward anger, but not this wise, old woman. Through her glasses, Mrs. Hardwick saw more than just the student in her class. She saw a student of life who needed to learn how to handle the curve balls which get thrown in life. This woman had been an angel, and if anyone had looked closely, they might have seen her wings and halo.

Kayleen hadn't seen them at first, but by the end of her visit, the wings and halo were shining brightly.

Too few people take the time to really listen to a person. No one had listened to Kayleen. Until now. Mrs. Hardwick had stayed with Kayleen for hours that day in the hospital. She had stayed long and listened hard, which allowed Kayleen to share all of her story—from beginning to her parents' end. Only when Mrs. Hardwick had been certain that Kayleen was done and emotionally spent, did she do the unimaginable.

Through tears of her own, Mrs. Hardwick had knelt down on the cold, hard, tiled floor, had taken Kayleen's limp hands into her own warm ones, had looked into her eyes . . . and had asked for forgiveness on behalf of Kayleen's parents! The heart-felt apology had covered all the sins of Kayleen's mother and then her father, having nothing unaccounted for.

No one had ever done such a love-filled gesture for Kayleen. Her father had never, not even once, apologized for any harm that he had done to her and their family. And, her mother had done nothing except apologize, but it had been for things which she was not responsible.

Mrs. Hardwick's offering had been more than just an apology offered from a kneeling position. It carried with it some sort of power, healing power which she had never before felt. Later, Kayleen had learned that her words had been escorted in by the Holy Spirit, through prayer first, and then obedience to say the very words God wanted her to hear, and accompanied by the only One who could offer that type of healing.

It had unburdened her, and freedom had never felt so good. The healing of her soul had felt like a gentle, cool spray of water on a stinging, red-hot sunburn. But, it had done more than just provide immediate relief. It had been like soothing aloe cream on a boil, penetrating and healing each layer of pain.

From that day forward, Kayleen had no longer seen the walls of the hospital as stark and clinically white, without emotion. She had come to view the white interior as the color of a flying dove, or possibly the color of light, puffy clouds surrounding and lifting her up. The hospital had no longer imprisoned her, but simply held her while she completed her healing.

Years ago, Kayleen had felt led to share her experiences with Natasha when the timing was perfect. The healing which Natasha had experienced as a result of Kayleen's sharing had been monumental.

So, what had gone awry? Why had Natasha returned to a lifestyle which would feed her addiction and destroy her life?

After hearing the harrowing details of Natasha's relapse, Kayleen gave her opinion, whether she wanted to hear it or not.

"Addictions always carry with it the possibility, actually probability, of relapse into old behavior which usually led back to your use. I'll bet you thought you were bullet-proof, didn't you?"

Shaking her head, Natasha added, "I really didn't even see it coming. Not all the stuff that went with it. It just got so bad so quick."

"Which is why it's referred to as the most baffling disease ever, girl. You *know* that. We've been through this before," Kayleen explained. "You got complacent in your recovery."

Natasha started to argue, but she stopped herself.

Kayleen could see right through her. She could see that Natasha still was not convincved. So, she rifled off a spray of questions.

"Okay. Tell me this, then. When did you stop going to meetings?"

Before Natasha could answer, Kayleen shot a few more questions towards her target.

"And, when did you stop calling your sponsor? And, when did you make that very first phone call to your old buddy? And, when did you start believing that you were cured from this disease—that because it had been a long time since you had used, maybe things would turn out differently this time?"

"Okay, okay! Stop. I know everythin' you're saying is true. I **know** it, okay?"

The long pause allowed Natasha's brain the time to process her questions. She had been in this place before and had sworn that she would never, e-v-e-r, be there again. What happened to the promise? Why did it all fall apart? And, how did it fall apart that badly? These were questions which Natasha asked herself a mere nanosecond after Kayleen had asked hers.

Kayleen recognized the glaze in Natasha's eyes. Now, it was time to act.

"Alright, Natasha. Time for your brain to stop thinking. You know, fixing your thinking is only part of recovery. You gotta decide what it is that you're gonna do with it. Quit trying to fix this with logic. You're thinking about it too long, and sometimes what Satan wants is to keep you so focused on the whys that you don't do the things you should do. Ok, quiz time: what do you need to do next?"

"Huh?" Natasha answered almost in a fog.

"Pay attention, girl. You just have to do the next right thing. So, what is the next right thing that you should do?"

"Wow. Can you gimme a minute here?" Natasha pleaded.

"Uh, NO. That's how you open a door for Satan. You know, that little worm doesn't need much of an opening to get inside your heart. Quickly, now. What do you need to do now?"

Natasha knew what she needed to do. She'd been resisting for a few months, but now there was no escaping it. Kayleen wasn't going to let up until Natasha was back on track.

Relenting, Natasha finally said, "Get myself to the nearest meeting."

"Ahh, that's my girl. You got that right. Now, get to it." And, without saying another word, Kayleen stood, grabbed her purse, and headed for the door. At times, it was difficult to catch up with her.

Never one to lag when action was needed, Kayleen glanced over her shoulder.

"Ya comin' now or are you waiting for Jesus to return?"

Sometimes, the longest and biggest sighs precede choosing to stay stuck in denial or laziness. But, not this time. By the time Natasha had ceased exhaling, she had noticed that Kayleen was almost to the door. Natasha would have to hurry to catch up, and since they had come to the restaurant in Kayleen's car, she figured she'd better move quickly if she was going to get a ride.

Natasha knew her ride was not going to be taking her home, though.

Next stop, the nearest meeting.

And, brutal honesty with others was the task awaiting her. She would get her desire chip (noting the desire for sobriety) and begin counting her sobriety days. Again.

CHAPTER 10

The thing about relapsing is that there's always a mess to clean up. Sometimes, the messes are barely noticeable. Maybe you miss just a few days of work, or you have a big fight with your boyfriend, or maybe you're just out a few hundred dollars. At other times, the messes are gargantuan. Natasha's relapse was closer to this latter side than to the former.

Restitution needed to be made in a number of areas. There was no way around it. Not in a good recovery program, that is. And, certainly not with someone who has a sponsor and mentor who were worth their weight in gold. Natasha had both.

She could handle having been in jail and now huge fines to pay; she could even handle the fact that now she had a rap sheet. There were many things for which she was thankful: having her apartment and furniture; having her sponsor and mentor on her back; having Cathey and Randy to support her. But, there was one piece that she dreaded having to face: Jenny. Her baby girl (she referred to her as *baby* even though she was her oldest). The boys would be fine. They probably hadn't noticed her absence anyway.

But, Jenny would, and did. Though Jenny's adoptive parents had kept her safe, warm, happy, and secure, she had always seemed to be the most affected by Natasha's actions.

Having to look into those big, brown eyes again and tell her why she had been absent in her life these past few months was enough to cause her stomach to twist. But, she had to make amends to her, like she had the others. It was a critical part of her recovery program and sanity. The hardest things in life are the ones which cause the fork in the road. She could take the easy way out and avoid having to deal with Jenny at all or she could face this head on.

She'd just have to suck it up and deal with it. Natasha was the one who had done the harm, caused the alarm, and now she must recover from the storm without her usual charm. She could do it. She'd done it before. Though, for some reason, this time seemed different. Natasha couldn't quite put her finger on the reason why, but she somehow knew that facing this would be like trying to surf in a tidal wave. There was a greater than big chance that she was going to take an emotional beating on this one.

Twelve-step programs are a pain, she thought. *Sobriety sucks.*

Natasha had thought this many times over the past few years. But, then, she'd recall all the consequences her disease had caused and would, once again, remind herself that, actually, her *addiction* was what had sucked, not sobriety. Sobriety was the only way she could live in reality with hope, not despair.

But, right now, Natasha would rather not face cleaning up her mess as far as Jenny was concerned. No use in fighting it, though, or procrastinating any longer. She'll just take the first step and see what damage there really was. Maybe, just maybe, Natasha was just imagining the worst. It might go better than she expected!

"Hello?"

"Um, hi Cathey. It's Natasha."

Pausing for a moment, Cathey gathered her strength and asked God for more.

"Hi, 'Tash. How are you doing?"

"Well, don't know. Scared, I guess."

Cathey knew from their previous conversations that Natasha had called to speak with Jenny. Not knowing exactly how to prepare Jenny for this, um, discussion, Cathey thought it best that she just let Natasha handle it.

"Have you called to talk with Jenny?"

"Um, no. Guess I'd better get it over with."

"Alright then. I'll go get her. Just so you know, I haven't told her that you would be calling. Just so you know, while you all are talking, I'll be praying,."

"Thanks. I'm gonna need all the help I can get."

Before Cathey put the phone down on the counter, she heard a long sigh on the other end. There was nothing she could say to Natasha to make her more comfortable. So, she just went to call Jenny.

"Jenny?"

No response.

"Jenny, honey. The phone's for you."

"Okay, Mom. Hang on. I'm trying to get my hair fixed. Who is it?"

Pause.

"Who is it, Mom?"

"If that's Elisha, tell her that I'll call her right back."

"Um, no, honey. It's not Elisha. It's Natasha."

Pause.

Longer pause.

Cathey's eyes darted around the room while waiting for her to answer.

"Honey? Jenny, don't keep her waiting."

Cathey realized that her last comment was probably less than the best choice of words, and wondered if Jenny was ever going to answer her back. As Cathey attempted to climb the stairs, she was met with a voice that was not the usual sweet Jenny.

The words came from Jenny's mouth, but without her usual cadence and tone. Instead of perky and smooth, her voice was low, slow, and devoid of any compassion. Standing at the top of the stairs, she addressed her mother.

"Mom," she said very slowly. "Please tell her that she can wait until you-know-what freezes over." She turned, and then disappeared into her room.

Cathey was appalled! She had never before heard such rudeness from Jenny—or any of the other kids for that matter. She was stunned. Walking back to the phone, she wasn't quite sure what to say, but she had to tell Natasha something.

"Natasha, um, Jenny said . . . ."

"I heard what she said. I got ears, ya know." Natasha hated when she became so defensive. "Wait, I'm sorry, Cathey. Jenny's got every right to be mad at me. I wouldn't wanna talk with me either."

"I'm so sorry. I-I don't know what to say."

"Don't worry 'bout it. I'll call her another time. At least she knows that I called."

Still shocked, Cathey was still empathetic.

"Natasha, I'll talk with her and see if I can get her to . . . ."

Suddenly filled with that old, familiar attitude, Natasha's level of maturity dropped to match Jenny's.

"Ya know what? You tell her what you wanna tell her. But, if she were here with me, why I'd slap her big across that sassy little face of hers.

But YOU'RE her mother, so do what you want." The phone went silent. Natasha had hung up.

Stunned, yet again, Cathey thought to herself, *That's part of the reason you lost your kids in the first place,* but would not dare say that aloud to her. Natasha's comment unleased this wave of protective and righteous anger toward Jenny. *How dare she think that she could slap my daughter! Before she can see Jenny, Natasha'll have some explaining to do and some boundaries to agree to.*

Cathey was convinced that, given this new turn of events, she should not allow Jenny to see Natasha alone. Maybe they could talk in front of Liz, the therapist, but it would only be with the agreement that either Cathey or Randy, or both, would be present. Cathey said a quick prayer thanking God that her children were no longer with their birth mom. How different, and sad, their lives would have been had they continued to be raised in an environment of such abuse.

However, there was still the matter of Jenny. Cathey still had to address Jenny's attitude. Silently praying, Cathey heard in her heart that the issue must be confronted with an attitude of love and compassion, and firmness, but not anger.

Cathey noticed how hurt Jenny had been during these months of Natasha's absence, especially around the Christmas season. She had grown weary of her abrupt and sporadic absences. Natasha's last relapse had broken something in Jenny. Due to the length of Natasha's silence and this special time of year had ripped apart the last strand of their bond.

Jenny had found it challenging to stop worrying about her birth mother. She loved Natasha, of course, but this was precisely why she worried so much—because she DID love her. Jenny had never had to worry about Cathey, her second mom. Cathey had never given Jenny any reason to worry. Stable, steady, and present—that's who Cathey was. Always. What a relief this had been for Jenny's heart! She always knew where Cathey was, what she was doing, and when she'd be back.

Jenny would tell you that trust was a precious commodity and not one to be squandered or treated haphazardly. Cathey had often said that people should say what they mean and mean what they say. And, you should always keep your promises. Well, Natasha didn't subscribe to the same theory and Jenny was tired of it. Jenny would tell her mother just that as soon as she came upstairs—as she knew very well would happen.

When Cathey entered Jenny's room, she found her on the bed holding her favorite pillows tightly and looking down.

Cathey came over and gently sat on the bed next to Jenny. They sat in silence for a bit until Jenny looked up at her mom's eyes. Jenny felt the guilt as her heart softened.

"I'm sorry, mama. I really am. I don't want you mad at me. That was lame."

In Cathey's presence, Jenny never found it difficult to admit her mistakes. She never had to worry about being slapped, hit, or abandoned. Over the years, Jenny had learned that Cathey and Randy were different from Natasha. They did not want to hurt her or her brothers. They just wanted to teach their children how to treat others, as Christians.

"Thank you for owning your wrongs. I'm proud of you for doing that, and so quickly, too," Cathey affirmed as she gently took hold of Jenny's hand.

"Your relationship with Natasha is really hard, isn't it?"

This was another thing about Cathey. She always seemed to understand the hurt underneath the anger. Just one more thing she loved about her mother. Jenny loathed disappointing her.

"Uh-huh. I just don't know what to think about her anymore. She frustrates me so much. What am I supposed to do, Mama?"

"Just what we're doing, sweetie. Talk about it, tell me how you feel, and then at some point you'll know what to do and how to forgive her."

"Ohhh, Mama, I don't know if I can do that. I mean, how many times am I supposed to let her get away with it? How long is Natasha gonna do this stuff?"

"I know how much she has disappointed and hurt you. She has not been there for you when you have needed her—like for the Christmas Eve service. But, she's really not doing this TO you. This is part of the disease of addiction. Remember what the therapist told us—that relapse is to be expected in a disease like this?"

Jenny said nothing as tears formed in her big, brown eyes.

"You wouldn't feel this way if she had cancer and it came back, would you?"

"Well, no. Of course not! But, this is different." Her welled-up tears began to spill over her cheeks.

"Not really, honey. This is a disease, just like any other disease." Cathey knew that she was really pushing Jenny beyond her limits to understand that the devastating effects of this disease. Sometimes, Jenny understood the concept like a thirty-year-old; at other times, she understood only as much as her chronological years would allow.

They had attended family therapy sessions with Liz, the CPO therapist, during the adoption transition and again when Natasha had begun her series of relapses. Cathey thought Jenny and the boys had understood the origins of addiction. But, Liz said that they would probably go through phases where they would gain yet a deeper understanding of it and the effects on the family.

"Jenny, do you want me to call the therapist and set up a time where we can go see her again? Liz said that we could call her anytime."

Jenny's saddened tone turned into a whine. "Mom, I don't wanna go see her again. I mean, I like Liz and all that; it's just that I want Natasha to stop using those drugs and getting in trouble. Liz is just gonna tell me the same thing she told us last time. I *know* what she's gonna say."

Continuing to stroke Jenny's hair, Cathey sat with her and began to smile at her whine. Hoping to add some levity to the grave situation, Cathey said, "Oh, Jenny, would you like some cheese with that whine?"

That always got Jenny. She began to smile. "Mom, I'm serious here."

"I know, I know. Except, it's hard to take you seriously when you whine like that. I'm thinking yellow cheese; or maybe some pepper jack. We haven't had that in a long time."

Both broke out into laughter. Jenny was able to step outside herself and hear how she sounded. She didn't know what else to do except laugh and continue the joke.

"Ohhh, that reminds me, Mama. I'm hungry. Really, do we have any cheese and crackers?"

Fluffing the top of Jenny's head, Cathey grabbed her hand. "C'mon. Let's go down and see what we can find."

Jenny went willingly.

Yet, both knew that this discussion was far from finished. They just needed a break.

In the meantime, Randy had arrived home with boys in tow. Randy had taken them to see a movie, but Jenny had not felt like joining them.

The twins saw the cheese and cracker plate and immediately ran to the table to claim their share, shoving the others out of their path. Jenny and Cathey were making sandwiches while warming up some vegetable soup for dinner.

"Hey boys, slow down," Randy said. "There's enough for everyone."

Randy made his way over to Cathey and kissed her on the cheek.

"I guess you can tell that we're home, huh?"

"Uh, yeah, we got that," Cathey said jokingly.

Next, Randy searched for a way to get to Jenny, to give her a hug. "Hi, princess. How was your afternoon?"

Jenny glanced at her mother before answering. "Um, it was okay."

Taking off his coat and gloves, Randy caught the exchange. He looked at Cathey with raised eyebrows. "Is it something I need to know?"

Jenny answered first. "Nope. We got it all handled, Dad."

But, Cathey's look contradicted Jenny's response.

"Hmmmmm. I see," Randy silently mouthed. "I guess we'll talk later, huh?"

Cathey nodded silently while Jenny stirred the soup.

Later that night, after Cathey and Randy had talked about the situation between Natasha and Jenny, Randy went to tell Jenny goodnight and see how she was doing. The door was open but the room was dimly lit. One small lamp allowed enough light so that Randy could see her face. He noticed that her face looked lost in thought. So engrossed in whatever she was thinking that she did not hear Randy as he approach her room.

"Knock, knock, Jenny. Can I come in?" her father asked.

"What? Oh, daddy, it's you. Sure, come on in."

"A penny for your thoughts."

Looking at him for a few moments, she knew that her dad had come to talk and she wasn't really looking forward to the discussion. Wanting instead to joke, she made a joke out of her dad's question.

"Well, the rate's gone up, ya know. It's a dollar now," she giggled.

"Wow! That's some increase! Wish my job would give me that kind of raise."

Jenny sighed while her smile began to slowly fade. Each was waiting for the other to broach the subject of Natasha, but neither initiated it. At least, not for a few minutes. Randy gathered up the covers around her and gently sat beside her.

"Sorry you had a rough afternoon," Randy eventually said.

Jenny knew better than to let the conversation drop. It needed resolving and it would not happen magically.

"Daddy, I just don't know what to do. I get so mad at Natasha sometimes. I just don't want to talk with her. Are you gonna make me?"

"I'm not going to force you, honey. Actually, I don't want you to talk with her by yourself. Either your mom or I need to be present. Natasha's not in a good place right now, but that doesn't mean that you can be that rude back, especially towards someone you love."

Jenny started to say something, but remained silent.

"It's okay to be mad at someone," her father continued. "That's not what I have a problem with. Any relationship is going to have its problems, but when you have a problem with someone, don't avoid talking about it. That can be a big mistake. You can start making assumptions about what the other is thinking and feeling, and it usually turns into a big mess because the assumptions are usually wrong. But, when you *do* talk, don't be rude about it. You can be angry, but you just can't sin. *H-o-w* you work out your problems with another makes all the difference in the world."

Jenny was very surprised that her father didn't want her to talk with Natasha alone, and wondered what had happened to change this.

"Why don't you want me to talk with Natasha?"

"No, it's not that we don't want you to speak with her, but any conversation between you two needs to be monitored right now. I think both of you are upset, so there needs to be some guidance to turn this thing around. I hadn't realized that you were this frustrated with her, and vice versa."

"What d'ya mean, vice versa?"

"Well, Natasha seems to be upset, too, especially after hearing your little comment earlier on the phone. Both of you got your feelings hurt, and sometimes it's difficult to resolve things without help."

"Oh," Jenny said quietly, shocked that she actually cared whether or not Natasha was hurt by what she had said. And, of course, Jenny immediately felt guilty. With Natasha, guilt seemed to always be her default mode. Jenny had always felt responsible for Natasha. For many years, Jenny tried to make her happy; and, when that didn't work, she tried to remove or handle what was making her miserable. But, it never seemed to work. Jenny could never do enough, say enough, or be good enough so that her birth mother would be happy and loving and want to stay home.

"But, you haven't ever said that Natasha and I couldn't talk alone. So, why now?"

It was a good question, but Randy did not want to tell Jenny that Natasha had threatened to slap her. Just thinking about it made anger's poison course through Randy's veins again. *Nobody, repeat nobody is going to ever slap my little princess again. Ever! He was going to see to that.*

Randy had paused almost too long before answering Jenny.

"Sometimes when people get upset, they can be unpredictable. So, your mother and I think it'd be best if we were present during any face-to-face conversations you have with Natasha. Either that, or you can speak with her in front of the therapist. Your choice, unless you have a better idea."

"Do I *have* to talk with her at all?"

"Only to apologize for what you said."

"Why do *I* have to apologize? Doesn't she have to do it, too? Actually, Dad, she should be the one to say it first since she's the one that's been acting stupid for so long. I wouldn't have said what I said if she hadn't been acting so crazy."

"Nice try, sweetheart, but that won't fly," her dad said knowingly. "You're not getting' off the hot seat on this one. Regardless of what Natasha said, you are responsible for what you say and do. So, how do you want to approach this?"

At least Jenny had given it a try, but she couldn't get that one passed her dad.

"Well, how 'bout I just send her a card. Can I do that? Or, do I have to face her?"

Her father thought long and hard about this. Apologies are always better when they are done in person. Apologies offered face-to-face are much harder to do because it keeps our pride in check. However, sending a note means that the person has taken the time to think about what they've done, and that it meant enough that they would send a card.

Randy was torn. Suddenly, he felt inadequate as a parent to advise his own daughter on a subject matter. He couldn't decide if it was Jenny's intention to avoid Natasha altogether or if she was trying to take the easy way out. Maybe emotions were too volatile right now to have either of them address the matter now. Maybe he should suggest that they wait a week or so before getting together.

Wow, he thought, *parenting is tough.* He wanted to teach all of his children to do the right things and do the hard work. But, Jenny's big brown eyes made his heart melt. He didn't really know which the right answer was, but something in his spirit told him that his suggestion would have far-reaching consequences.

Why don't children come with an instruction manual? Note to self: search the internet for one such manual, and pay whatever enormous price to get one or twenty.

Jenny stared at her father while patiently waiting for his answer. What was taking him so long and why was this a big deal? It was just an apology, right? It's not like it was a matter of life and death or cancer or anything. It was just an apology. So, why was her father taking so long to respond?

"Jenny, why don't you spend time thinking and praying about how you'd like to handle this. I've told you that your mom and I need to be present if you choose to do it in person. I don't know what the best way would be—for you. I know what I would do, but you have to make your own choices and live with them. No regrets. Just think it through. Think of each possibility and the likely outcome, and then make your decision."

"Dad, what's the big deal?"

Oddly enough, her father stammered.

"I-I don't know. I just want you to think about this. It's important somehow. I mean, apologies in general are important, but this one is different in some way. Just pray about it, okay? Then, you can let us know in the morning what you've decided."

Shrugging her shoulders, Jenny agreed. "Sure, Dad."

What was all that about, Jenny wondered. She didn't really see that this was a situation which called for thought and prayer. Bigger circumstances, serious ones, called for thought and prayer, but not this little thing. It was just an apology.

Yes, she assured herself. *This just calls for a written note.* That was the logical choice.

Might as well get it done, she thought, as she reached for her stationery which was a Christmas present from her Grandma. She loved writing and drawing on special stationery, and always had as far back as she could remember. One particular stationery contained her favorite colors and designs. Big geometric designs in various shades of brown, orange, tan, and green. Another set celebrated the pages with pink and purple circles of all different sizes.

The biggest decision about this situation was which stationery to use. After several minutes, Jenny decided that this apology note should not be written on happy sheets, but on normal, plain pages. Walking over to her desk, she reached for the plain, ruled paper and returned to her bed to write.

It didn't take her long to write out her apology letter.

Well, that wasn't as bad as I thought it was going to be, she thought, relieved that the task had been finalized.

Jenny placed the tri-folded page on the corner of her black desk near the door so that she could remember to give it to her mom in the morning. They would determine how to get it to Natasha and the mission would be complete.

After she had read for awhile, she began to get sleepy. Closing the book after marking the page with a piece of green yarn, she placed it on her bedside table. Before turning off her light, Jenny's eyes rested on the letter across the room. It held her attention for a moment or two, though she was unsure of the reason.

It's just an apology note, she told herself. There's nothing she could do about the issue that night other than writing the note.

And, then, it will be finished.

But, for some unknown explanation, Jenny had difficulty getting to sleep that night. Her spirit seemed restless. Her stomach churned. Something seemed unfinished, but she couldn't quite put her finger on it.

Jenny tried several things to put her to sleep—methods her mother had taught her when she first came to live with the Abbotts. She hummed several songs as she tossed and turned; recited the Lord's Prayer; and, visualized places she'd like to visit someday. Tonight, it was the beach with white sand and rolling waves.

The rolling waves were the last thing she remembered before finally falling asleep.

Rolling waves, much like rolling thoughts that turn over and over in one's mind.

Rolling waves . . .

Unsettling thoughts . . .

Unsettling . . .

Rolling.

Rolling.

Rolling.

CHAPTER 11

The sound of the phone ringing rocked Jenny out of bed.

She had slept in since she was still on Christmas break. But, she only had a few more days in which to do so.

The time away from school had been refreshing, but it was quickly fading. Jenny thought she would have been able to do more things with her friends, but schedules had just not cooperated. They had met only once at the mall and it had been for a mere three hours.

So, when Jenny heard that Monica was on the phone, she quickly jumped out of bed to answer the phone.

Monica Beasley had been a good friend to Jenny over the past few years. They were in the same grade and in many of the same classes. They were usually seated next to each other due to the assigned seating in alphabetical order. Otherwise, Jenny would have had to sit in front of that annoying, pimple-faced, tuba-playing Darrin Bigsly.

She could tell Monica anything and it was kept in confidence. Over the years, they had enjoyed plenty of conversations about boys, interests, classes, life, purpose, and family. She understood Jenny's confusing and complicated feelings about Natasha, for which Jenny was forever grateful. Monica seemed to just accept her feelings and never cast judgment. Jenny was the same way with Monica. They were good for each other during these difficult years.

Monica, like Jenny, had been frustrated because they had not been able to spend any time together over the last two weeks. So, when her parents asked if she wanted to invite Jenny to go with them to visit her grandmother, Jenny jumped at the chance. She was so excited she could barely eek out the words.

Running down the stairs two at a time, Jenny ran to her mother to get permission. Cathey could hardly understand her excited words which sounded like babbling by the time she was through.

"Mom, I have to go! Please? Please? Please?"

Her mother considered the invitation as she tried to remember any family plans that might have been made. Searching the calendar and her memory, she could find nothing, so she agreed she could go—with one exception. If she was going to be gone the entire weekend before school started, Jenny would have to clean her room before she left. Randy was at work, but she knew he would have no problem with allowing her to go.

Cathey and Randy knew Monica's family well and neither would have any difficulty with her spending the weekend there, just as she had done on countless previous times.

"Thank you, thank you, thank you, Mama," Jenny said excitedly while swirling around her mother. Giving her a big hug before running upstairs to accomplish the task, Jenny grabbed a black garbage sack. The trash in her room could not outrun the welcoming, enfolding arms of a good, flexible trash bag. Kleenex, gift receipts, tags from new clothes, pieces of cardboard, half-used sheets of paper, crayon wrappings, pencil shavings, all got swept into the bag. Running into the bathroom, she did likewise, emptying the counter of used cotton balls, stridex pads, Q-tips, tissues, and three empty toilet tissue holders. After pulling hair from the shower drain and wiping up toothpaste spillage, Jenny ran to pack her overnight bag. At least she wouldn't be bored this weekend. They would have a great time laughing, listening to music, talking, and trying to get a good look at her grandmother's good-looking next door neighbor. They figured he must be about eighteen years old, maybe nineteen, much too old for them realistically, but his presence certainly made for some good fantasies and conversations.

Making sure she had everything she needed for the trip, Jenny took one last look around the room to see if she had forgotten anything. In facing her room, though, Jenny's back was to her black desk—the one holding the letter to Natasha.

In all the excitement, neither Jenny nor her mother had given one thought to what she was going to do about the note. It stayed on the corner of the desk waiting to be noticed, addressed, and sent. But, the words of apology would spend the weekend in the dark on the plain paper.

About an hour later, Jenny had been picked up by Monica's parents in their tan SUV heading for their destination three hours away. Cathey stayed out on the porch with her arms wrapped around herself, shivering and wondering if the weather would hold up for their trip. Monica and her parents said they were aware of the approaching storm, but were not concerned because it was nothing that their SUV couldn't endure.

Waving good-bye and smiling, Cathey glanced again at the bright, wintry sky and noticed the building up of clouds off in the distance. She waited until the SUV had rounded the corner before re-entering the warm house which smelled of hot tea and half-eaten egg dish. Though it was late morning, she still had not cleaned up the breakfast dishes or run the dishwasher. She guessed she needed to do that before the boys would want lunch.

Shesh! These boys sure do eat a lot, Cathey thought to herself.

But, before she attempted to bulldoze the kitchen, she wanted to check the weather channel to see the forecast conditions for the northern part of the state where the Beasley family and Jenny were headed.

NATASHA HAD JUST HUNG UP the phone from Cathey when the phone rang again. The first call was from Cathey who had called to find out how Natasha was doing and to let her know that Jenny had gone on a weekend trip with her friend's family. Natasha's white-hot anger towards Jenny had weighed heavily on Cathey which had caused a major increase in her anxiety. To be truthful, Cathey had, in part, called to gauge Natasha's mood and to determine if an adjustment had been made towards Jenny.

One of Cathey's gifts was that she was a peacemaker—and had been all her life. She had a spiritual gift for being able to discern people's moods, even the slightest of changes. It was certainly a gift of social sensitivity and discernment, but it may have come with the territory of being the eldest child in her own family.

Sometimes Cathey considered it a gift; at other times, she thought of it as a curse. She loved being able to read others correctly, but found no way to turn it off when she didn't want to be so aware. She could never find the *off* button. The switch to this gift was continually *on.* But, Cathey had always made the best of it and thanked God for allowing her to have such a special gift which served to minister to others and glorify Him.

Cathey used this gift during the phone call to Natasha. The conversation went well; that is, until the subject of Jenny was broached. The shift in Natasha's mood paralled this day's approaching wintry storm: gradual, but definitive.

Though Natasha responded with only a few words on the subject of Jenny's weekend, the tone was as icy and heavy as sleet. *Well, I hope she has a good time*, Natasha had said. There was nothing wrong with what she said; rather, *how* she said it—with such sarcasm—which had indicated that their relational storm had not blown over yet.

Having obtained the sought-out information, Cathey quickly wrapped up the conversation and hung up. Cathey had determined that it was still not safe for the two of them to work out their differences alone. They were definitely going to need the help of the therapist—with Randy or Cathey present in the session.

Natasha rolled her eyes when she heard the phone ring again and wondered if Cathey had forgotten to tell her something else about how much fun Jenny would be having on this trip of hers.

"Did you forget something?" Natasha said as she answered the phone.

"Huh?" came a confused, but familiar voice. "Wha' are ya talkin' 'bout? Forget what? I didn't forget nothin'."

"Oh, Dyno. I thought you were someone else. Nevermind. Where are you? Are you out of jail?"

"Yeah, I'm out. Cost me a fortune, too. I'll be payin' back people for years, so I'll have to be creative in how I do it, though. I got no money, but I do have one thing that people want," Dyno said with a slimy, cheeky grin, "if ya know what I mean."

"Stop it right now, Dyno. I don't wanna hear nothin' about that. You are nothin' but trouble to me, you know that? You almost cost me everything."

"Me?" Dyno yelled as he smirked. "What did *I* do? *You* were the one who was drivin' the car. I was just sittin' back, mindin' my own bidness, and all of a sudden, you gotta go to ya kids' home and check on them. Then, you even forgot how to drive. Ran into a stupid mailbox thingy. That's why the police stopped us. Ain't nothin' that was *my* fault."

"You birdbrain! I swear you ain't even got a brain big enough to fit into a hummingbird. Did you forget that it was YOU who took the car? YOU stole it, Ace, not me. So, don't go blamin' nothin' on me."

"Oh gimme a break. You can't even . . . ."

"Why are you even callin' me?" Natasha interrupted while flustered.

"Well, if you'd just shut up a minute, I'd tell you. But, no, you gotta go flappin' your mouth, bustin' my chops for nothing. I was jus' gonna tell you that I was out and that we oughtta get together. Ya know? Jus' chill, maybe come over and we'll smoke us some weed."

"You idiot! Have you lost your frickin' mind? I ain't gonna do anything with you. You shouldn't even be talkin' about smoking anything, fool. You just got outta jail and you're already talkin' 'bout smoking? I can't even believe . . ."

Dyno had had enough of this conversation. He was getting dogged on too much. He certainly didn't need this from her. This was his first day out and, like always, all she wanted to do was whine and complain. How could she fault him for just wanting to have some fun now that he was as free as a bird.

"HEY, SHUT YOUR MOUTH. I'm hangin' up on you since you're gonna jack me around like this. But, don't go comin' to me when you need you some weed. As far as you're concerned, this store is closed."

"I DIDN'T EVEN SAY I WANTED ANY. Don't you listen at all, fool? Jus' go smoke yourself to death, dingo. And, don't come whinin' to me when you land in jail again."

The next sound she heard was silence, which she considered the best response.

Natasha admitted to herself that going over and getting high did sound good. After all, she had been angry and frustrated ever since her little encounter with Jenny—or, more precisely, her lack of encounter since Jenny had not wanted to talk with her.

How dare she treat me that way! You know what, I certainly don't need that in my life when I'm trying to get my act together. Jenny knows better than to talk to me that way.

Suddenly, Natasha heard it.

She caught it.

She got it!

She was doing that thing again.

She was escalating herself into a frustrated frenzied emotional state so that she could make an excuse to get high.

Her years spent in NA meetings, counseling, and support group, had paid off. She was aware of the damage her own thoughts were doing to her.

Stinkin' thinkin' is what NA called it. And, she was filled with it. Blaming, complaining. Murmuring and grumbling, just like the Israelites had done in the Bible.

Wow! Where did that insight come from? Natasha wondered, but she knew. She knew it was the knock of God on her door. The Hand of the One who had saved her before.

Aware of how sad she had suddenly become, Natasha began to cry. She began to wonder how she had wandered so far away from God. She had sworn that she would never do that again. For her own sake, for her mentor's sake, for her sponsor's sake, for her children's sake—for Jenny's sake—she no longer wanted to be a co-conspirator with her feelings, the false feelings which she, herself, had ignited.

Natasha wanted to break the pattern—again. She wanted to stop this cycle, once and for all. Wasn't she worth it? Weren't her kids worth it? Wasn't her little Jenny worth it?

Wasn't God worth it?

"Yes, God is worth it. They all are," Natasha said aloud with new resolve.

She wondered how she could have been so stupid as to allow this cycle back into her life so quickly, like a long, lost, destructive friend. Or, had it really been quickly and suddenly? No, she reminded herself. This had not begun overnight. From counseling and meetings, Natasha knew that relapse happened over a long period of time, beginning with the smallest of thoughts and decisions.

Natasha sat on her couch for the better part of an hour recounting what she had forgotten about getting one's self back on track. Though she knew to keep doing 'the next right thing,' she hesitated, though she had no understanding of why.

Recovering from such a bad relapse was very difficult work. She could 'think' all day long on her good choices, but it counted for nothing as long as she took no action.

"Okay, 'Tash. Get 'hold of yourself. You know what do you," she encouraged herself aloud. "Now, just do it!"

The couch hung onto Natasha for dear life, as though it had its own agenda. It took such energy to get up. She could feel the heaviness of the spiritual battle fighting over her. Satan's voice was the loudest, but Natasha knew from past experiences that God's still, small voice contained more power in one brief word than Satan's entire vocabulary.

Had the room darkened in the last hour or was it just her imagination? The slightest movement of her hand felt impossible. Blinking her eyes seemed as though it was the only task she could accomplish.

Satan must really want me to fail, she thought, *if he's putting this much energy into holding me back—a simple, average, young woman who has little to offer anybody.*

"THAT'S A LIE, SATAN!" Unexpectedly, Natasha became angry. "I am somebody that has something to offer, and you're not gonna lie to me anymore. You hear me you little worm? Now, shut up!"

As though Satan was trying to launch one last attack on Natasha, he dealt her one last blow with one last lie.

YOUR CHILDREN WILL NEVER FORGIVE YOU.

CHAPTER 12

Recovering from the startling, emotional slap from Satan, Natasha gathered her wits about her and yelled aloud the only thing she knew that would transform her situation.

"JESUS! HELP ME!"

Immediately, Natasha felt as though the seemingly invincible, yet invisible, chains which had held her hostage were broken. With those few words, Jesus had set her free, and with her new-found freedom, Natasha raced frantically over to her phone which she had thrown on the floor after her conversation with Dyno.

Speed dial number nine quickly rang her life rope.

"Hello?" came the voice.

"Kayleen? This is Natasha," she said through tears and fears.

"Hey, girl. What's wrong?"

"Where are you?" Natasha asked almost frantically.

"Calm down, hon. Are you alright?"

"Yeah . . . no . . . I don't think so. I need to talk."

"Well, I'm at my brother and sister-in-law's house right now having dinner, but I can talk a few minutes."

Natasha knew that a few minutes over the phone might uplift her spirits briefly, but she was going to need some long, face-to-face contact with one of the safest people she knew—her mentor, friend, and fellow recovering alcoholic.

Kayleen had been through everything with her and had always been there for her. She even knew enough not to put up with any of Natasha's mind games, excuses, justifications, or ridiculously stupid attitudes and moods.

"No, Kayleen. You don't understand. This can't be taken care of with a few minutes over the phone. Can you meet me somewhere?"

"Sure. Um, can it wait until I'm through with dinner, or do you need me to leave right now?" Kayleen was beginning to wonder if she shouldn't just leave. Natasha's tone was disturbing her.

"Okay, um, yeah, that's good. That's fine. As long as I know that we're gonna meet. Just name the time and place and I'll meet 'cha there."

Kayleen looked at her watch trying to estimate when they would be through eating and when she could politely get away. Her husband and the girls could stay awhile and play with their cousins who would give her time to meet up with Natasha and return before anyone became too bored and before any disagreements erupted. She'd have to check out the plan with her husband, though.

"Natasha, I need to run this by my husband and everyone here. Hang on a minute and I'll be right back."

Suddenly feeling like a burden, Natasha nearly changed her mind. But, this was too important for her sobriety and sanity to let her pride get in the way of sanity. Natasha was just too fragile, so she just ignored her first instinct to hang up.

Waiting for Kayleen to return to the phone, Natasha paced a new path in her apartment. The worn, tan carpet needed replacing someday, but her landlord didn't seem to be in much of a hurry for that. She figured it was somewhere on his priority list, right below eating donuts, smoking a cigarette, and flirting with young women in her complex.

Keeping her mind focused on sane thoughts was challenging, to say the least. Her thoughts were bouncing all over in her head, like a pinball machine. Ding, ding, ding, ding.

The conversation with Dyno came rushing back into her mind. Ding.

Then, the problem with Jenny ran another bell. Ding.

Again, the words from Satan crashed into another bell, this one being the loudest one of all. Ding, ding, ding.

Noticing her increasing anxiety, Natasha began picking off the piles of her used, dark orange sweatshirt. As her mind began to wander, she looked at the colony of little piles she made on her pant leg. *How ironic*, she thought. *I'm making a mountain out of a molehill.*

What was taking Kayleen so long? Was she coordinating her entire calendar year with her family?

Calm yourself, she thought. Ding. Natasha began to understand how people with attention-deficit disorder felt. Further, she began to wonder if she, herself, had it. Maybe that was the problem.

"Hello? Natasha? You still there?"

"Finally," Natasha sighed. "What took you so long? I thought you'd driven to Canada." Then, feeling badly for her remark, Natasha apologized. "I'm sorry. I don't know what's wrong with me, but I'm about to jump outta my own skin!"

"That's okay. I'm sorry it took me so long. I had to discuss everybody's schedule, which seemed to take forever!" Kayleen remarked.

"Uh, e-YAH," she fired off with attitude.

"I'm not going to acknowledge that sarcasm because I know you're having a hard time right now. So, how about we do this: we'll finish dinner here, I'll get my girls settled, and then I can meet you in, say, about an hour or so, or maybe just a bit longer. Does that sound alright to you?"

"Fine with me. Thank you for changing all your plans around to fit mine," Natasha said with newly-found humility. "Ya know, I wouldn't ask if I *r-e-a-l-l-y* didn't need to see you," Natasha explained with just a touch of guilt.

"I know you wouldn't, Natasha. I do have history with you, remember? But, my husband said to be careful of the weather that's coming in. He's checking it right now, but he heard on the forecast this morning that an ice storm is moving in, so we'll just need to be aware of that. Now, where do you want to meet?"

"You're way across town, aren't 'cha?"

"Yes, but I can come over to your apartment, if you'd like me to. It will take me longer, but I can do that. Or, we can meet at McAllister's, our regular spot, which would be a bit closer."

"Yeah, let's meet at McAllister's," Natasha said feeling claustrophobic. "I need to get outta here. I'm just driving myself crazy and I have so much energy that I don't know what to do with myself."

"Will you be okay until then?" Kayleen asked cautiously.

"Yeah. I need to take a shower anyway. I've been such a slug all day. If I still need t' waste some time, then I'll drive around for awhile or go to the mall, or somethin'. So, just call me on my cell phone when you're leaving."

Still not convinced that Natasha would be alright, Kayleen asked again.

"You know, I can leave right now and be there in about thirty minutes. That sounds to me like a better idea."

Natasha took in a big breath and let it out slowly. "No, really, I'm gonna be okay. I'm jus' lettin' some stuff get to me—stuff about Jenny that has me upset."

"Jenny? What's going on there?"

"Oh, it's such a long story. But, I might as well tell ya, Dyno called and wanted to let me know he had just gotten outta jail and wanted me to come smoke some weed wi' him. 'Course, that really got my thoughts racing."

Natasha knew that she'd better say these concerns aloud—which would be the next right decision in her recovery—or else, they'd just intensify in power if left to swirl in secrecy.

"But, you know what? I think I got a handle on it. I called you, didn't I? I did the right thing. I'm not, I repeat, I AM NOT going back to my ol' ways or that stupid lifestyle. That's it for me. I'm feelin' stronger and stronger just since we been talkin'. And, as far as Jenny's concerned, I'm gonna go clean up some of my mess with her, too. I get so tired of havin' to clean up my messes," Natasha said laughingly. "So, just go and finish your dinner and get everybody settled. I'll meet up wi' you in an hour or so. Just call me when you're ready, okay?"

Kayleen pondered the situation for a minute. Natasha did sound like she was doing better than she was at the beginning of the conversation, so after quickly thrashing it around in her head, she decided to go with their original plan.

"Alright then. If you're sure. I'll call you when I'm ready to walk out the door and we'll meet up at McAllister's. But, promise me that if you change your mind, you'll call me. Agreed?"

"Agreed," Natasha replied. "Sounds great to me. I'll see you soon, then."

"Bye." Kayleen almost flipped her phone shut, but thought better of it.

"Oh, Natasha? You still there?"

But, she had already hung up.

Kayleen wondered whether or not she could call her back. Oh well, she had already mentioned the weather once earlier in their conversation. She was going to remind Natasha to be careful on the ice, but she had already told her that the storm was coming. Natasha certainly didn't need to be badgered about it.

Clicking off the phone, Kayleen paused before returning to her family and the half-eaten dinner which awaited her.

She tried to finish dinner, but something deep within her was as unsettled as an unpredictable snow storm.

THE BEASLEY'S SUV WOUND ITS WAY around the mountainous turns. Though the weather had turned colder and sleet had begun to fall on the windshield, Monica and Jenny giggled in the back seat, unaware of the change. For two hours, they had been nestled in blankets and pillows while whispering, laughing, and writing notes to each other. The girls certainly did not want the parents to know that both of them had a crush on Monica's next door neighbor. When parents discovered such things, they usually intervened and cut off all hope of a wonderful future with such a god; or, at least, with the hope of even a conversation with him.

Would they see this fine specimen when they first arrived? Would they be able to talk with him? What would he be wearing? How long would his hair be now? Did he still smoke? *Ewwwww*, they giggled, *they wouldn't think about that*. Neither liked anyone who smoked. That was just *gross*. It didn't fit with their fantasy of him, so they just wouldn't think about that. Anyway, even if he did smoke, it probably wasn't all that much. But, what if he already had a girlfriend? What then? Well, if he did have a girlfriend, she'd probably be some old, skanky girl who didn't deserve him in the first place.

Their notes to each other were filled with questions about lover-boy. And, neither of Monica's parents had even the slightest hint that they were discussing such things. How much better did it get than this!

For the past few years, Monica had stopped asking such childish questions as, *How much longer 'til we get there?* And, *Are we there yet?* She had developed mile-markers of her own so that she could tell where they were along the way. For the last thirty minutes, the road had become bumpier, which meant that the estimated time of arrival to Grandma's house was approximately twenty minutes. Not long now.

The flat areas of their state had never held much interest for Monica, but this particular area, which was mountainous, had always grabbed her attention. Jenny liked it, too. She liked the winding roads, the steep hills, the greener grass in spring, and the scarcity of people year round. Country living! Jenny hoped that one day she would be able to live in a place like this.

The city contained certain good things, like her family, friends, and church, but not huge boulders on which to climb, or steep hills down which she could run. Jenny had made this trip with Monica and her family a number of times. Her favorite time to visit was during the spring. The waving, knee-high grass punctuated by the vibrant colors of the flowers swept Jenny away into a fantasy world of her own. Oftentimes, Monica and Jenny ran wildly in circles with arms outstretched so that they could feel the tops of the thin blades of tall grass. Then, when their lungs and limbs were exhausted, they would lie down on the cool, green soil, close their eyes, and listen to the wind as it whispered freedom in their ears. Such was life in the country in the spring.

But, this was not the spring. This was the dead of winter. Fields were brown and barren, and leaves had been plucked from the trees. White snow and black ice replaced the multitudes of colors from the flowers. Every living thing hid from winter's harsh climate.

The skies were no longer sun-filled but cloud-covered. Winter wept its freezing rain onto the winding roads causing slippery spots and dangerous turns. The predicted storm had unexpectedly intensified in the last hour. Temperatures had plummeted into the teens.

Conversations in the car changed from casual to somber as Mr. and Mrs. Beasley glanced at each other with looks of caution and concern, which did not go unnoticed by Monica and Jenny. Silence from the backseat marked the sudden awareness of the gravity of the situation.

"Dad, are we gonna be alright?" Monica asked softly.

Though her father had heard her question, he hesitated in answering.

"Well, looks like the weather turned sour on us, doesn't it? We'll make it okay. It's not too much further anyway. Grandma's expecting us, so she'll have the front porch lights on and a fire in the fireplace."

"But, Dad," Monica continued somewhat impatiently. "I don't like the roads when they're like this. When is it gonna stop?" Knowing her father could not predict the forecast, she asked if they could turn on the radio in hopes of picking up a radio station which could give them the needed information.

"I'll turn it on," Mrs. Beasley responded quickly. She and her husband had been married long enough for her to read his stress signals. The tightening of his hands on the wheel and the clinching of his jaw told her that she needed to intervene in the parenting. "Monica," her mother said quickly, "let's be quiet so that your father can concentrate on the road."

Jenny looked at Monica with compassion. The curtness with which her mother had spoken had slightly embarrassed Monica, but fear reigned.

Jenny took Monica's hand as both looked silently out the window for some sign of clearing weather.

Each could feel the back tires slip and slide as the engine revved at the loss of traction. Mr. Beasley remembered that he had put the tire chains in the back, and planned to put them on at the next turnout. He realized that he should have stopped earlier, but he had just kept hoping that they would drive out of the storm. Rarely had the weather been this bad when they traveled, but the area had been known for receiving more snow than down south. Ben Beasley much preferred traveling in snow than this horrible storm. How could the weathermen have missed the forecast by so much? If he had known that it was going to be this torturous, they wouldn't have come this weekend—at least, not that day.

Where is that blasted turnout anyway? Ben grumbled silently. Visibility was down to a few feet and there were no signs that it was going to let up anytime soon. They had passed very few cars. Most people had the good sense to stay home that evening, probably in front of a warm fire, sipping hot chocolate, and reading a good book. But, not the Beasley family. *No, we had to go today instead of waiting one more day!* They usually left on Saturday mornings, but Monica wanted to go one day earlier. Ben had agreed since it was the last weekend of winter vacation before returning to school. He wanted them to have a longer, fun-filled weekend, but his feelings of excitement and anticipation for them had quickly turned to dread and exhaustion.

Suddenly, Amy Beasley's cell phone rang. It had been tucked away neatly in the pocket of her purse. Barely audible, it was on its fourth ring before Amy could reach it.

"Hello?" Amy answered. Turning around and looking towards Jenny, she pointed to the phone and mouthed the words, "It's your mother."

"Yes, hello, Cathey. I can barely hear you. Must be the storm or the poor reception we're getting out here. Can you speak up?"

Jenny could only hear Mrs. Beasley's side of the conversation.

"Yes, Cathey, I can hear you now. This storm has really gotten bad. Is it bad there, too?"

Mrs. Beasley nodded to Jenny.

"Well, we would have arrived earlier, but the slick roads have slowed us down quite a bit."

Jenny wanted to speak with her mother, so she unbuckled her seat belt and scooted towards the edge of the seat. Mrs. Beasley could see how anxious Jenny was to speak with her, so she interrupted the conversation.

"Cathey, I have someone here who *really* wants to talk with you. Hold on."

Grabbing the phone, Jenny hurriedly asked, "Mom, you there?"

"Yes, I'm here, honey. How are you doing?"

"Well, okay, I guess. It's kind of scarey. These roads are really, really slick. But, Monica and I have been holding hands, especially when we bumped into a rock or something back there."

Ben and Amy glanced at each other wondering what Cathey must be thinking.

"Okay, Mom. Yeah, I love you, too." As she handed the phone back to Mrs. Beasley, Jenny inhaled deeply, sat back in her seat, and buckled her seat belt before reaching over and grabbing Monica's hand again.

Jenny overheard Mrs. Beasley explaining to her mother about the bump they had experienced earlier on the road.

"We don't know what that was. We slid a bit, so we may have grazed a rock or maybe caught something underneath one of the tires. We haven't stopped yet to look at the car, so we're just not sure what happened. When we get to the next turnout, we're going to stop and put the chains on the tires. That should help quite a bit. We just hate to stop in the middle of the road. We're not seeing many cars, but you never know when one could come. Are you watching the weather? Can you tell if we're almost out of it?"

More was said from the other end of the phone.

"What? Cathey? What did you say? How long did you say? You're breaking up . . . . I can't quite hear you. I was asking if you could see whether or not we're almost out of the storm. Cathey . . . . ?"

The call was dropped. Not unusual for being out in hilly country. Amy stared at the phone and her gut twisted. She did not like what she read on it.

No service.

CHAPTER 13

Mrs. Beasley glanced at her husband before slowly turning to look at Monica and Jenny who were fearfully huddled together in the back seat.

"What is it, Mom?" Monica asked frantically. "Why aren't you talking to Mrs. Abbott? Can she not hear you? Keep talking, mother. She can't hear you if you don't keep talking."

Mr. Beasley searched his wife's face for an answer as to why she was silent. It was then he knew that they had lost the cell phone signal. This long stretch of somewhat crude, back road offered little chance of getting any coverage.

"I can't understand why this storm isn't letting up," he said looking ahead at the blinding snow. Clicking his headlights on high beam seemed to make matters worse, so he switched them back to low.

Jenny remained quiet. Wishing she were home instead of out in this mess of a storm, she closed her eyes and began humming. She had always been a hummer for as long as she could remember. Occasionally, the humming had been a source of trouble at school. But, she had never stopped; she had just lowered the decibel level.

For Jenny, humming served a number of purposes. As a child, it kept her company, like a good friend; it passed the time more quickly when she was bored; it cheered her up when she was sad; and, most importantly, it soothed her when nothing else would—and when no one else was home.

Jenny liked to think that she had learned it from angels and had often imagined angels humming with her.

But, humming was seen differently by Natasha. In Natasha's presence, it had always irritated her, but Natasha had been constantly irritated in Jenny's early years. Cathey had the completely opposite opinion. Cathey had told her that it was a wonderful thing to do and encouraged her to do it whenever she felt the need.

Cathey had discovered Jenny's critical need for humming on the very first night she was placed in their house. Throughout that first night, Cathey had checked on her—on all the children—several times. The boys had fallen asleep fairly quickly, but it had taken Jenny awhile to doze off. Actually, it had taken Jenny many nights for her to feel comfortable enough to let go of her anxiety. But, when all had calmed down that first night, Cathey had quietly checked on Jenny, only to hear a young, sweet voice humming. No words; just humming.

The next day, Cathey had asked Jenny if she wanted to learn songs, which would put words with that adorable sound. Jenny had immediately fallen in love with singing and singing fell in love with her. Jenny was utterly delighted that there were so many songs in the world, and she had vowed to commit to memory as her young brain would allow.

Jenny had learned so many and was still continuing to learn them in her church youth choir and at school whenever they had music class. Jenny had learned that songs (really, humming *with* words) allowed her to experience such a wide variety of emotions—sadness, joy, peace, anticipation, healing. It was a place where she met God.

And, that snowy, dangerous night, in her fearful state, Jenny really needed God's calming presence.

Monica knew how much Jenny loved to sing, so she was surprised when she heard Jenny humming in the back seat.

"What song are you singing?" Monica gently asked.

Jenny opened her eyes to see Monica's fearful face close to her own.

"I can't remember any, so I'm just makin' up something," Jenny said. "Wanna hum with me? We don't even have to sing the same notes or even put any words to them. We can just hum whatever comes to us."

"Um, sure. I can't think of any song either. But, my mouth is so dry. I don't think I can do it."

"Here's what I do, just follow me," Jenny offered in her familiar role as caretaker. Jenny pulled Monica back into the seat, wrapped her up with the blanket. "Now, scoot down low with me, 'n close your eyes."

Monica started to tell her that she couldn't because of her near-paralyzing fear, but decided instead to follow Jenny's lead.

"Close your eyes and keep 'em closed. Shut 'em real tight."

Mrs. Beasley heard these words and turned around just in time to witness the most tender, compassionate act of kindness she'd ever seen. She watched the calming care with which Jenny attended to her friend.

Watching Jenny with Monica was like watching a mother offer comfort to a small child, yet Jenny and Monica were not small children and were the same age. Amy had never before seen this side of Jenny. She knew Jenny was sweet, kind, loyal, and nothing but the greatest friend to Monica, but this mothering role was an added delight to observe.

As Amy watched and listened, she felt such gratitude for her daughter's friendship with Jenny, yet this feeling was tinged with an unexplained sadness. Amy wondered where she had learned this caretaking role. It seemed to come to Jenny as easily as her own mothering instinct. Amy knew very little about the situation from which she came before living with the Abbott's, but had a suspicion that this behavior had to have been learned quite early in Jenny's already-young life; quite possibly from having to care for her younger siblings for whatever reason.

Smiling slightly while watching the girls, Amy had welcomed any relief from worrying about their current situation. But, that brief interlude was quickly broken when she felt the car begin to slide sideways. Amy gripped the door handle with her right hand and seat belt with the other.

Though he was quite familiar with the road, he had lost sight of where he was because of the blanketing snow. The landscape was all so different looking in these conditions. Suddenly, a sharp, ninety degree, left-hand turn had come upon Mr. Beasley quickly; so quickly that Ben had to jerk the steering wheel unexpectedly. The white-out conditions blinded him from seeing the turn.

"HOLD ON, GIRLS," Ben said with more force than he had intended to convey.

Immediately, everything went into slow motion. To the car's four occupants, it seemed as though they were watching a nightmarish movie of someone else's life. Their outstretched hands, contorted faces, and young screams took so long to produce.

Then, for the longest time, they heard nothing but silence; or, maybe their ears had become numb.

Multiple questions from all four seemed to float out of their minds and into the atmosphere. *Was it possible for ears to become numb? Are we all going to die? When is the car going to stop? Why didn't I put the chains on the tires? I can't feel anything! Am I gonna ever see my mama and daddy again? I wish we would have picked another weekend to visit Grandma. What's going to happen if we crash?*

The four of them waited for the impact. *What was taking so long? They should have hit something by now. Maybe the snow will cushion our impact, like protective, plush cottonballs.*

Ben gripped the steering wheel so hard that his knuckles felt numb and turned white. Trying to remain calm, but anticipating contact, he felt as though his racing heart would pound its way out of his chest. He couldn't panic, though. He had precious cargo on board. Ben had good driving skills and had certainly developed strategies to deal with snow, but ice was always unpredictable. Ice had a mind of its own. And, this ice could not, no, *would* not, be tamed.

As they prepared for impact, suddenly there was a change in direction. Initially, the back of the car was sliding to the right. However, they must have hit a gravelly spot because the car immediately righted itself, if only for a brief second, but in that second, Ben pushed the steering wheel to the right. Though it appeared that they were only creeping along, the sliding had evidently gained enough momentum for the car to quickly overcompensate, and the car began to spin.

Never before had Ben been in such a difficult and capricious situation. He anticipated sliding, but not spinning in three-hundred-and-sixty-degree circles. The narrow road would not allow them to continue their circling motion for long and, for that, Ben was thankful. Or was he?

Yelling at the girls to make sure their seat belts were securely fastened, Ben shouted at them to cover up with blankets and pillows, but could say no more due to the fear that choked his throat. Glancing hurriedly at Amy, Ben saw stark terror in her eyes.

Silence marked an impending crash. Realizing where they were, Ben's mouth gaped. They were at the last turn-out before their final destination, a particularly tight spot and one peppered with bolders. The edge was outlined by a short, weather-beaten, dingy-white fence, initially designed to keep cars from careening off the road and falling down a short cliff onto a surface resembling a crater-filled moon. But, the dilapidated fence couldn't save a rabbit from sliding off much less a heavy-ladened SUV!

Ben focused intensely on navigating over the ice. Slightly aware that Amy was praying for God's divine assistance and mercy, Ben joined her.

Bracing for the harsh impact, it seemed like time was briefly suspended.

The girls' blood-curdling, foreign-sounding screams were muffled by the blankets and pillows. Having hit the fence from the passenger side of the vehicle, Amy was instantly hurled into her husband's strong presence.

When finally airborne, Ben shouted, "Hang on, girls!"

How long could it possibly take to fall twenty feet? The whole thing should have been over long before now, but they just kept falling for what seemed like an endless amount of time.

And then the steel-collapsing, people-crunching hits began.

SHOWERED AND DRESSED, Natasha left her apartment donning her coat and scarf. The biting wind had come up in the brief time it took for her to hang up from Kayleen and get out the door. Checking her pockets for gloves, she closed her apartment door and locked it before quickly putting them on. The wind was piercingly cold and she could already feel the hard sleet pricking her face.

Cautiously descending the stairs so as not to slip and fall, Natasha gripped the handrail. The wind almost blew off her thick, orange scarf. Wrapping it around her neck secured it until she could slide her way over and into her car.

Anxious to retreat from her emotions and her apartment, Natasha had dashed out forgetting to check the weather report. She vaguely remembered Kayleen telling her something about a storm coming in, but she paid it little attention. From her psychological vantage point, Natasha's need to process emotions was, by far, greater than checking any precarious weather report. She was surprised that she even remembered to wear her gray coat and orange scarf though she would have been immediately reminded the second she opened the door.

Grateful that her windshield did not yet need to be scraped, she jumped into the car. Rushing to get heat in the car, she immediately turned the key in the ignition and heard it start, thanks to the new battery which she had to have installed last month.

The parking lot of her apartment had begun to develop patches of black ice but Natasha was certain that the main roads would be fine to travel. Besides, she could see people driving out on the roads which meant the weather must not be too bad.

Though the car was still cold, Natasha decided to start driving anyway, hoping the action might encourage the heater to work faster.

Knowing that she was running early, Natasha decided to drive towards the mall. Exiting the parking lot went fairly smoothly, especially since she was only traveling one mile per hour. From her apartment, the mall was only several miles away. Before meeting Kayleen at McAllister's Deli,

Natasha wanted to first get Jenny a small gift. And, she knew exactly what she wanted to get her.

There was a cute, little stationery store at the mall which sold a vast array of notecards in a multitude of colors and designs. This would be a perfect gift to bring her when she went to make amends to Jenny.

Natasha had so many things to say to her little Jenny. So many apologies to make! So many things to tell her about life's hardships. If only she could save Jenny from having to go through what she, herself, had to blindly manage her way through, it would be worth hatcheting her own pride and self-righteousness to do so. She hoped that Jenny would listen. Their relationship over the years had been very tricky. Natasha had had so many issues that being around her was, often, as challenging as negotiating her way through land mines in a war zone. Jenny had run into so many of them which had blown up in her face and caused collateral damage that she had often wondered how she could simultaneously love and hate Natasha.

Aware of all the confusion and hurt which she had caused Jenny, Natasha made the decision to no longer be divided in her desires. Divided loyalties were destructive and lethal.

For the first time in months, Natasha had, once again, grasped clarity in her hands and was committed to clutching it eternally!

When she had been baptized six years ago, she had asked Jesus into her heart and the Holy Spirit to clean her up—to teach her, guide her, comfort her, and confront her. He had done just that, but then five years later, she had begun to rebel. She thought she had all the answers. But, bit by bit, decision by decision, feeling by feeling, she had crawled away from God. From the very One who saved her! Not only had Jesus given His life for her, but he had, again, saved her from her addictions. She wondered why and how she had fallen so far away from Him.

Well, today was a new day, she determined. Kayleen had often told her that sanity (and sobriety) was only one right decision away. For that matter, her addictions were always just one bad decision away, she had discovered yet again.

However, today, she was going to choose health, sanity, and sobriety. Today, she was going to make a decision to stand on faith. To worship God. God alone. No more juggling all of her idols like drugs, men, food, and laziness. No more worshiping other gods. As for Natasha and her household of one, she would worship the Lord!

Natasha could not believe how enboldened she began to feel with each thought. She began to feel alive again, much like she did when she was first baptized. She felt a fire beginning to burn within her. A burning desire to love and to serve. She felt so good that she couldn't help but say these things aloud to the other empty seats in her small car. She wondered how she could feel so differently than just an hour ago. She hadn't felt this way in such a long time. If only she could feel like this all the time!

No longer able to contain her increasing joy and excitement, Natasha decided that she had to tell someone about this newly-felt transformation. Her chest could no longer contain these thoughts. She had to let Kayleen know. Kayleen would understand this work of the Holy Spirit. Maybe she didn't need to meet with Kayleen tonight after all. In the last hour, things had turned around completely. Besides, the weather was getting worse. Natasha began to feel guilty for asking Kayleen to get out in this mess. Yes, she would just call her and tell her not to bother getting out in it.

Approaching the busy street where the store was, she waited in the far left-hand turn lane for a green arrow to signal that it was her turn. She was first in line and didn't have much time before the light changed, but she wanted to call Kayleen. With wipers blazing and hands shuffling, Natasha quickly reached into her purse and grabbed her black and chrome phone.

"Hey, Kayleen! Have ya left yet?"

"Hi! Natasha, you okay?"

"Sure! Actually, I'm great. I just had to call ya and tell ya that I feel so totally awesome. It's snowing like crazy on this side of town and I just wanted to tell you not to get out in this mess. Just stay put. I really am okay."

"Natasha, what has happened to you, girl? A couple of hours ago, you were so low that I thought you might end up . . . well, I thought you might hurt yourself. And, now, you're saying everything is fine. You're not making any sense at all."

"I KNOW," Natasha exclaimed. "It doesn't make sense at all, does it? That's how I know that God has gotten ahold of me and has shaken my heart up. Right here in the car."

"Where are you?" Kayleen asked concerned.

"Over here by that stationery store. You know the one in the mall that Jenny likes so much?"

"What in the world are you doing over there?"

"I was just fixin' to tell ya. I'm gonna go pick up some cute little notecards for Jenny and then maybe tomorrow, or I don't know when, I'm gonna go over to the Abbott's and apologize to Jenny. There's so many things I gotta tell her. I've been so stupid and prideful and screwed up 'n all that I had really forgotten about my little Jenny and how important she is to me—how important ALL my kids are to me."

With an eagle eye on the stoplight, Natasha noticed that the arrow for her had just turned green. Changing the phone from her right hand to the left, she continued expressing her curiously exciting insight.

"I tell ya, I haven't felt this good since the day I got baptized. You remember that day? I remember feelin' SO good and that's how I'm feelin' . . .

S-C-R-E-E-C-H . . .

CRASH!

The call was dropped.

"Hello, Natasha? Are you there? Natasha? ANSWER ME! What happened? I can't hear you. NATASHA?"

Kayleen could hear nothing . . . nothing but dead silence.

CHAPTER 14

Kayleen demanded that her husband hurry.

"I can't drive any faster than this," Darryl said.

In the distance, they could see what looked like a landing strip of red tail lights. The entire mile before the intersection was a parking lot of car after car, stopped due to the traffic accident ahead. And, they were certainly getting in the way of being able to reach them without traveling up the back of their cars and down over the front. But, Kayleen and Darryl were determined to find a way to reach it.

"Surely it can't be Natasha," Kayleen pleaded. "Do you think it is?"

"Sweetheart, you've asked me that twenty times and I'm telling you that I have no idea. We'll see when we get there. That's all I can say. I don't have x-ray vision or some alien whispering in my ear about who's in the cars ahead. Now, do me a favor and stop asking me. I'm nervous enough as it is trying to manoeuver my way through this traffic in this storm."

Kayleen was holding on to Darryl's right arm in a death grip. The only thing which protected his arm from bruising where her hands were was the grey, fluffy down coat he was wearing.

"I know, I know. I'm sorry, dear. I'm just so scared that it might be Natasha. First thing I knew was that Natasha had called me sounding on top of the world. She was going on and on about how great she felt, how it was God who was doing a work in her, and how she was going to meet up with Jenny to tell her . . . . . things. And, the next thing I knew there was a loud sound and a scream. I don't know if her phone went dead after that or not. I thought I could hear something after that, but Natasha wouldn't answer me back."

"How did you even know where to go?" Darryl asked.

"She said she was heading over to the little stationery store in the mall to get Jenny a present. We've been to that store before many times when she wanted to get Jenny something. Then I heard this crashing noise and now I'm seeing all these lights up there, right by the mall. I'm counting two firetrucks and one, two, three, four police cars. This doesn't look good, Darryl. Surely, it can't be Natasha."

Darryl grumbled something.

"Nope, I'm just NOT going to believe that it's her. She must have been nearby the wreck for the noise to be so loud and she's probably just standing around gawking or maybe trying to help somebody. That's what it is. And, that's why she won't answer her phone. Her phone probably dropped on the floor or something and just broke. Just broke right then and she hasn't gotten to a phone yet to call me back."

Stretching her neck to see over the cars in front of her, Kayleen couldn't sit still. Becoming exasperated, Kayleen blurted out, "What is wrong with all these people? Why are they going so slow? Haven't they ever seen a wreck before?"

Now, Darryl was beginning to get anxious. As they approached the intersection in the far right lane, where police were directing the through traffic, they could begin to see specific cars involved in the wreck. The snow was nearly blinding and visibility was only about twenty car lengths ahead.

Bile from Kayleen's acidic stomach began to churn as she recognized a car very similar to Natasha's. Whereas before, she could not stop her mouth from spewing streams of endless, anxiety-ridden words, Kayleen could no longer force words from her mouth. In the depths of her soul, she knew that Natasha was somewhere in that horribly twisted wreckage.

Kayleen's body began to grow numb.

"Darryl," she said in an almost eerily calm voice. "I need to get out of the car now. Right now. Just pull over here and stop just long enough for me to get out." As she unclicked her seatbelt, she glanced at Darryl who was staring back at a woman who seemed to have lost her mind.

Several police were standing in the cold, blanketing snow, directing traffic with whistles and flashlights. The one standing next to their car gave Darryl several tweets through his whistle demanding that he follow his instructions to move along. As Darryl stopped the car and rolled down his window to inform him that they might know someone in the wreckage, he noticed that Kayleen had already exited the car and was crossing lanes to get to the car which could be Natasha's.

The policeman who had been talking with Darryl noticed that his wife was trying to make her way over to the wreck. He spoke directly to her, but she didn't seem to hear him.

"Hey, lady! You can't go over there. Ma'am? Excuse me, ma'am," he yelled as he finally reached her. Brushing the snow out of his eyes, he again tried to convey his instructions that she not get involved.

It was then when he noticed that her face had begun to contort. Kayleen was close enough to the cars to know that one of them was, indeed, the one belonging to Natasha. She became frantic.

With arms flailing and voice screaming, Kayleen began to dart over to the car.

"NATASHA! NATASHA!" she shrieked.

Nothing could have prepared her for what she was about to witness.

Two EMTs from the ambulance were attempting to obtain vitals from a young, black woman from the wreckage while the policemen and firemen worked frantically to remove chrome and chassis to better reach the trapped people in both vehicles.

From across the road, another police woman had viewed Kayleen's face and movement toward one vehicle and ran over to stop her. Standing in front of Kayleen, the police woman grabbed both arms and tried to make eye contact in hopes of gaining some control over the situation. Speaking calmly, the woman asked Kayleen her name.

"What? Um, Kayleen. Kayleen's my name and I think I know the woman in this car. I just need to get to her. I think it's Natasha," she reported trying to contain her anguish and terror.

Meanwhile, somehow Darryl had managed to park his vehicle in the vast parking lot not far from the intersection and make his way over to his wife. As if it held any weight at all to the officer, Darryl informed her that this was his wife.

The police woman quickly glanced at him and said, "Then I'll say the same thing to you that I said to your wife. You can't be here. You're not safe in all this. You've got to move over to the side."

"But," Darryl interrupted, "we think we know the girl in the wreck. Please let us see if it's her. Please, officer."

"Are you two related to the woman?"

"Well, um . . ."

"Yes," Kayleen interposed. "I'm her sister. Um, an *older* sister."

The officer wasn't entirely convinced, but she wanted to do the right thing just in case. Who knew for sure whether or not they were related, but she didn't want it on her conscious if they were and she withheld information from them.

"You're gonna have to wait here. Get me? Stay right here and I'll see what I can find out."

As they watched the officer walk away, both noticed that reality seemed to go in slow motion. Darryl wrapped his arms around Kayleen as if trying to keep her simultaneously protected and warm, yet feeling like a failure at both.

Both Darryl and Kayleen strained their eyes and necks in hopes of catching a glimpse into what was happening, yet were unable to glean one single truth from the chaos. So many people were working around the cars that it was difficult to determine the number of involved drivers and vehicles. The snow wasn't helpful either.

After what seemed like hours, Kayleen said, "What's taking her so long? I can't stand this anymore. I have to go over there and see."

"Just stay here, Kayleen. She said she'll be right back with some information."

"I can't, Darryl. I just can't."

Breaking lose from her husband's arms, Kayleen sprinted over to the crushed cars. Suddenly, she stopped just feet away from the rear of the car.

Slowly and cautiously, she stepped closer to the vehicle. She, too, felt herself begin to move in slow motion as she caught glimpses of vague but familiar sites.

The first thing she saw that made her stomach lunge was the familiar face of a beautiful black woman whose neck was bent over in an unnatural way.

Somewhere, off in the distance, Kayleen heard a low-pitched voice telling her to step away. Another voice, to the right and back of her, was telling her to come back. But, all of these sounds were distorted and not making any sense at all.

Another step closer. Slowly, as if against her will. Yet, a presence was drawing her closer and closer to the nightmare. She began to feel her eyes stinging with wetness.

From behind, Darryl ran to her, grabbing her arm. "No, Kayleen. Stop!"

But, both knew that stopping was an irreversible act. There was no backing off now. Kayleen had to know. Had to see for herself.

The dullish, gray coat was questionable and certainly not confirmation that this was, in fact, Natasha, but there was no denying the truly distinguishable orange scarf which draped partly around her neck and partly over the seat. Seeing the scarf was the one thing which caused her to stop dead in her tracks.

Suddenly, reality returned to normal pace. Some raced to tend to the occupants of the cars while officers paced off a wide, protective circle which would prevent intrusive gawkers.

The sobs from Kayleen confirmed to others that she was not merely a gawker, but a loved one of one of the crash victims. She was shouting the girl's name repeatedly while EMT's worked on her while waiting for the jaws of life to arrive and fetch her out of the wreckage.

Darryl gleaned from the two EMT's faces who were working on Natasha that this was a critical situation. He felt so helpless. There was nothing to do but wait. And pray. Darryl turned Kayleen around and held her. As they clutched each other, they both began to pray, demanding that God save Natasha's life. Their prayers were heartfelt and fervent. No prayers could have been more boldly pleaded or passionately stated before the throne of God. Natasha's life simply must be spared.

"JENNY! OH, MY LORD!" Kayleen thought of Jenny and the boys. Turning to Darryl, she implored him to call Cathey and Randy. The kids need to know. They will need to meet us at the hospital, just as soon as we find out which one. They've got to know, Darryl. Call 'em. I can't do it."

"Calm down, Kayleen. Let's just wait until we find out whether or not . . . ."

Kayleen shot him a terrified look.

"I mean, let's find out what the situation is and then I'll call them. Let's not get them all riled up before we even know what's going on or where to go."

The occupant from the other car now seemed to beg for attention. He wasn't trying to get *their* attention, specifically, but his odd behavior pulled their eyes. They couldn't get a full view of him, but could certainly hear loud shouting coming from the direction of his car.

Kayleen recognized that there was something about his voice that wasn't quite right. His words were barely understandable, not because he was hurt but because he sounded as though he was slurring. And, he was yelling in the direction of Natasha's car.

As she began to put the pieces of the ugly puzzle together, a boiling broth of rage stirred deep within Kayleen. She couldn't believe what she was hearing. This other injured "victim" seemed to be hurling insults at Natasha, blaming *her* for the accident, for ruining his new, burnt orange mustang, and for causing him such inconvenience. Swear words streamed from his slimy mouth landing atop Natasha's broken and battered body.

Though he was covered in blood, he was at least able to walk around. He was mobile! But, not Natasha. She was still being assessed by EMTs.

They were still unsure about the extent of the damage to Natasha, and his outrageous behavior was certainly not helping the situation. The police tried to subdue him, but had difficulty due to the unusual strength of this young man. Kayleen knew that alcohol was the culprit. From her own experience, she knew that, for some, alcohol acted like liquid power. Curbing one's anxiety and igniting one's rage could make a deadly cocktail in these situations.

Man-handling the young, drunken assaulter, the police grabbed his arms, turned him around, shoved him up against the car and cuffed him. While watching the action, Kayleen also heard the strong words from the police.

"Sir, please calm down. Sir? Please stop struggling. You are under arrest. You have the right to remain silent (but, obviously not the ability), you have the right to an attorney . . . ."

This was all happening so fast and yet it seemed as though they had been at the scene for hours.

Darryl tuned into what some of the passers-by were yelling.

"Hey, get that drunk off the road, will ya?"

"Are you all alright?" another called out.

But, the driver who touched his heart the most was the one where the man and his wife looked upon them with such compassion that it made his spine tingle. The male driver removed his hat while the woman seemed to whisper something with bowed head.

Darryl was touched that the couple would offer their prayers for him and his wife. That is, until Darryl realized that they were not looking at Kayleen or him. Their stares stretched over them to focus on Natasha's car.

Darryl followed their line of site to the target. Natasha. The EMTs were performing life-saving measures on a body that had seemed to go limp. There was a rush of activity around Natasha.

"GET HER INTO THE AMBULANCE, NOW!"

Another flurry of activity had completed this command and Natasha was whisked into the back of the ambulance and doors shut.

Kayleen broke free from her husband's grasp and ran over to the ambulance yelling frantically, "What's wrong? Where are you taking her? Is she dead? Can I go with her?"

"Ma'am, stand back," said the policeman. "Give 'em room to work."

But, Kayleen would not be so easily dissuaded.

"I need to go with her. I need to find out how she is," she pleaded. "We were just going to meet for some coffee. Please, I *need* to go with her."

Hearing the impotent pleas from his wife, Darryl rushed to her side.

"Kayleen, honey, let them work. They're just doing their job."

One of the men in the truck flipped on the siren, triggering an avalanche of anxiety.

"Where are they taking her?" Darryl asked the EMT.

"Wait here. I'll find out." Turning to Joe who was climbing in the driver's seat, the policeman asked, "Hey, Joe, where ya takin' her?"

Without so much as a turn of the head, the EMT driver called back over his shoulder. "Taking her to County General." The door shut and the ambulance began to move.

Without another word, Darryl grabbed Kayleen's arm and began to run towards their parked car. Kayleen didn't know which sight would be harder to handle: the current one or the one they were about to encounter.

Either way, they were going to see this horrible thing through with Natasha.

Kayleen knew what she must do.

She had to make a difficult phone call.

She had to call the Abbott's and have them head for County General immediately.

"What do I tell them, Darryl? I don't know what to say. This is all so awful. How am I gonna explain this horrible thing to them? To the boys? To Jenny?"

Ever the logical one, Darryl calmly said, "Just say that Natasha's been in a wreck and they're taking her to the hospital. Just keep it simple. We really don't know anything more than that."

"But, but, they were doing CPR on her. Should I tell them that? Should I let them know how serious this is?"

"Would you like me to call them, honey?"

Trying to calm herself down some, Kayleen reached for her phone. "No, I'll call. You just drive."

Dialing the number, Kayleen waited for a voice.

"Cathey? This is Kayleen . . . ."

Kayleen's mouth went as dry as the Sahara desert and her mind went utterly blank. Tears formed in her eyes and she began to sob.

Darryl took the phone from her.

"Cathey? This is Darryl, Kayleen's husband. I'm afraid I have some bad news."

CHAPTER 15

Off the icy road and into the dark abyss, the mangled car could hardly be seen. Two of the occupants inside were moving, but only two. The other two were still.

Silence.

After some moments, Ben groaned as he turned towards his wife. Reaching for her in the dark, he began to whisper her name. Inhaling was painful due to the air bag which had deployed into his chest and lungs. He wondered how long they'd been there and if he had been unconscious. Thoughts spun slowly, as though in a vat of molasses.

Oh, yes, he remembered, they had been on the icy road, and then they started sliding, and then he saw the fence and . . .

"OH, MY GOD! Amy? Kids? You okay?"

No movement from the back seat, but Amy stirred.

"Ohh, ouch," Amy said before opening her eyes. Suddenly filled with panic, she yelled for her husband and children. "I can't see anything. Ben? Are you okay? Monica? Jenny?"

Ben strained to see into the darkness, but failed to find even a speck of light. But, then he suddenly remembered that the glove compartment could offer the gift of a flashlight. Reaching in, he felt around and finally bumped into it. Hope! He was grateful that this was not just an ordinary flashlight. No, this was a big one; one fit for a big truck or SUV.

Upon flashing it upon Amy's face, Ben was startled by the blood running down the right side of her face. She had to have taken a fairly good blow to the head to release such a stream of red.

Ben looked around for something to put on it to stop the bleeding. Finding his gloves, he gingerly placed one on the open wound and told her to continue putting pressure on it.

"I-I can do it. Just check on the kids," Amy blurted out with a frightened tone.

Turning around in his seat caused a myriad of pain in multiple places on his body. Both air bags had deployed causing burns to his arms and face. He figured the same would, quite likely, have happened to Amy. But, additionally, the tops of his knees ached and felt badly bruised, probably due to the steering wheel having somehow slammed into them. Both sides of his face stung—still more collateral damage from the air bag. But, his left wrist was the place which demanded his most immediate attention. It may be broken, he thought, but he couldn't tend to that injury just yet. The girls' lives were his utmost concern.

Reaching with his right hand to open the car door was quite awkward, but his left hand hurt far too much to use it. The door was somewhat uncooperative, so the adrenaline pumping through his veins in addition to a few good pushes with his left hip opened the crushed door.

"Monica! Jenny! You guys okay?"

Hearing moans from the backseat charged him with hope.

The back door was much easier to rip open than his own.

"Daddy!" Monica shouted.

"I'm here, baby girl. You alright? You hurt anywhere?"

Shining the flashlight on her gave him immediate relief. No blood! That's good. He tenderly unfastened her seat belt as she began to slowly move her body parts.

"Where does it hurt, Monica?"

"Um, I don't know. I don't think anywhere. We had all these blankets and pillows around us." Remembering her dearest friend, Monica whipped her neck around to see how Jenny was.

"Jenny?" No response. "Jenny, you okay?"

Fearing the worst, Ben instructed Monica to move off to the side so that he could see more clearly. When Monica began to cry, her father told her to carefully climb into the front seat and stay with her mother.

Straining to hear any type of sound, Ben kept calling out to Jenny. Please, God, let me find her safe and alive.

Gently, he began to peel back blanket after blanket. His hand bumped into something, but he couldn't tell if it was a body or another blanket. Why wasn't she answering? Please, Jenny, answer me!

"Jenny, honey, I need to know that you're alright—that you're not hurt in any way."

Making his way through more clutter, he discovered a small suitcase that had bounced into the back seat and some other unidentified items.

With more determination and dread, Ben frantically reached across the entire seat. One way or another, he was going to get to her this time. Punching his right hand into the dark abyss, he felt his knuckles strike against an opposing force—something very large, cold, and hard.

"What is this?" he cried out.

Shining the bold flashlight on the foreign object, Ben's jaw dropped in horror.

Hearing his gasp, Amy shouted, "Ben? What is it? Ben?"

"Oh, my God," his voice oozed slowly.

"Ben, you're scaring me. What is it? What did you find?"

Grasping for the calmest voice he could find, he said, "It's a big boulder."

"What? A what? Did you say a boulder?" Amy began to panic. "Monica, sit over in Daddy's seat for a minute. I've got to get out and help him." But, as she tried to open the door, she could not do so past an inch. Ben turned the flashlight onto Amy and the obstacle she encountered—a boulder almost identical to the one which had invaded the back seat. The very seat Jenny had occupied just moments earlier.

Ben looked at the heap where Jenny should have been. The shards from her broken window crumpled against each other as he moved the pillow away from the door making an unwelcome tingling noise. The pillow contained no heat from a small child's body, but that didn't really mean anything, right, he wondered; or, did it? All of the items in the back seat were cold by now; blankets, seat belts, pillows, all having come in contact with the freezing rain. It was all stone cold.

As he began to back his way out of the seat, Ben's left elbow landed atop a soft object on the floor giving way under the weight of his body.

"JENNY?" He began to frantically discard the debris which covered a small body.

"OH, GOD! PLEASE. PLEASE KEEP HER ALIVE! PLEASE LET ME FIND HER ALIVE! JENNY?"

The other two waited with baited breath to hear the plight of the child.

Amy couldn't stand it anymore. He was taking too long. She turned around in her seat to help though she was in much pain.

Monica began to scream and cry simultaneously. She felt so helpless and so scared. Her mind began to spin with questions. Didn't she feel Jenny next to her just moments ago? Wasn't she just talking with her? How long ago had it been that Jenny had instructed her to hunker down under the blankets and pillows? And, why wasn't she moving? Why can't Daddy hurry so that he could tell her something about her friend?

Reaching the bottom of the pile, Ben discovered Jenny's limp body.

"Okay, everybody, I found her," he said to Monica and his wife.

"Well, get her out, Daddy!" Monica cried. "Pull her up. Is she okay? Is she dead? Is she hurt?"

"Just a minute. I can't just yank her up; I don't know if she has a broken neck or back. I have to be very, very careful. So, just hang on a minute." Turning to Jenny, Ben grabbed his flashlight and pointed it on her. What he saw both surprised and relieved him.

"Jenny? Can you hear me?" Then he yelled to the others, "She's alive. Thank God, she's alive."

Amy's gratitude prayer was simple and barely audible, but heartfelt. Looking over her seat and down at Jenny, Amy saw a petrified little girl who was having difficulty saying anything.

"Maybe she's in shock," Amy said. "Put one of those blankets around her, carefully though."

What scared Ben the most, though, was not what he *could* see, but what he *couldn't* see. There was no blood. Shouldn't there be blood when a boulder smashes into you? Or, does it mean that if you're not bleeding on the outside that you might be bleeding on the inside? And, if this was the case, then she would need to be taken to a hospital immediately.

First things first, though, Ben considered. He had to see if he could get through to Jenny somehow, especially since he had no cell phone coverage.

"Jenny, honey, can you hear me?" Ben reached his right hand towards her face and gently placed it on her cheek. He could see that she was following his hand with her eyes now, which gave him great hope.

"Is she conscious?" Amy asked Ben.

"Um, I think so. She's watching me," he responded. "Jenny, are you hurt somewhere? Can you understand me?" No response. "Honey, if you can hear me, squeeze my hand." Waiting for a response, he grimly focused on his right hand. Come on, Jenny, he cheered silently. Squeeze my hand. SQUEEZE IT!

After what seemed hours, he finally thought he felt something. Was it a squeeze?

"Jenny! Did you squeeze my hand? Can you hear me?"

Then it happened. Jenny began to move. She looked directly into Ben's eyes as her own came alive. She opened her mouth as though she might say something.

Ben waited.

But, Monica couldn't stand it anymore.

"Daddy, what is she doing?"

Smiling, he replied, "Jenny's with us. She's trying to get up."

Grabbing ahold of Ben's arm, Jenny began to lift herself up.

Ben tried to spot any damage to her small frame, but found none.

"What happened? And, why am I down here?" she asked.

Ben was never before so happy to have been asked such a question. As he continued to help her up on the seat, Ben explained the turn of events as best as he could remember. He inspected her arms, legs, and head and was glad to report that she had no injuries.

"Do you feel alright, Jenny? Do you feel any pain? Are you nauseous?"

"Um, no," she replied while checking herself over. "I think I'm alright. I don't especially hurt anywhere. My neck's kinda sore, but it doesn't really hurt a lot."

Thankful beyond words, Ben sat back in the seat and thought about what they should do. The storm seemed to be letting up a bit and he wondered if he should walk to the nearest house—which was probably Grandma's—and call someone. But, he didn't want to leave anyone behind in the cold.

As Ben was trying to recall how far it would be to his mother's house, he heard something outside the car.

Appearing from nowhere was a person with a flashlight.

"Hello? Anybody in there?" this voice asked.

The voice was unfamiliar to Ben yet sounded friendly and concerned.

"Yes, yes, we're down here. Can you get us some help?" This person seemed to come from out of nowhere. Was this man on foot? Was he driving? If so, Ben had not heard the vehicle approach.

"Help's already on the way. I already called the ambulance, but it's gonna take 'em a bit to get out here."

Help's on the way. Best words Ben had ever heard!

"Thanks. I appreciate it. I think we're all fine . . . I mean . . . as good as anyone can be after what just happened. But I think my wife needs to be checked out. Her head's bleeding and I don't want to take any chances."

Wondering if he could trust this man-from-nowhere, Ben tried to get some information about him. He certainly didn't want some axe murderer coming after them, especially having just survived an accident like this! At least this man was still up on top of the road above them. A bit of distance between them relieved his wavering anxiety.

"You live around here?" Ben called up to the stranger in the night.

"Yup. I live just right up the road a piece. Not many people get out here on this road."

Ben did not find comfort in his last statement, though he knew it to be true.

The ironic part about this situation was that this helper-man was feeling similarly. He, too, wanted to know more about these people. He didn't know whether or not to go down and help or just wait for the ambulance to arrive. Maybe he, too, could gain some insight into this family.

"Yeah, not many people come up in this part of the woods. Y'all from around here?"

Ben wondered how much information he should give this guy, but then decided that he could offer a bit about them because this stranger was, at least, helping them.

"No. We're not from here. We came to visit my mother when this storm came up over us."

"Your mother? You mean your mom lives around here—way out here? Shoot, I probably know her then. What's her name?"

Ben decided to take yet another chance.

"Her name's Mrs. Beasley. Margaret Beasley. You know her?"

"Why, shoot yeah. Mrs. Beasley's my next door neighbor. She's lived there for, oh, forever I guess. She was in that house when my family moved in next door."

"Oh, my gosh," Ben said to Amy. This is Mom's neighbor!"

Amy breathed a huge sigh of relief.

"Are you Tom? Tom, isn't it?"

"Oh, no. Tom's my dad. I'm Tommy. Well, Tom, Jr. actually. But, everybody 'round here just calls me Tommy."

Tired of yelling, Tommy decided that it would be safe to climb down and join them. "Hang on, I'm comin' down."

"Be careful, Tommy. This is really slick, and there're boulders down here. Don't hurt yourself."

Monica and Jenny looked at each other in stark terror and sudden amazement. They had just realized that this stranger, this man who had been helping them was, in fact, Mr. Hunk who lived next door to Monica's grandmother. Mr. Hunk! THE Mr. Hunk! The same one who had captured, and held, their attention previously on numerous visits. This idol, who had been the subject of numerous late-night conversations between the two young girls, was coming down the hill to rescue them. *What a hero!* they both sighed simultaneously.

Suddenly, their physical pain no longer held their attentions' first place.

* * *

CATHEY AND RANDY ABBOTT could hardly believe their ears when they heard the news from Kayleen about Natasha. They both stared at each other for what seemed like an hour before one of them finally said, "Get the children ready. We're going to the hospital."

It took another thirty minutes to round up their boys, dress them in warm coats and mittens, and get out the door.

Cathey found it hard not to panic, but she focused on the children and explaining where they were going in such a hurry.

Randy focused on carefully racing to the hospital. He knew that the hospital was a good ten miles from them, but he would try his best to arrive before . . . well, before the worst could happen.

Questions swirled in Cathey's anxiety-filled mind, but she dared not begin to ask even one question. One question would summon the next, and so on, until they would arrive in exactly the same place—not knowing anything more than they already did.

Randy's cheeks were bright red, but not from being warm, though he had his warmest coat on. They were red from adrenaline streaming through his system. It was the old "fight or flight" response. And, this was certainly a trauma which would trigger just such a needed response.

Because of the weather, it took the Abbott family about forty minutes to arrive at the bustling hospital. One ambulance pulled away as another took its place under the awning of the Emergency Room doors.

Not knowing exactly where they should go, Cathey called Kayleen as Randy gathered the children from the back seat.

"Be careful, kids. The parking lot is slick," Randy called out.

Cathey grabbed Randy's arm with one hand as she motioned with the other for the children to quickly follow. Kayleen had told her that they were in the waiting area of the ER just inside the door.

Meeting them as the sliding door swished open, Kayleen hugged Cathey. She did not want to look into the naïve faces of the children. All they knew was that Natasha, their birth mother, had been in a car wreck and that it was fairly bad.

"Where is she?" Cathey asked.

"They've got her back there," Kayleen explained as she pointed to the trauma area.

"How long have you been here?"

"Not long. But, it seems like forever. No word yet. They're not telling us anything," Kayleen said.

"Well, they've got to tell us SOMETHING!"

Randy placed a calming hand on Cathey's shoulder.

"I'll go up and ask. You and the boys stay here with Kayleen," Randy volunteered.

The boys became unusually quiet. They knew, somehow, that their mother needed them to be on their best behavior.

Kayleen sat down, but more than ever, she wanted to pace. But, she would sit with Cathey and they would pray. Together, prayer was enforcing. Certainly strengthening. Empowering for whatever awaited them. Rocking back and forth, Kayleen closed her eyes and prayed nearly inaudibly. Cathey joined in prayer, but her eyes needed to act as radar for the children.

Cathey's mouth moved and, suddenly, she heard an odd question from Jeremiah, their oldest son's, mouth.

"Mama? Does God hear your prayers when your eyes are open? I think you're s'posed to shut 'em real, real tight, like Miss Kayleen. Otherwise, the prayers won't work. Close your eyes, Mama; close 'em!"

Both Kayleen and Cathey paused and gazed into the young boy's pleading eyes.

Wrapping him up with both arms, Cathey turned his head towards hers and reassured him that God most certainly hears all prayers, whether or not eyes are opened or closed, whether one is standing or kneeling, and regardless of the words being prayed. She explained that we needn't say fancy prayers, as some people are prone to do. God just wants an open heart; one which searches for His face. All her children understood that

God was huge and loving, but Cathey knew that the children needed to be reminded that God was with them all the time. They were not going through this alone.

Jeremiah, having been reassured, meandered back to his chair next to his brothers. His brother, David, had found a small fleet of cars in his pocket and was utterly delighted to see that he hadn't lost them. The cars were only "on loan" to his pocket from his room's play garage. The twins, having witnessed David's discovery, began to transform the magazines on the nearby table into the Old West's bumpy, winding, and treacherous roads. They always found a way to convert any normal-looking environment into magical mountainous or raceway roads. Creativity surely ran in their genetics, for all the children displayed large dollops of it.

As the boys were playing, Randy returned with no news.

"They're still working on her, I guess." "There's nothing else they can tell us. So, I just reminded them that we were as close as any family member would be, as far as they were concerned, and they should let us know as soon as possible when they got any kind of word on her. I don't know if they will or not. But, if we haven't heard something in fifteen minutes, I'll go back up and ask them."

Sitting down next to Cathey, Randy looked at the boys playing around the coffee table in front of them, and then glanced cautiously at Kayleen.

Darryl returned from having parked the car and visited the restroom. Sitting beside Kayleen and placing an arm around her shoulder, he asked, "So, what did I miss? Have we heard anything?"

"Nothing. They haven't told us anything yet! I'm just almost beside myself with worry."

"Now, Kayleen, maybe *no news is good news.* Know what I mean?"

"I know. It's just so hard to wait."

Cathey was having difficulty waiting, too. They had still been unable to reach Jenny or the people she went on a trip with. Turning to Randy she asked, "Have you tried calling again?"

Sighing heavily, Randy responded, "No, I called just a bit ago. Still goes straight over to voicemail. I'm tired of leaving messages. I'll call again here in a minute. I just want to sit down for a bit. If I can't get ahold of them within the hour, I think I'll call the highway patrol and see if they have had any reports of wrecks up there."

"This is all just too, too much to handle. I don't know how much longer I can stand this."

"Okay. I'll call in a minute, but I just want to find out more about the wreck." Turning to Kayleen, he asked, "So, can you tell us what you saw or what happened?"

Keeping her tone low so as the boys wouldn't hear, Kayleen passed along all she knew and had seen.

About two l-o-n-g hours later, the doctor emerged from behind the doors. The clerk at the front desk had pointed the way towards her "relatives."

Approaching their group, Dr. Larson asked, "Are you the family of Natasha?"

Everyone stood except for the kids who were playing on the floor. But, even they turned their heads towards the man in the funny, sky blue scrubs who had stopped to address them.

Randy responded by telling the doctor that they were all here for Natasha.

"What can you tell us?" Kayleen asked urgently.

"Is one of you a family member?"

Kayleen was afraid that they weren't going to tell them anything about her condition if there wasn't a family member present.

Stepping forward, Kayleen spoke up.

"I'm a family member. She's my younger sister." Kayleen had lied.

Dr. Larson looked over at her suspiciously.

"My, um, much younger sister." Kayleen had lied again.

Pausing momentarily, Dr. Larson gazed at her before continuing.

"I'm afraid it's not good news." Noticing that everyone in the waiting room was staring at them, Dr. Larson asked them to step over to the side and into a small room.

"She's lost a lot of blood. There were many external abrasions and bruisings. She also received a nasty blow to the head."

All waited with baited breath for recognizable and formidable words of hope. Words like, "optimism," "out of danger," "in recovery," but none of these words were uttered.

"What are you telling us, doctor?" Kayleen begged.

The children joined the adults leaving their cars wrecked in the magazine mess.

"What's wrong, Mama?" asked the youngest of the brothers while making his way over to Cathey.

The man in the sky blue scrubs continued his explanation, though his words were impossible to fully comprehend.

Scratching his head, Dr. Larson searched for words.

"We knew Natasha's external injuries were widespread. Several of us had been working on her when her vitals crashed."

Dr. Larson expected them to comprehend what he was telling them, but he could tell that they were dazed. After deeply inhaling, he looked straight into Kayleen's eyes and, with a softening voice, continued.

"The internal bleeding was extensive. We worked on her for a long time, but it was impossible to stop her from bleeding out."

No response from the group.

"We tried to revive her, but were unable to."

Less response.

This part was the most difficult and hated part of the doctor's job. He hated delivering such bad news to families. *Why did I choose to be a doctor?*

"I-uh, I'm sorry to have to tell you this, but your sister has died."

Slowly, the doctor's words became a hideous reality, first to Kayleen and Darryl, then Cathey and Randy, and finally the children. Never in a million years would they have thought their evening would have turned out this dreadfully.

Physical pain coursed through Kayleen's veins. Falling into her husband's arms, she wailed aloud. Nothing could have prepared her to cope with this amount of grief.

Randy and Cathey felt the need to contain their sense of deep loss due to little childrens' eyes searching theirs for answers. Their parents rallied around the boys. Randy knelt beside David, Nathaniel, and Nehemiah, the youngest ones. Cathey sat down in the hard, worn, connected seats and pulled Jeremiah in close. Hugs could not make this pain flee. Cathey felt helpless as she looked into Jeremiah's big, brown eyes which were beginning to fill with tears. He was nine years of age and old enough to know about death. Not everything, but enough to know that he would not be seeing his birth mother again. Not in this life anyway. His small, stoic frame communicated to his father that he was mature enough to *keep it together* for the sake of the younger ones.

Little David, who was five, searched everyones' faces for guidance and direction. *No one his age should have to face this,* Randy thought. *Actually, none of them should.*

How was he going to explain this to them? At seven years old, the twins, Nehemiah and Nathaniel, were not old enough to comprehend all of this. They knew that something had gone terribly, terribly wrong, but were waiting for their parents to fill them in on what had happened.

Dr. Larson helplessly stood by. This was the worst part of his job. He knew adults were far more eqipped to handle this type of loss than children. And, it was the children, in particular, for which his heart hurt. Losing his own mother when he was in his early teenage years had developed compassion and empathy for the grieving. In fact, this was the sole reason Dr. Larson went on to become a doctor. He wanted to help heal the injured and sick so that they would be saved from the life-altering grief which always companioned loss. If he could prevent just one person from experiencing this heart-wrenching sadness and emptiness, then all his hard work would have been worth it.

But, this night, with these people, Dr. Larson was unable to prevent it. As tears pooled in his eyes, he took off his blue head wrap and extended his condolences.

"I'm so very sorry for your loss," was all he could utter. Empty words, though heart-felt, could never erase what he had hoped to save them from.

Suddenly, Jeremiah stepped forward.

"Um, exuse me," his young voice said. "Dr. Larson?"

Turning towards the young boy, Dr. Larson stopped to address the lad. "Yes?"

Lifting his chin up, Jeremiah asked, "Can we see her?"

Tilting his head as though not to understand the young boy's request, Dr. Larson's eyes begged the boy to repeat what he had just asked.

Can we see . . . . I mean, may we see my moth . . . um, may we see Miss Natasha?"

Dr. Larson searched his parents' eyes for their opinion.

"Ohhh, honey, you don't know what you're asking," Cathey answered. "That would be very, very difficult for you to see, don't you think?"

"I agree," said Randy out of love and concern. "I don't think you're ready to do that."

But, Jeremiah would not be so easily deterred.

"But, Daddy, I want to see her."

Randy continued with his concern.

"Jeremiah, son, listen to me," Randy said kneeling down so that he could look Jeremiah in the eyes. "Do you understand what you're asking? Do you understand that Miss Natasha is . . . not with us anymore? She's passed on to eternity to be with Jesus."

"I know, Dad. I know she's dead. I just want to say good-bye. That's all."

Randy and Cathey were truly stumped. They knew he would be able to see her body at the viewing in a few days. They turned to the doctor for direction.

"What do you think, Dr. Larson?"

Dr. Larson's expression softened as he turned to the young boy.

"You must understand, young man, that this woman is not ready to receive visitors yet. She would want you to wait a couple of days before seeing her. Then, you can take all the time you need to say good-bye. How does that sound?"

Cathey and Randy were touched by the doctor's careful and sensitive response to their son's request. In fact, they all wanted to see Natasha but certainly not looking the way they had imagined.

Jeremiah thought about it a minute before answering.

"Well, okay. As long as I get to say good-bye."

"I'm sure your parents will be certain to make sure that happens. I know how important it is to say good-bye to a loved one. You trust your parents, don't you?"

"Of course!" Jeremiah quickly responded.

"Then, let them handle all the details and they'll let you know when you can go see her. It'll only be a day or two. Deal?" Dr. Larson extended his hand to Jeremiah for a man's handshake as if to close the deal.

"Deal," Jeremiah said before turning to his parents to make sure they were in on this deal.

Randy nodded his head. "We'll make sure of it, son. We all want to say good-bye to her."

The young doctor winked at Jeremiah before again giving his condolences to everyone.

Their group huddled in the waiting room while life in the hospital halls and outside world continued as if life was supposed to go on as normal.

Turning to Randy, Cathey said, "We have to find a way of getting hold of Jenny."

Jenny.

Their sweet Jenny. The one who would be most affected by Natasha's death. The oldest of the sibling bunch who had come six years ago to make and complete Randy and Cathey's family. This same little child who had previously been placed so often in the position of taking care of Natasha, her birth mother, and her brothers.

How would she take this news?

And, where was she?

Why couldn't they get ahold of her?

CHAPTER 16

The night was dark without a moon shining largely above them. Though the snow storm had finally lessened, it surrounded them with chilling presence. The wrecked car was impossible to sit in comfortably and the big boulders were harder than the ice.

Far off in the distance they could hear the ambulance's siren. No one knew how long they had been waiting. Maybe an hour. They had tried climbing the boulders up to the road, but it was too slippery. *No more injuries*, Amy had said.

The red lights became quickly visible once the ambulance rounded the hill. It would take them only a bit longer to arrive.

When they did arrive, the EMT's said they were able to locate them due to their waving flashlights. Tommy had given them great instructions, but they wouldn't have known exactly where the vehicle had departed the road.

Bringing each passenger of the car up onto the road was challenging, but they completed the task in less than half an hour after quickly assessing them for broken bones. Finding none, the EMT's knew they would be able to get them into the ambulance for further assessment.

After treating Amy's slight head wound, Ben's sprained hand, and finding no apparent injuries on the young girls, the EMT's suggested they go to the hospital for x-rays and further observation.

Ben and Amy agreed. They were certain that they had no further, hidden injuries, but were worried about Monica and Jenny who had barely said two words in the last hour. Monica's parents had no idea that the reason for their silence was not because of any injuries, but because they were in the presence of *Tommy*.

With stomachs twisted and tongues tied, Jenny and Monica spent the last hour or so looking at him before turning and smiling at each other. At one point, Tommy had approached them and asked if they were hurt.

121

The only sounds that escaped their mouths were two grunts and a nod of Monica's head.

Confused by Monica's nod, Tommy searched for clarification.

"So, you *are* hurt then?"

Appalled at her stupidity in his presence, Monica stuttered.

"Y-yes. Um, I mean, n-no, I'm not hurt. I'm f-fine is what I mean."

As Ben glanced oddly at the girls, Amy suddenly became aware of what was going on between the two, and smiled. It was as clear as running stream water that the two had become quite enamored of him. She had even suspected as much last summer when they visited, but didn't want to say anything to the girls. Amy had noticed then that they had been studying Tommy in between bouts of giggling. She could now see that their crushes on him had not ended with that trip.

Tommy's medium, stocky build and tight, worn jeans caused enough of a stir in Monica's and Jenny's souls, but his tanned face and long, blondish hair were what had tickled their hearts the most. They hadn't seen him since last summer so they took time to survey him to detect any differences. His full mustache was the only noted change—and, to them, it was a good change indeed! It made him look older and more sophisticated which, in turn, made them feel older than their brief eleven years of age.

Never before had they been given the chance to touch his thick hair, but on this snowy night, both had been allowed by the hunk gods to touch his hands. Tommy had helped the girls up the embankment while the EMT's assisted Ben and Amy. Jenny and Monica had become aware that his hands were those of a working man; rough, strong, big hands able to fully engulf their small hands and lift them up quickly.

Tommy had muscles, too, from what they remembered. They had seen them last summer as they watched him lift bales of hay and large machinery on their property. Jenny and Monica had spent hours staring out the guest room's window which overlooked his property. Such a hard worker! Took orders from his father pretty well. From what they had seen, Tommy's father would show up, bark an order or two, pat him on the back, and then leave. Tommy would then shake his head, laugh at something his father had said, and return to his work.

Jenny and Monica had concluded that, though his father looked tough, he enjoyed a good, working relationship with his son. And, it had not escaped the girls that Tommy had received his build and good looks from his father. Though Tommy was a bit taller and more muscular, he shared many features with big Tom.

The ambulance escorted the four of them to the hospital. Tommy left in his own truck and he and Ben had agreed that they would try to tow his SUV out tomorrow or the next day—whenever the weather would next allow. They had also agreed that Tommy would stop by Ben's mother's house on his way home to apprise her of the situation. Tommy would try to assuage any fears of hers and inform Mrs. Beasley that Ben would call his mom from the hospital.

Saddened that they couldn't ride back with Tommy, Monica and Jenny plotted how they could show their gratitude. In whispered voices, they brain-stormed ideas. Maybe they could bake something and personally take it over; or, maybe they could make a card and hand deliver it to Tommy; maybe they would just do both, they decided. Using this latter plan, each would then be given the opportunity to carry something over to their hero, the hunk.

What an evening, Jenny thought to herself. *Who would have thought that this early-evening disaster would have ended in a monumental blessing!*

Interrupting Jenny's thoughts, Amy told her that they would give her parents a phone call as soon as they arrived at the hospital.

Earlier, Jenny had thought of nothing other than wanting, no, frantically needing, to talk to her parents. But, now, after these later events, her thoughts drifted to . . . other, far more pleasant things.

*   *   *

LATE IN THE EVENING, Cathey had decided to take a break from attempting to reach Amy's cell phone. The phone immediately went over to a stranger's voice, informing them that the caller that they had dialed was out of the area.

The Abbott family was able to arrive home safely and intact, though it felt as if they were operating on auto-pilot. Still dazed from the horrible events of the evening, Cathey and Randy tucked the children in, one by one. Neither of their parents had offered to read them a book, which indicated to the children the degree of seriousness of the situation. They couldn't remember a time that their parents had not read them at least one book at nighttime.

Jeremiah had quietly dressed in pajamas, brushed his teeth, and slipped under the sheets and blankets of his bed while Nehemiah, Nathaniel, and David needed more direction and participation in the goal. The chaos of the evening had dropped a good deal of adrenaline into David's little system, so he required extra efforts in calming down. The twins, Nehemiah and Nathaniel, asked a few questions about the car wreck, but none about Natasha. Randy was aware that neither fully understood the ramifications of tonight's events, but they certainly understood anything having to do with cars for they had each received multiple little muscle cars for Christmas presents. He imagined that, over the next few weeks, the boys would repeatedly play out the wreck until their young minds could make some sense out of it. He dreaded the thought of watching his children grieve the loss of their birth mother.

"They're just too young to have to face something like this," Randy said angrily.

"I know, honey," Cathey responded. "This whole thing seems like such a horrible, horrible nightmare—like it couldn't have really happened, and that I'll wake up and this whole thing will be over."

Suddenly, their phone rang.

"Why would someone be calling this late?"

Cathey rushed over to it and answered it quickly.

"Hello?"

"Cathey? Oh, good! This is Amy Beasley."

"Oh, thank God. Are you all alright? I have been trying to call you and haven't been able to get through," Cathey answered frantically.

"Yes, we're all okay. There's been a huge snow and ice storm up here and we'd lost all cell phone coverage in this pocket. It's pretty remote, but now that we're at the . . . I mean, now that we're in town, my phone works. But, Cathey, I need to tell you something, though. Jenny's fine; she's just fine, but we're at the hospital."

"The hospital? What happenend?"

As far as Cathey was concerned, Amy couldn't talk fast enough.

"Is Randy there with you?"

"Of course he is. Now you're scaring me. What happened?"

Amy recounted the details of the day's horrors while Cathey listened disbelievingly. Randy ran to the study to listen in from that extension.

Relieved to hear that everyone had fared fairly well despite the severity of the accident, Cathey then took her turn explaining their evening's deadly outcome.

Amy had wandered down the hospital hallway, out of earshot of the girls.

The shudder from the shockwaves coursed through Amy veins as she listened to their night's account.

Ben had been looking for Amy and, having seen the expression on her face, began to run to her. Tears fell over her cheeks as she listened and as she thought about how this would affect Jenny. Amy briefly mouthed the words to Ben whose face, in turn, dropped as low as Amy's.

Gathering her wits about her, Amy asked how they wanted to handle telling Jenny.

"We first need to first make sure that Jenny's alright," Cathey said.

"She's going to be checked out by the doctor. Monica's in there with her and they're acting just fine. Ben will go back in there with them in a minute."

"Actually," Ben piped in, "They're more than fine. They're whispering and giggling and all kinds of strange, girly things."

Amy encouraged Ben to return to the room with the girls.

"Before I forget," Amy said, "the hospital needs to ask you some information about consent for treatment, that sort of thing. Why don't you talk to them first and then you can talk with Jenny when she comes out. I'll have her call you on my cell phone."

Wretched bile suddenly began to stir in Cathey's stomach at the thought of telling Jenny about Natasha. She briefly weighed her options before realizing that she must tell her over the phone even though it was, by far, the much less desirable option.

Randy and Cathey took the opportunity to discuss how to best handle telling her. Both agreed that it had to be done immediately so that she wouldn't feel left out or excluded in any way. Randy led them in a brief, yet desperate, prayer.

"Give us the words, Lord, to say to this sweet child—*your child*, Father. Give us the strength and courage to tell her and then give her peace and comfort, the kind that only comes from You, as she struggles her way through this. In Jesus' Name, Amen."

Waiting for Jenny's phone call was excruciating. Cathey rehearsed several versions of the story, but couldn't find one without pain anchored to it.

The phone finally rang.

Your words, Father. Please.

"Hello?"

"Hi, Mama," Jenny said enthusiastically and quickly. "You'll never believe what we've been through. Guess what happened. Oh, well, I guess you know since you already talked to Mrs. Beasley. She said you were worried about me, but I'm fine, Mama. Really, I am."

"I'm so glad, sweetie. You don't know just how glad I am to hear that. I've worried so much about you. We kept calling and calling and couldn't get through."

Jenny was so excited to be talking with her mom that her words almost tripped over each other.

"I know! It was awful and I was so scared, Mama. But, now, well I'm not scared anymore. Monica and I, well, we have plans to . . . ."

Stopping suddenly and cueing in on the concerned tone of her mother's voice, Jenny knew that something was wrong, and it wasn't just worry for her being in a wreck. This tone was a more-than-concerned one—more like a somber one.

Fortunately, and unfortunately, Jenny had always been good at reading people's voices and faces. She had had six years as a child with her birth mother, and being able to read her was a matter of survival. It was highly useful in those young, unsafe years, but, now that she was safe, she had no ability to shut it off.

"What's wrong, mama?"

Cathey hesitated while gathering her words.

"Mama, I *know* something's wrong. What is it?"

Cathey shook her head, again realizing how mature she actually was —well ahead of her chronological years. Stalling was not helping either of them. *Words, please, Father!*

"Honey, I have something to tell you."

Jenny stopped breathing as her mother inhaled deeply before speaking.

CHAPTER 17

Their visit would have to be cut short. Neither Jenny nor Monica wanted to leave, for they had other fantasies they wanted to pursue, but all of them had come crashing down with the news of the tragic death of Natasha. Jenny must return home as soon as possible for the memorial service.

Monica's parents worked diligently at their plans to return. Their SUV needed to be pulled out from the crash landing site among the rocks, but would they even be able to drive it?

At the hospital, the doctors had completed the tests on all of them and had allowed them to leave. Few cabs were available in this small town, even fewer still on a night like this. Somehow, they needed to make it out to Monica's grandmother's house for the night. In the morning, Ben and Amy would initiate new plans for their trip home, but not before some well-deserved sleep.

Ben had contacted his mother, Monica's grandmother, to apprise them of their situation. She had indicated that there was a small hotel nearby which would get them through the night until they could look at their circumstance in the morning with fresh eyes. Knowing that this was the best idea, though far from most desirable, they found a cab driver who was willing to drive two miles to the Motel 6 where they stayed overnight.

For the rest of the evening, Jenny was quiet. Seeing Jenny in such emotional pain was difficult for Monica and her parents. There was no way to help her except to be there for her in case Jenny needed ears to listen.

When they arrived at the motel, Amy ordered in pizza from the local Pizza Hut though she was surprised that they would deliver in this weather. The Eggs 'N Biscuit restaurant next to the motel remained open, but few customers were eating out at this late hour. Ben noted that they would eat there in the morning, but, as for tonight, it would be pizza.

The girls gobbled two pieces each before hopping into their double bed. The television was on the late-night talk show though no one was particularly listening. After Amy had cleaned up their dinner, she looked over at the girls who were sound asleep already. This day had taken its toll on them—on *all* of them. Sleep now beckoned for Amy and Ben, who were delighted to answer its call.

* * *

THE FOLLOWING MORNING GREETED THEM with sunshine and the promise of a better day. The storm had passed but, in its wake, had left a snowy wonderland with ice-ladened streets. City crews had been sanding streets since before dawn, but there was much more work to be done before this city would be dug out. For this small town, it had been the snow storm of the decade.

The Beasleys and Jenny had just returned from the restaurant next door when Ben noticed the red button flashing on the phone. Ben's mother had left a message telling them to call Tom and Tommy who would pick them up and bring them out to her house when they were ready. They would then tackle the problem of retrieving their wrecked vehicle.

Ben was delighted at having received this message. He was feeling largely overwhelmed with the day's details. He quickly made a phone call to the number his mother left on the voice message and made plans for Tom to get them. Evidently, Tom owned an old 4 X 4 which had been able to rescue any car and survive any test he had put it through so far, so he was feeling confident that pulling Ben's SUV out of the ditch would not be the first obstacle to overcome it. Now there was light at the beginning of the tunnel for them as far as removing his car.

Though Jenny was not as energized as she was at the beginning of their trip, she and Monica began their secret whispering again while her dad was on the phone to Tom. First, Monica would say something, and then Jenny would respond with something evidently equally as funny or silly. The girls wondered if Tommy would come with his father or if they would have to wait for the opportunity to see him when they arrived at Monica's grandmother's house. Either way, the wait was going to seem long.

Though Tom was the only one in the vehicle when it finally pulled up to the motel, there was still the matter of how they would thank Tommy for saving them. The truck ride over there would give them the opportunity to discuss options laced with fantasies.

When Tom arrived, Ben jumped in the front passenger seat while the women piled into the back seat.

They arrived safely at Grandma Beasley's house though there had been some slips and bumps from the ice and snow covered roads. Tom's truck lived up to his expectation and its reputation. They carefully piled out of the truck hanging on to one another to prevent falls. Over a foot of snow had fallen in the last twelve hours preceeded by several inches of ice. *Quite a storm*, Tom had said, *but it can't beat me!*

Grabbing each other's arms, Jenny and Monica somehow remained vertical in the snow where they thought the sidewalk might have been. Glancing over at their neighbor's house, they were disappointed when they saw no one (translate, Tommy) outside. They thought he would be shoveling snow or coming out to greet them. However, convinced that Tommy would help retrieve their SUV, the girls guessed that he would be coming over soon, and knowing they would have to return home soon due to Natasha's funeral did not deter the girls in their plan-making. One way or another, they would be assuredly seeing Tommy again. It wasn't a question of '*if*' but '*when.*'

All were able to walk into the small, single-story white stone house without falling or slipping. Hugs were generously given to all from Monica's grandmother. The smell of hot pancakes, bacon, and coffee hung heavily in the air, wafting through the kitchen to their nostrils at the front door. Late morning breakfasts were golden in Grandma Beasley's house. Though they had eaten just two hours ago, they would certainly not turn down such a feast. All sat down to eat and recount the details of their adventure to Grandma Beasley.

The large front room and kitchen windows were wet with perspiration due to the meeting of inside humidity and outside cold. Monica had been here previously several times so the quaint house was quite familiar and comforting to her. Grandma Beasley's floral sofa and matching love seat framed the small living room, leaving just enough room for an end table, a small, maple-colored coffee table, and an oddly colored, well—worn chair which had belonged to her own grandmother. It didn't coordinate with the rest of her furniture, but was obviously a cherished piece and one which would be always honored in her living room.

The small master bedroom was on the west side of the house while the two guest bedrooms occupied the east. A light, yellow bathroom split the two bedrooms and was one of only two bathrooms in the house. The other bathroom was, of course, in the master suite. In it were color-coordinated, floral towels, wash cloths, and shower curtain, much like you would expect at any grandmother's house.

The house was small compared to Jenny's and Monica's, but the feeling of love was huge. If love was a contest, Grandma Beasley would easily win first place. Jenny loved being there. But, this visit was tinged with darkness and death. Natasha's death. These feelings were a crime and death was the intruder to this soft, comforting house. It was a crime of breaking and entering which deserved a life sentence which should have no chance of parole.

Thoughts carried Jenny back to the many recent times when she had felt the emptiness and void from Natasha's unexpected absence— whether from church, or a birthday celebration, or a promised shopping trip. Jenny's sadness morphed into a disturbing anger, resentment, and bitterness towards her birth mother. Again.

The last instance of disappointment had not yet worn off. And, now this!

Jenny felt guilty for not feeling differently towards the woman who had birthed her. Yet, in thinking about not having to dread future pain regarding Natasha, Jenny sensed a feeling of relief surround and enfold her. *Finally,* Jenny thought to herself, *Natasha could no longer cause any pain—ever! She was gone from this earth, was in Heaven, and would no longer bother her again.*

How horrible that sounded, Jenny thought once again.

Jenny was ashamed and reluctant to share her feelings with anyone for fear that they would not understand the roller coaster relationship they had experienced over the years. Honestly, she felt horrible for feeling such relief, but then quickly reminded herself of how these negative feelings had come into existence. Water now under the bridge. Too much *tainted* water under the *collapsed* bridge.

Everyone at the table was looking at Jenny as she emerged from her daydreaming. She hadn't realized that they had been asking her questions, trying to determine what she wanted to do about attending Natasha's funeral. They had all assumed that she would want to be home for that sad occasion but had not wanted to assume.

"Maybe now would be a good time to call your mom, Jenny," Monica's mother said. "I told her that you'd call her after we got settled in here."

"You can use the phone in my bedroom, honey," Grandma Beasley said lovingly. "That'll give you some privacy in talking with your mom. That way, none of our big ears will distract you." With the last comment, Grandma Beasley winked.

"Oh, um, yeah, okay," Jenny answered.

Getting up from the table and heading towards the master bedroom, Jenny glanced back towards the kitchen table.

"Now, go on, honey," Grandma Beasley said, motioning with her hand. "We'll be right here when you come back and you can tell us about your conversation with your mother, or anything you want—or nothing, if you'd prefer. We just want you to know that we love you and are here for you." Tears had formed in the corners of Grandma Beasley's eyes. She was very fond of Jenny and hated that Jenny had to experience the death of a loved one at such a young age.

When Jenny had disappeared around the corner into the master bedroom, Grandma Beasley shook her head and said in agony, "This just kills me. This sweet little child . . ." Her voice trailed off as she dabbed her eyes with tissues.

"We'll just have to figure out a way to get her back home," Ben said, glancing outside at the tall snow drifts. "Not sure what we'll do with my SUV. Yesterday, Tom said he'd come help me get it out of the ditch, but it's not going to be drivable by any means. We may have to rent a car from town somewhere so that we can get Jenny home. Anybody know what the weather's supposed to be?"

"No, I haven't paid attention to it—at least not today anyway. Was glued to it all day yesterday anticipating you all getting here. Wore out my eyes staring at that thing for so long," Grandma Beasley said. "Monica, dear, why don't you go on over and turn on the television. Let's see if we can find a weather channel where somebody will tell us what the weather is gonna be."

Monica jumped up and ran into the front room towards the T.V. She was glad for something to do besides sit and stare at each other. Monica was sad, too, and she didn't know how to comfort her friend, so having a task to focus upon helped her out.

Amy and Ben began clearing off the breakfast dishes and placing them into the dishwasher.

It wasn't long before Jenny entered the kitchen.

Her face was not downcast as they had anticipated. Instead, it was lifted and scanning the room looking for Monica.

The adults looked at each other trying to guess how she was doing and what she had decided. Since no answer was forthcoming, Amy decided to take the lead.

"Jenny, honey, how was the conversation with your mother?"

"Oh, fine, I guess."

Jenny turned her head towards the television and began watching the weather channel with Monica.

Silence continued for a few minutes before Amy spoke again.

"Jenny, do you mind my asking what you and your mother talked about? What did you two decide about coming home for the funeral?"

With a confident voice and uplifted chin, Jenny answered, "Nothing. I'm not going."

And, with that answer, she and Monica ran into the bedroom to continue their "vacation."

Stunned, Amy turned to look at Ben who was, in turn, staring at his mother.

"What?" Amy asked. "Did I hear her correctly? Did she say that she was NOT going to go to the funeral?"

"T-that's what I heard," said Grandma Beasley. "Oh, dear. Poor little thing."

"I'd better step into the other room and call Cathey. I just can't believe that this is what they have decided. Imagine not attending your birth mother's funeral. Why, that's just crazy. She must have misunderstood. I'll go call. Be right back."

"There's something more to this than meets the eye," Grandma Beasley offered, shaking her head. "A person just HAS to attend the funeral of a loved one. She'll regret it if she doesn't go."

"I agree," Ben responded. "This is strange. I'm sure that Jenny must have twisted up the information. Maybe they're just going to wait a week before they have the actual funeral."

Hearing the girls giggling in the back room only confirmed that this was the perfect time to make a private call.

The girls came running from their room to ask Grandma Beasley if they could make a cake or something. Obviously, the girls had revisited their original plan to bake a "thank you present" to personally deliver next door to Tommy—well, and his father, Tom, of course—for all their help in this matter. It was the courteous thing to do. It was the right thing to do. Somebody had to make the gesture, and they were going to rise to the occasion, sacrificing their time and energy to make it up to them.

"For crying out loud," Grandma Beasley said. "Why do you want to bake a cake now? What's the hurry? You two seem as excited as two girls going to Disneyland or something."

The girls settled down a bit after discovering that their excitement conveyed a little too much information. The adults might suspect their impure motives for baking this cake if they were too excited, so Monica turned to Jenny and gave her "the look" to tone it down.

By the time Grandma Beasley had given permission for a cake to be baked, the girls had already run into the kitchen scouring the pantry for a cake mix. There were several from which to pick, but they chose a yellow cake mix with dark chocolate, fluffy icing. The white cake sounded too pure and the chocolate cake mix sounded too naughty, so yellow was the perfect compromise.

Amy returned from her telephone call to Jenny's mother and noticed the girls busy with bowls, beaters, and a baking pan. She hated to interrupt their obvious excitement, but needed to talk with Jenny privately.

"Jenny, can I speak to you for a moment in the other room?"

Jenny looked at Monica. They were right in the middle of this delicious task, but Jenny agreed.

"I just spoke with your mother," Amy explained. "I hope you don't mind. I was just so concerned about your not attending the funeral. So, I decided it would be best to call and discuss it with your mom. She said that she had concerns about you—about how you are handling your birth mother's death. Or, not handling it. I admit you don't seem to be too upset."

Blank stare.

Amy waited a moment before continuing.

"Anyway, your mother said that she really would prefer that we bring you home as quickly as possible. Actually, for a number of reasons she said. Weather is a main concern and your whole family is going through this thing without you and she said they want you home."

Amy wasn't going to continue without first receiving a response from Jenny.

Jenny gathered her thoughts.

"I know Mama's worried about me. But, I'm fine. Really, I am. I don't wanna go home right now. I'm having a good time."

Attempting to add humor to the conversation as a way of furthering this discussion, Amy responded.

"Well, if you can call being in a huge snow storm, in a bad wreck, and going to the hospital, a 'good time' then you are quite easy to please." Jenny smiled.

"Think about it, Jenny. Your birth mother just died. You must want to be around family right now. Don't you? Don't you want to be with your parents and brothers?"

The last sentence stung Jenny's heart. Her thoughts began to race. A lifetime passed in those few emotionally-ladened moments.

How could I be so selfish? My brothers would want me there with them. They can't go through this without me. They need me there.

Jenny's shoulders dropped, her smile disappeared, and her shoulders straightened.

"Okay, Mrs. Beasley. You're right. I should go home." Sigh. "When do I have to go?"

Relieved by her consent, Amy pulled her in close and hugged her around the shoulders.

"I'm so glad, honey. I know you won't regret your decision. Now, let's go tell Monica. She's the one who will be disappointed, but we'll see what we can do about that. Maybe you can come back."

After several phone calls back and forth to her mother, Jenny was pleased to learn that she didn't need to return home immediately. She could have another day there if she wanted. Besides, Ben needed some time to retrieve his vehicle and discuss their options as well. Ben could drive Jenny back in a rental car or the whole family could go and return in a few weeks for another weekend. Maybe they could even find a small plane that could fly Jenny home.

After some dialogue on the matter, Ben and Amy decided that they would all return home together when the roads allowed and a car could be rented. The other options weren't even a close second.

It was Saturday. They wouldn't have the memorial for Natasha probably until Monday which gave them some leeway to get home. They could leave by Monday morning when the roads were cleared and the temperature above freezing.

Grandma Beasley called Ben and Amy over to the television. She had been watching the weather channel which had indicated that the temperature was going nowhere fast. The weather forecaster said that their neck of the woods wouldn't see above freezing until sometime next week. And, another storm, though much less intense, was expected Monday. It might bring freezing rain, sleet, or snow, or all three depending on where the jet stream fell. Weather in that part of the state was highly unpredictable. It could be sixty degrees one day and twenty degrees the next.

They had convinced Jenny to return home for the memorial service, and now they didn't know if they could even make it.

Delicious smells wafted through the kitchen, into the front room, and into their nostrils.

"Hmm, that smells good in there," Grandma Beasley called to them. "Any of that for us?"

The girls giggled.

"No, Grandma. We're baking it for someone else."

"Like who? We're the only ones here, so I guess we'll just have to eat it."

Monica sighed loudly. She was going to have to explain it to everyone now.

"Well, we thought we'd bake the cake and take it next door. As a way of saying thanks, ya know?" The girls waited for their responses.

Ben's eyebrow rose as he looked at Amy.

"Oh, quit, Ben. They're just being sweet girls. There's nothing to it. Do NOT do your eyebrow thing."

"What eyebrow thing?" Ben said with playful, knowing sarcasm.

"You know what I'm talking about. That thing you do with your eyebrow, where you lift one of 'em up and then you frown, all at the same time."

Ben smiled.

"Oh, you think you're so cute, don't you?"

Ben loved the way he could play with Amy. They had always had this wonderful ability to kid with each other.

"Okay, you two," Grandma said smilingly. "Just quit while you're ahead. One of ya's going to have to go tell those girls about the weather."

When Amy told the girls that it looked like the weather was not going to cooperate for getting them home to her parents and brothers, Amy noticed an immediate strange look appear on Jenny's face. It wasn't one of disappointment. Was it fear?

Suddenly, Jenny blurted out that she had to call home. She had come to terms with the plan of having to go home—and the real reason for it. Her younger brothers would need her there for all they would be experiencing. *She* had *always* been there for them before, long ago when they were with Natasha, and she *had* to be this time as well.

Jenny began her usual task of kicking herself, mentally, for being so selfish before and thinking only of her own desire to stay here with her friend.

I have to talk with my brothers now, Jenny thought to herself. *Why didn't I do that after talking on the phone with my mom? How could I do that to them? They've probably thought I've forgotten about them. I am such a bad person. I blew it.*

Somewhere within her mind, or was it coming from the depths of her troubled and pained soul?

A voice, dark and ugly, inserted itself into her being. Was she hearing her own voice? Was it someone else's voice? Whatever the case, she was certain that she heard it as clearly as someone was standing beside her. And it reverberated within her like an imploding sonic boom.

You are just like HER.

At that moment, Jenny knew.

I have turned out to be just like Natasha.

I am just like my birth mother.

I am her.

CHAPTER 18

The funeral chapel was beautiful. Not what Jenny had imagined. She had assumed that the place would be dark, dingy, and almost death-like. But, this small chapel was filled with sunlight streaming through the windows which, in turn, enhanced the light wood interior. There was no altar in front. In its place was a single, small podium, made also of light, heavy wood. None of Jenny's siblings had been to a funeral before. Neither had she, but no one could detect that from Jenny's action. She appeared as though she had been to a thousand—calm, poised, and always watching to see who needed comforting.

Jenny insisted on sitting between her brothers and sat with her arms around them, like a mother hen gathering her chicks.

Cathey commented to Randy that she had not seen such protective behavior in Jenny since they first came to live with them.

"I wonder what's going on with her," Randy asked.

"I don't know, but she's got her protective wall back up again," Cathey replied. "Just makes me so sad to see our Jenny that way again. It took us so long to penetrate it—for her to trust us to take care of her and her brothers. How easily she has slipped back into her old role!"

Though Jenny stared at their pastor, Pastor Dave, for the brief service, she allowed herself to only grasp certain phrases in his homily.

"Some people live troubled lives . . . who have difficulty accepting the gift of Good News . . . when Natasha was at her lowest, she made such a brave, courageous, selfless decision to allow Cathey and Randy to adopt her children, at a time when she couldn't parent . . . addictions are strong, and they consume everything . . . but her sins were forgiven, and not only forgiven, but forgotten, forgotten by Jesus . . . and our own sins can be, too . . . we pray for those who have been hurt by Natasha's past behavior . . . we pray for those who have hurt us . . . and, only by God's power can we strive to forgive them . . . there, but for the grace of God, go any of us . . . Natasha had accepted Jesus as her Savior; . . . she had been baptized in the nearby lake if any of you will remember . . . we know where she will spend eternity . . . we will see her again someday . . . we pray, especially, for her children . . . for all who have loved Natasha . . . for those of us remaining here on Earth until our Savior comes in the clouds to take us with Him . . . we must continue to be servants of Christ, to be a cloud of witnesses to encourage one another, especially now during this painful time . . . and we pray all this in Jesus's Name. Amen."

People gathered in the back after the service for just a bit, talking, shaking hands, hugging, while wiping away tears. The boys were getting antsy and had obviously reached their limit of their ability to sit still. Randy gathered them up and escorted them outside. Their hearts seemed fine, though Jeremiah seemed a bit subdued.

Jenny would not make eye contact with anyone. She felt if she did, then all of this would become a reality to her. And, not only reality, but a nightmare. She felt such conflicting feelings towards Natasha, though anger seemed to rule lately.

Kayleen had, somehow, been able to inform Natasha's siblings and Grandmother Mae. Though only two of her siblings came, the other three sent their condolences to Jenny and the boys.

Natasha's grandmother approached Cathey with gratitude mixed with caution. They had not conversed much over the past few years and Grandmother Mae was ashamed for her lack of follow through. However, she wanted to connect with Cathey and Randy to ask permission to visit them occasionally.

Feeling protective, Cathey was gracious, polite, but hesitant. She told Grandma Mae that she'd have to talk with the children before making any final decisions. Cathey had not understood why the grandmother, and Natasha's other siblings for that matter, had not kept in touch. Family was so important to Cathey and Randy. She couldn't imagine moving through life's peaks and valleys without them. They had been a vital element in the adoption, especially in the initial stages. The transition from no children to a full household had been extreme, but they wouldn't have changed a thing about it.

After briefly talking with Grandma Mae and Natasha's sisters, LaVerne and N'collette, Cathey developed compassion for them. After all, they had lost a family member. Natasha had been a daughter and sister to them. Approaching Grandma Mae, Cathey extended her hand again.

"I'm sorry for your loss. Can't believe I didn't say that earlier. Where are my manners?"

Appreciating the gesture, Mae enfolded Cathey's hands into hers.

"Thank you so much. It means a lot to me to hear you say that."

Cathey extended the same to LaVerne and N'collette.

"I'm sorry for your loss, as well. You lost a sister. I don't believe anything can replace a sister," Cathey said with much empathy. Cathey couldn't fathom life without her sisters and brother.

Feeling suddenly embarrassed and guilty, LaVerne apologized for her husband's absence as well as her other siblings.

"Um, the others couldn't make it today. My husband had to work and . . . well . . . her brothers, well . . . . I haven't heard from them in awhile. I'll have to wait until they contact me."

Cathey continued her grace. "I'm sure it must be hard not having all of your family together for this, but I'm certainly glad you three could come."

Kayleen had been watching from afar and decided to come join them. She had been the one to have called Mae in the first place. Mae smiled at Kayleen as she approached.

"Mae, it's so good to see you again. It's been so long, but you're looking mighty good. You feeling alright?"

"Well," Mae responded. "You know how things are. My memory don't function well, my knees ache, and my hands have arthritis. But, other than that, I guess I'm alright."

Turning to LaVerne and N'collette, Kayleen extended her condolences to them as well. All felt momentary awkwardness tinged with regret.

"This most certainly is a difficult reason for a gathering, isn't it?"

All agreed. Silence interrupted their short conversation.

Cathey's thoughts overtook her. She knew that these were her children's biological Grandmother and Aunts, but the full impact of that had not hit her until now. *These were important people in the lives of the kids*, she thought. *And, they must continue to be involved.* At least, she would invite them to remain a part of their lives.

"Mae," Cathey began. "I'd like to see if I can gather up my kids and bring them over here to say hello. Would that be okay?"

They all seemed delighted by this at first; that is, until fear gripped them. Mae and Natasha's sisters looked at each other. N'collette whispered to them; something like, *What if they hate us?*

Cathey did not know how the children would react to meeting them, but she was willing to find out.

Bringing the boys and Randy back inside, Cathey steered them over to Mae and her daughters. She introduced them while the boys just stood there staring at them. For a brief moment, Cathey wondered if anyone was going to say anything. Nobody did, so she took the lead.

"Boys, this is your Grandma Mae and your Aunt LaVerne and Aunt N'collette," she said encouraging the boys to shake hands. Then, she introduced her sons.

"This is Jeremiah. He's nine years old. These are the twins, Nathaniel and Nehemiah. They're seven. And, this is our youngest one, David. He's five. And, of course, this is my husband, Randy."

"It's good to see you again, Mae. I'm just sorry for the occasion," Randy offered. And, to the sisters he said, "Nice to meet you, ladies. I'm so sorry for the loss of your sister. I can't imagine the pain you must feel."

The young boys stayed quiet. Grandma Mae made a big to-do over how handsome they were and such fine young men. Jeremiah seemed tense and stiff when shaking their hands, but the twins and David giggled and hid behind Randy.

"Here we go again," Randy said as he watched the boys' energy escalate. "Excuse us, ladies; I think I'll take them back outside again if you don't mind. Nice to meet you." Excusing himself, Randy exited the building following his sons.

Jeremiah stayed with Cathey. Though he said nothing, it seemed important to him to be with these people. He knew that they were part of his biological family, but he had spent no time around them. He wanted to hang around, listen to them talk, watch their hand and facial motions, and hear what they had to say. It's not as if he felt any specific feelings against them, but thought it odd that he felt nothing *towards* them.

Jeremiah thought the situation was worth examining. He was the only one of his sibling bunch who had a passion for science and engineering. To Jeremiah, life was one big puzzle to be solved by reasonable and logical methods. This situation was clearly a puzzle which had yet to be solved. So, he stayed, observed, and gathered data.

Cathey wanted Jenny to come talk with them. Jenny would certainly remember her grandmother and aunts.

"Jenny's around here somewhere. I just saw her," Cathey said looking around the room. "Hmm, maybe she's gone to the restroom. Jeremiah, have you seen your sister?"

Jeremiah pointed to Jenny who was standing at the opposite end of the room with Monica and her parents. The Beasleys had attended the funeral, but had not planned to stay particularly long. But, when Jenny latched onto them, Amy and Ben had changed their minds, sensing that Jenny needed them there.

Motioning with her hands for Jenny to come join them, Cathey expected her to come right over. But, Jenny did not move. She had noticed that Jenny had barely looked up from the floor for the last half hour.

"Excuse me just a minute," Cathey said to Mae. "I'll be back in just a minute. I'm going to check on Jenny and see how she's doing."

Jenny glanced up long enough to see that her mother had approached her.

"Honey, are you doing okay?"

"Sure, Mom. I'm doing just fine," Jenny replied with a hint of sarcasm.

"I know this is difficult for you. I'm so sorry, honey. Is there anything I can do for you?"

"I just wanna go home," Jenny admitted.

"I know, sweetheart. We'll be just a bit longer. Come with me, first. I want you to say hello to your grandmother and aunts."

Jenny looked at her mother as though he had lost her mind.

"Really, Mom? You seriously want me to go over and talk with them? You want *ME* to make the effort when they haven't made any effort all these years? Do I have to do ALL the work with that family?" All that was missing from this pre-teen scene was the eye-rolling look.

Cathey was stunned. Never before had she heard such pain and anger spew from Jenny—that is, except for when she last spoke with Natasha.

"Jenny! Listen to me," Cathey said in a soft, yet very firm voice. "I know that you're hurting and you're very angry, but nothing gives you the right to be disrespectful. If you do not want to talk with them today, then fine, we can work something out another time maybe. In the meantime, they can read your body language and it's pretty loud right now." Cathey took a minute to inhale deeply. "Look, honey, I just don't want you to regret anything. Like it or not, these people are part of your family, which means that they are a part of ours." Cathey allowed a minute for this to sink in.

Jenny's ire began to subside as she glanced at Jeremiah. A twinge of guilt invaded her heart, messing up a good ol' fit she was going to throw. Her attitude could not hold up under the pressure of what this could be doing to Jeremiah.

Taking a moment to gain composure, Jenny inhaled deeply, lifted her chin, and grabbed hold of Jeremiah's hand on one side and Cathey's hand on the other. They approached them as though they were an army group obeying an order to charge the enemy.

Steeling herself for a personal encounter with a piece of her old life, Jenny stretched out her hand and shook her Grandmother's hand.

"Hello, Grandma Mae. So nice to see you again," Jenny said as though she were the epitome of Miss Manners.

The intentional formality did not escape the aunts and grandmother. Over the years, Jenny had developed hard feelings towards them, and she was right to do so, they thought, but was at least being polite.

"So good to see you again, too, Jenny! How have you been? You look so grown up and so beautiful," Mae offered. The aunts chimed in with their own comments, speaking in a very friendly manner yet respecting her physical and emotional boundaries.

Glances to Jeremiah encouraged Jenny to continue with her path. Her polite conversations with past family members was one more way she could help meet the needs of her siblings. Though she was seething inside, she let on to no one.

Mae wanted to offer her condolences to Jenny for losing her birth mother, Natasha, but was unsure how it would be received. LaVerne took advantage of the lull in conversation to offer their condolences.

Jenny took it well, mostly politely, and in response said, "Same for you. I'm sorry your daughter's dead." And, with this blunt comment, Jenny asked to be excused from the group, taking Jeremiah with her.

Stunned, Cathey said, "I'm so sorry for Jenny's last comment. I don't know what in the world has gotten into her. That was rude and she needs to apologize for that."

Mae shook her head and cried. LaVerne assured Cathey that they all understood that the death of Natasha must be tremendously difficult for her, especially being so young and having to deal with such loss.

"It doesn't give her permission to be rude, though. We have not taught her to act like this," Cathey said. "Pardon me while I go get her and have her apologize to you."

"No, no, no. Please don't do that. It'll just make matters worse. We'll talk with her another time. M-maybe we can see all the children sometime soon, and once, or *if*, we get our relationship back on track, then her feelings will change," Mae said sadly. "M-may we see them again?"

"Of course! Absolutely you can," Cathey said enthusiastically. "I think it would be very good for the boys, and it will give Jenny a chance to deal with her feelings about the past—since she obviously has some!"

Cathey tried to keep their conversation light-hearted.

"One of the things my husband and I like best about open adoption is that everyone can meet and develop a relationship with each other. The kids don't have to do without their extended birth family. And, it would give Randy and me a chance to get to know you all as well. Unfortunately, I haven't heard very much about any of you, so I would very much like the opportunity to get to know you."

Instantly, Cathey regretted saying the last part. Cathey did not wish to hurt them with that comment, but it was true that none of the children talked very much about Natasha's parents, sisters, brothers, or anyone else from her past. Admittedly, Cathey had found herself wondering, from time to time, why Natasha's family had not contacted her, but she didn't want to judge them.

She immediately followed up with saying, "Getting all of us together would probably be healing for everyone involved. You all have missed out on the last six years. We can fill you in on what they've done during that time. We can show you pictures and video. Would you like that?"

With tears in her eyes, Mae was decidedly elated about the invitation. LaVerne and N'collette were a bit more subdued and cautious, but took Cathey up on her offer.

After the service, Cathey and Randy gathered up the children and took them home. On the way, they noticed that Jenny had become very quiet. Not that she was at all talkative before or after the service, but she seemed to be even more somber than previously.

"Sweetheart? Is everything alright?" Cathey asked.

"Fine, mom. Just fine," Jenny quickly retorted.

Cathey started to respond but stopped when Randy touched her hand, whispering, "Give her some time."

Nodding her head in agreement, Cathey wondered how their conversation would go later when she would approach Jenny with these issues.

Why does life have to be so hard? Cathey thought to herself. *And, how can I help my children handle these gut-wrenching situations? How can I, myself, navigate through these thorny briar patches of life? Lord, help me!*

She knew that this delicate situation must be handled perfectly; otherwise, if not, well . . . . Cathey shuddered to think where it could lead Jenny.

CHAPTER 19

Jenny's spring semester's frustration was about to melt into summer's instant relief. Over the semester, Algebra had been generally impossible; General Science, mostly tolerable; English, fairly enjoyable; and History, well that had been yawningly boring. Without Band and Choir classes, Jenny's sanity would have surely been surrendered. This semester just seemed to drag on forever. Endless assignments and tests filled each day of the week, and year-end papers in two classes were due in only a few weeks.

Jenny's ninth grade year had been very challenging, to say the least. Hard to believe that it had already been three years since Natasha's death. At times, it seemed as though it had happened only yesterday; at other times, it seemed like it had been nine lifetimes ago.

The now-distant semester of Jenny's sixth grade year had been a total blur to her. She had felt numb towards just about everything. She could remember that her parents had tried their best to help her through her birthmother's sudden death. They had always been ready to listen anytime she had felt like talking (which had been rare), bake her favorite meal, or offer lasting hugs which had so completely comforted Jenny.

Family was important to all of them, but especially to Cathey. And, in stressful times, Cathey would always draw in family more closely. After Natasha's death, Cathey and Randy's extended family had surrounded and showered them with love, good food, and activities.

Jenny loved her adopted family and wouldn't change anything at all about them. She knew that her parents had wanted her to help heal her past wounds—Natasha's death being the biggest one of all. But, Jenny hadn't *wanted* to feel better. She had wanted to remain angry, which had felt so much more empowering than sadness or fear, so she had just stayed angry and aloof for these past three years.

Her parents had taken her to counseling, but it hadn't helped because Jenny hadn't *wanted* it to help. She had appeared for every scheduled appointment; had been polite, and even friendly, with the counselor. She had talked freely about anything and everything—except any issues having to deal with Natasha. When the topic was broached, Jenny had constructed a thick, inpenetrable wall, much like the long, unforgiving Wall of China—built to keep certain things in and other things out. And Jenny was in control of both.

When the counselor had told Cathey and Randy that there was nothing more she could do at this point to help Jenny, they had agreed that she could stop going to counseling. The counselor had told them that the door would always be open to Jenny, or any of them, in the future. But, it would have to be Jenny's choice. And, at that time, Jenny simply hadn't chosen to do anything with her pain other than keep others away. Her parents conjectured that her stance had been to minimize the risk of getting hurt again, but the therapist had held a different hypothesis. Liz had watched and pondered over Jenny in each session. She knew that Jenny had been no stranger to pain from Natasha in her early years. Natasha had barely been present physically for her children, much less emotionally. Liz had seen it so often before. Emotional heartache could be a thief and a liar, taking away one's spirit, personality, and very presence. But, Liz also knew that love was stronger and could soften obstacles preventing nourishment to the heart and soul.

Though Jenny had denied it in a session with Liz, she had a touch of her birth mother's stubbornness in her. Having been responsible for her younger siblings when Natasha would disappear for hours at a time, Jenny had experienced little control and high frustration in her early years. Years later, she had found an unhealthy source of power, a storehouse at her fingertips, through unforgiveness. Of course, she had been too young to realize that refusing to forgive others would always backfire on her by deadening a piece of her heart—to say nothing about the obligation as a Christian to forgive. Nevertheless, she had grabbed on to that murdering mode and had refused to let go.

In a number of sessions, Liz had tried to explain the psychological dynamic to her and the spiraling consequences that unforgiveness would produce, but she had latched on to the strangler for a season. In due time, it would, no doubt, drop her to her knees, and she would be faced, once again, with the most important decision of her life.

After consulting with Liz, and discussing the situation with each other, Cathey and Randy had decided that more sessions with Liz would be futile at that time. But, agreed to keep a vigilant watch over their precious Jenny, wait for any further symptoms to emerge, and, in the meantime, pray that God would soften her heart so that He could mold her into the beautiful, strong woman of faith that was in His plan for her life.

Over the next three years, they had watched Jenny's joy vanish bit by bit. Classes became more frustrating, homework more demanding, and friendships more challenging. But, the one thing which had seemed to continually restore and re-strengthen her had been music. Whether she was singing or playing the piano or flute, Jenny's spirit had always been lifted and carried into another world when she engaged in it. It had a special, unexplainable hold on her, and Cathey had been very grateful for the moments of peace it seemed to bring her. Like a gift given from above.

The last few weeks of the school year seemed to drag on unrelentingly. But, not the weekends. Weekends were for friends, freedom, and fantasizing!

Though Jenny and Monica had remained best friends over the past couple of years, Monica had noticed slight changes in Jenny's demeanor and personality, especially after Natasha's death. Monica hadn't said much to Jenny about it, but she knew that Jenny had been through a painful ordeal and thought she would, in time, recover on her own.

Over time, Jenny had become more irritable, impatient, and quick to anger, yet they had still been able to laugh together, especially when discussing the daily essentials of life—boys, dreaded homework, boys, friends, boys, movies, boys, chores, and boys.

Monica had developed a crush on Mike T. Mindenhall who was, by all accounts, one of the best-looking guys in the school. He was older by an entire year! And, a football player. Most of the freshmen girls ooh-ed and ahh-ed over him as he passed through the halls from class to class. They'd watch as he'd glide through the halls as though he was walking on clouds in slow motion, and intentionally smooth down his long, dark, wavy hair back with his hand. The gasps from the girls were amost audible.

Mike was certainly aware that he was being ogled by dozens of female eyes everywhere he went and he used it to his advantage. You see, Mike dated. He dated a *lot*. Because he *could*. Had a reputation for it and everyone knew it within the first few weeks of class. He had one particular girl whom he kept bouncing back to, but they'd soon have another fight, and then their on-again, off-again would be off again. So, during their "off" times, other girls would be given a once-in-a-lifetime opportunity to go out with him, at least for a few dates anyway before he moved on to other victims, which is what girls were to him. Mere victims to be owned and then destroyed.

Though he was a year older than Monica, they shared biology class together. Monica sat in the second seat of the first row and Mike sat across from her two rows, second seat back. And, since the teacher positioned himself at the front in the middle, Monica could stare at the back of Mike's head, and sometimes his profile, during the entire hour. Enough to give a reason to live every day!

"Why don't ya go talk to him," Jenny would ask several days a week.

"Are you kiddin' me?" Monica often repeated in horror. "He's not someone you just walk up to and just start talking! No, no. I need to wait for just the right opportunity, just the right time, to make my move."

Jenny rolled her eyes.

"Just make your move. I'm sick of hearin' 'bout him. Besides, he's got a reputation. I don't think you outta mess with him. You'll get your heart broken," Jenny warned.

"Well, what about you? I don't see you making your moves towards Jimmy," Monica mimicked.

"Leave Jimmy outta this," Jenny said irritatingly.

"Oh, so you can push me about Mike, but I can't push you?"

Again, Jenny rolled her eyes and walked away.

"Gotta go to class," Jenny said while walking away.

"Wait, Jenny!" Monica said. "I was only kidding. What's wrong with you? Can't take a joke anymore?"

But, Jenny had already turned around and walked off.

Monica shook her head wondering why she and her friend couldn't joke like they used to. Shrugging her shoulders, Monica walked away hoping they would talk at lunch and smooth things over. Again.

As Jenny walked to her next class, she was haunted by Monica's statement about her over-the-top sensitivity. She didn't know what was wrong. Sometimes she and Monica would joke and talk about guys and she wouldn't be bothered at all. At other times, Jenny just didn't want to be pushed. Maybe what everybody said was true—just hormones working overtime every month. *Sheesh, great!*

For the rest of the day, Jenny's mind wandered off to fantasyland. Thinking about Jimmy did nothing except make her emotional. True, she did have a crush on him. Who wouldn't? He may not be a football player, but he was the cutest and best drummer in the marching band. He even played in his own band on weekends, along with a singer, guitarist, and a bass player. She hadn't heard them play, but she was certain that they were good.

They were such opposites, Jenny and Jimmy. But, maybe that explained the attraction she felt for him. She was a short, dark-skinned, curly haired girl, and Jimmy was a tall, skinny, white kid with long, straight blonde hair. *What a pair we'd make*, Jenny thought as she smiled. And, off into fantasyland she went; that is, until the math teacher called on her.

"Um, I-I don't know how to do that problem," Jenny stuttered in response.

"I t-h-o-u-g-h-t not," the short, plump teacher said slowly while peering over her dark-rimmed glasses. "Maybe you should pay more attention to what the class is doing."

Rolling her eyes at the teacher's back, Jenny returned to her fantasy. Fantasy was most assuredly much better than any Algebraic problem. Jenny figured she'd just call a classmate later to help her *understand what the class was doing with that problem*!

Fantasies were the only thing she could enjoy in regards to any real or potential relationship she could have with Jimmy. Her parents had made sure of that. When they found out that he was a senior, they had about blown a gasket. The age difference was what got them. A difference of a mere four years. No big deal, right? After all, she and Jimmy were both in the same band class, so he really couldn't be THAT much older. Her parents had talked like he was twenty-nine years old or some age equally as bad. No, the difference was *only* four years. Her mother had explained to Jenny that, in high school, four years' difference was not just four years, but more like eight years. *They have other things on their minds, Jenny. More adult things that you're just not ready for.*

Sheesh! What did her mom think she was gonna let him do—like, rape her or something? Jenny concluded that her mother just did not trust her enough to let her go out with Jimmy. Not that he had actually asked. But, what if he did? She'd have to tell him that her parents wouldn't let her go, which made her feel like a baby.

Though she had honored her parents' rule against dating someone four years older, Jenny had at least talked with him some and even flirted a little as well. Their talks had not been *during* class or rehearsals, but rather before or after.

Band rehearsals were required every Monday night for all band members during marching season. In addition, the band practiced every morning from 6:30am to 9:30am, which included first class. Normally, they ended just in time to run upstairs for second hour classes.

Actually, as Jenny thought more about this situation, she and Jimmy spent a great deal of time together, thanks for band class. Though they shared no other classes, at least she spent several hours a day—well, maybe not one-on-one time, but time which counted for a possible dating relationship.

Then, like the sharp sound from a lightening bolt, she heard her mother's voice . . . . *No dating!* Not a senior anyway.

There are so many other boys at your school, Jenny. Why don't you look around? Her mother had tried constantly to shift her attention away from Jimmy. *If you gave any other boy **your age** half as much thought as you give that other boy, well you'd have more attention than you'd know what to do with.*

Her parents wouldn't let her date anyway. Not as a freshman. She could go places if there was a group, but no individual dating. And, certainly not in a car. Not until her sophomore year.

Jenny often wondered why she didn't like boys her own age. Maybe there was something wrong with her. Maybe there was something wrong with her parents, which was more like it. *It's not like I can command my heart to like someone else.* She had tried, but the boys her age were so immature. They laughed at stupid things, made fun of less-fortunate students, made footballs out of paper and shot them across the room at others, and hit each other in the stomach and then run away. *Such imbeciles,* she thought.

Not like Jimmy. Jimmy was serious. He took his music seriously and his classes, too. At least, that's what she had assumed. She didn't really know that for certain, but she did know that Jimmy wore a solemn expression most of the time—except when he was looking at her. During those times, he would flash a shy, slight grin which would barely expose his white teeth. Well, okay, maybe not white teeth. Jimmy was a smoker, so maybe his grin was not quite so fresh. But, she had cautioned Jimmy about his smoking habits. And, he would just take a drag off his cigarette, blow it away from Jenny, shake his head and then tossle her hair with his hand before walking away.

One day, Jenny ran downstairs to the band room after class. She was taking a chance on missing her bus home, but it was worth it to see if Jimmy was practicing on his drums. The drumline section did that sometimes. There were other students milling around the band room, but as soon as Jenny walked in, Jimmy looked up and smiled. He jerked his head as if calling her over to him.

"Hey! You going straight home today?" Jimmy asked.

Jenny barely knew what to say. She could feel her face turn hot.

"Um, no, I was just gonna see what was going on down here. Why?"

"I just thought," Jimmy said with a grin, "that if you were still here in about thirty minutes, maybe we could talk."

Jenny looked stunned. Never before had he been so direct. The thought shook her up for a minute. But, when she got her wind back, she looked straight into his eyes and smiled.

"I'll probably be here still," Jenny said flirtatiously.

"Great! Come find me in about thirty. Okay?"

"Uh, sure. I'll just get some other things done first and then I'll come back down," Jenny offered.

The other drumline members were getting antsy.

"C'mon, Jimmy. We gonna play or what?"

Jenny smiled and nodded knowingly. She mouthed, "I'll be back."

Jimmy grinned before sending her off to do whatever it was she was going to do.

Floating on cloud nine, Jenny exited the band room and went upstairs to her locker. Thinking about her schedule for the day, she took out only those books for which she had homework, and then talked briefly with some acquaintances before closing her locker.

At that moment, panic seized her. As she viewed her bus driving away from the school grounds, her thoughts screamed at her. *What am I gonna do now? How am I gonna get home? What am I gonna tell Mama? What was I thinking? How could I be such an idiot?*

Then, Jenny was seized with another twinge of panic. It had been thirty minutes! She had to rush downstairs before Jimmy gave up on her and left. She felt so stupid losing track of time.

Flying down the hall from her locker, she quickly prayed that Jimmy would still be there waiting for her. By the time she arrived down in the band pit (as some called it), she couldn't let Jimmy see her like this. Out of breath, her chest was heaving like she was going to die. Her hair framing her face had frizzed, and her rectangular, black-rimmed glasses had bounced askew on her face. What a sight for a future boyfriend to behold.

Get hold of yourself! Stop it! Just slow down and act natural!

Those who passed her in the small area before going in the band door thought she was having a heart attack or some other medical emergency. She assured them that she felt fine and was just in a hurry. Smiling awkwardly, Jenny allowed them to pass by without calling 911. Wow, she felt like a moron.

Having taken a few minutes to reduce her heart rate, fix her hair, straighten her glasses, and quickly slap on some strawberry lip balm, Jenny very slowly opened the door to the band room and glanced around. She zeroed in on Jimmy who was putting away his music and drumsticks. Others were in the room, but their bodies seemed to just fade into the background.

"Oh, hey, Jimmy," Jenny said casually while masking an approaching panic attack.

With a widening smile, Jimmy (being so cool) nodded his head.

"Are you gonna stay all the way over there or are ya gonna c'mon back here?"

What am I gonna do with these sweaty hands? "Oh, sure," Jenny said while remaining outwardly calm. "I can come back there. What 'cha doing?" *Oh, please do not trip over anything and make a fool of yourself in front of him.*

"Just cleaning up my area while waiting for you to come back down," Jimmy said as if he owned the universe.

Jenny wondered if he knew just how cool he really was. Jimmy was flirty, yet simultaneously shy, producing the perfect combination in a guy. Or, at least the kind of guy that interested Jenny.

"Let's go upstairs. I need a cigarette," Jimmy said as he motioned her.

Should I leave my stuff here? Should I take it with me? How long does it take to walk home? Jimmy didn't take his stuff, so I won't either. Oh, God, what am I doing?

"Sure," Jenny said trying to match the coolness of his tone.

They headed out the exit door and up the concrete stairs which led outside to the student parking lot.

Jimmy lit up and they talked for quite some time. He noticed which way the wind was blowing and made sure he stood down wind so that it wouldn't burn Jenny's eyes. Yet, there were times she saw smoke cover his own eye, causing it to squint and become teary and blury for a moment.

"So, uh, Jenny. How ya gettin' home? I mean, don't you usually take the bus?"

Oh, no, here it comes. What should I say? Don't say anything stupid. What if he thinks the bus is stupid? Maybe I shouldn't say anything at all! Oh, great.

"Um, yeah, I ride the bus, usually, but I just didn't feel like it today. Gets too hot on there. Other kids bug me. You know how it is. I just needed a break from it."

"Well," Jimmy said slowly. "I'm leaving now so I could give you a ride if you want. Where do ya live?"

Oh my gosh! He wants to take me home? In his car? Can I do that? Right? Should I? What if mom finds out? But, then, who cares? This is a once-in-a-lifetime thing. He may never ask me again! Ugh. Oh, wow, I think I'm gonna throw up.

"Jenny?" Jimmy thought she was taking way too long to answer. Little did he know that she was just trying to think it all through. "Hey, snap out of it, girl. You wanna ride or not?"

"Huh? Oh, yeah. Sure." *Stay calm.* "I think I'm about ready to go, too. Sure, I'll take that offer." She told him briefly where she lived. "Are you sure it's not outta your way? I mean, I could . . ."

"Nah. I just need to bring up my car, pack up some things, and then we'll be ready to go."

By the time Jimmy had retrieved his '57 Red and white Chevy, Jenny's hands had already begun to sweat. She watched him pull up, get out, and fill up the back seat of his car with music stands and other large items, leaving the front seat completely open. Suddenly, he popped his head up and asked Jenny where she thought he should put his snare drum—the last item to go into the car.

"Uh, anywhere it'll fit, I guess," Jenny answered.

Jimmy laughed. "I mean, do you want me to put it right next to me or next to the passenger door?"

It immediately occurred to her that he was asking, in effect, if she wanted to sit next to him or by the passenger door with the snare in between them. Palms, having gone from damp to dripping, she answered coolly, "Oh, you choose. I'm okay with whatever."

Jenny could barely wait to see where he was going to put the drum. Running back downstairs to the bandroom, Jenny called back over her shoulder. "I'll just go grab my purse and books. Be right back."

Jimmy nodded.

When Jenny returned, she discovered, to her amazement, that Jimmy had placed the snare drum against the passenger door, leaving the seat beside him as the only place in the entire car to sit.

Right next to him? I'm gonna sit right next to him! Her stomach did a series of disorganized Olympic flip-flops. *Okay, girl, don't blow it now.*

Pretending that she had not even noticed where Jimmy had wedged the drum, Jenny got in the car and scooted over. She sat in the middle of the white bench seat of Jimmy's car. *Life doesn't get any better than this, does it?*

Flicking his cigarette a few feet away from his car, Jimmy climbed in the driver's seat. His steadfast rule was, *No smoking in the Chevy. No one. Period.* Jimmy loved his car and treated it as well as he would a girlfriend. Lots of attention and tender loving care. Nobody drove the prized possession except Jimmy. That was his other rule. Many of his friends had asked, but no one had ever succeeded in manipulating Jimmy into letting them drive it. "She" was certainly a beauty. He didn't name her, but always referred to it as "she." Like, "She's ridin' real good today." Or, "She's as smooth as silk, and just as pristine."

Jenny knew that he always kept *her* clean and shiny on the outside, but this was the first she had ever seen the inside. Yup. Clean on the inside, too.

The ride home lasted only fifteen short minutes, but much was accomplished in that time. Jenny had inhaled his cologne, felt the leg of his jeans next to hers, and watched his hands handle the large, red steering wheel. She had been able to carry on a half-intelligent conversation, but had never allowed herself to be distracted from his features. Before she knew it, they were turning onto her street.

"Which house is yours," Jimmy asked.

"The two-story one, up on the right about six houses." Jenny began to panic. What if her mom was waiting for her for looking out the window? *It'd be my luck to have Mama outside watering the flowers in her robe or shorts or something equally as flattering. I'd just die.* "Um, don't go into the driveway. Just stop up here, just beyond the mailbox."

As Jimmy opened the car door, he hesitated for a moment as she gathered her belongings.

Jenny scooted across the seat after grabbing her backpack and purse with her still-sweaty hands.

"Well, um, thanks for the ride home. I really appreciate it." As she stood, her deep, brown eyes met the soft gaze of Jimmy's light-green eyes. Time should have frozen that moment forever. Jenny paused just long enough to entertain "forever" when, suddenly, she glanced at the windows of her house. Thinking she had seen her mother pass by, Jenny emitted a very brief, *Well, I gotta go. Thanks for the ride,* before running up the driveway.

Did her mom see? Was she watching? Did she seem to Jimmy like an immature, little girl? She thought that if she hadn't thrown up before, she certainly felt like it now.

Glancing back to wave goodbye to Jimmy, Jenny saw that he was smiling and shaking his head. He waved before returning to the driver's seat.

Waiting until he drove off, Jenny gathered her composure before entering the front door. Not knowing what (or whom) she would encounter when she stepped in, she held her breath. *I am so doomed!*

Jenny did not get in trouble that night. She, in fact, lived to tell about it! Her mother, who had noticed that the bus had come and gone, had, indeed, asked how she got home.

"A friend brought me home," was all Jenny had squealed out before running upstairs to her room and collapsing on her bed. Her mother had not tried to squeeze out any further information. *Whew!*

Jenny had escaped the bullet. That time.

CHAPTER 20

For weeks after that rivoting ride home, Jenny wanted nothing more at the end of each day than to re-live it, over and over, in her mind. As soon as she had raced upstairs, Jenny had quickly called Monica and pored over every single detail of the afternoon and the car ride home with Jimmy.

"I just can't believe it!" Monica had said so excitedly. And, then thought, *This had been the most Jenny had talked in months.* Monica was so relieved to have her gossip buddy back. They had spent the next two hours on the phone, each sharing the details of their crushes and wishes before finally hanging up exhausted.

Football season, freshmen year was beginning to go down in history as the best season of Jenny's life. The band spent countless hours practicing their routines and music. Memorizing the music was difficult enough, but playing while marching required both sides of her boy-crazed brain, making a perfect routine for Friday nights' games almost impossible.

The casual flirting between Jenny and Jimmy continued on and off the marching field. They usually didn't see each other during the day because their classes were in different wings of the school. So, band class was her only saving grace.

Jenny had wanted to ask Jimmy to attend church, but that was certainly out of the question—as far as her parents were concerned, she was sure. It would have been nice for her, though, to have had Jimmy witness her vocal and piano talents on those Sunday mornings when she was allowed to play for the youth choir. But, she had quickly tucked away that fantasy. Besides, Jenny didn't know whether or not Jimmy would have even been interested in coming to her church. *Was he a Christian? Did he already attend somewhere? Why hadn't we talked about their faith? Why haven't I shared mine, since my relationship with Jesus was the most important one in my life?*

There were certainly a number of reasons for that, Jenny convinced herself. She was busy, and it's not like they spent a LOT of time together.

She really barely knew him and his interests. Or, anything about his life, really. She had noticed that Jimmy had never really shared much about his family life. *But, that wasn't all that odd, was it?* Jimmy was just shy, that's all. And private. He didn't go spilling his life's details to anyone and everyone. *Maybe I should ask him about his family the next time we talk.*

Their high school football team had made it to the semi-finals this year. It was the talk of every class and at most tables in the lunchroom. The team was going to Midwest City for the playoffs in two weeks, and the principal had just announced that the entire band would get the privilege of going, too!

Jenny was filled to the brim with amazement. This meant that she (and, especially Jimmy) would get to spend a massive amount of quality time together. Midwest City was a few hours away, so they'd have to leave right after school to arrive in time for the game, and probably not arriving back home until after midnight.

For the next two weeks, Jenny could barely stand still. The time went by at a handicapped snail's pace, but the day finally arrived.

The band room was chaotic after school. Everyone was searching for their uniforms, making sure to gather all pieces, and instruments. The buses were parked upstairs by the outside bandroom door waiting for its occupants.

Jenny was so excited she could barely stand herself! Then, life intervened.

The band director decided to divide up the band members into certain buses. He placed the freshmen in one bus, the sophomores and juniors in the second, the seniors in the third and the percussion section in the fourth. There was no way that Jenny would be able to ride with Jimmy.

Glancing at Jimmy after the announcement, Jenny gathered up her flute and uniform and headed for the freshmen bus. How disappointing! And, she wondered if Jimmy was feeling similarly.

The buses didn't return to the school until well after midnight. The trips were long and unbelievably tiring. The game was great and they had won, but Jenny was still feeling the disappointment from the dream night that had held such high expectations. Jimmy and Jenny had been able to talk a bit during the game and had spent the entire third quarter together since the band always had that time off.

Jimmy had smoked a few cigarettes, which Jenny found disgusting, but she assumed that he would eventually get tired of such a foul-tasting habit and quit. Or, was she just being naive?

They sipped their cokes and ate nachos, which Jimmy bought. Leaning against a random white car parked next to the freshmen bus, Jimmy talked more than he had at any other time. Not a lot about his family, other than they were pretty financially poor, but mainly focused on how much he hated school. Couldn't seem to find any subject he was interested in other than just playing the drums in band. School had always been frustrating for him. Just didn't seem to fit in with the other brainiacs in school. He liked working on electronics, speakers and such, so he might pursue his interests in that after graduation. Until then, he would just keep dragging his feet through each class until it ended with a huge graduation party!

Jenny reassured him that he was very intelligent and that he would eventually find his niche. They talked about their love for music and how it had been the only thing that had captured their souls. Music was pure. Emotional and expressive. "And, healing," Jenny had added, to which Jimmy responded with a tilt of the head, a sad half-smile, and a long gaze at her before extinguishing his cigarette.

"C'mon. Let's go back," Jimmy said as he put his arm around her.

They walked slowly towards the stadium, across the gravel parking lot, listening to the crowd's cheers. Jenny didn't want to return to her seat. She wanted to stay and talk with Jimmy until the end of the game.

But, before they reached the stairs, Jimmy stopped and turned towards Jenny. Cupping her face in his cold hands, he sweetly said, "Jenny, you're very different from others. You know that?" Then, he kissed her. Gently. Sweetly. Briefly.

Neither said another word as they approached the stairs. Just a glance and a smile between them before separating and finding their sections in the bleachers.

For the rest of the evening, Jenny floated as if on air. As exhilerated as she was feeling, she would have to stoop *down* to touch cloud nine! She thought nothing could replace the experience as though she was in an air-tight bubble, protecting her from any other reality. Other sights, smells, and sounds were muffled as though they were far off. The football game, the crowd's cheers, the band's sound all seemed distant.

Reliving the events of that night certainly made the long bus ride home quickly squeal by. Having been the first to arrive at the high school, Jenny saw that her father was waiting in the car for her. Though she had to leave the parking lot, the memories of that night would never leave her heart.

The weeks following that one sweet night wrapped up the marching band season better than Jenny could have ever hoped. Concert and jazz band season would see her through the next few months with Jimmy since both of them had made the cut. Not as many hours as marching season, but enough to satisfy her.

However, Jenny's *satisfaction* was very short-lived. The night of the Christmas concert changed her life forever. Jimmy had arrived later than usual that night at the high school performing arts center. Jenny had waited downstairs in the band room as long as she possible. The flutes gathered upstairs in their chairs and tuned with each other successfully. The room was filling with people, and, just as the lights dimmed, Jimmy came rushing in, practically sliding into his place in the percussion section. The band director shot him a steely glare that communicated just how unhappy he was with his extreme tardiness.

Jenny tried to send him a reassuring glance, but Jimmy never looked around. She assumed he was embarrassed or mad about something. She kept checking on him throughout the concert, but Jimmy never once looked up. When he wasn't playing the drums, he was just staring into space, as if the world's weight was on his shoulders.

By the time the concert had ended, Jenny had become quite concerned about him. Her plan was to quickly run downstairs to the bandroom so that they could have at least a few moments to talk before having to leave with her parents. It was a great plan. Oh, how she wished it would have worked.

Jenny raced away from her friends after the concert and, though she was among the first to arrive in the bandroom, she found no signs of Jimmy. Upon putting away her flute, she quickly grabbed her purse and headed back upstairs to where he was last seen. Running into everyone else but Jimmy, Jenny had a brilliant thought to go outside to check to see if his car was still there.

And, it was, but he was not alone.

CHAPTER 21

Nothing could have prepared Jenny for what she saw that night.

As she ran outside into the cold, crisp air, Jenny stopped abruptly when she saw Jimmy's chevy up by the outside bandroom door. Beside his car stood a beautiful young woman with long, blonde hair, standing by the passenger door. It seemed as if she was waiting for someone. But, why would she be standing by Jimmy's car?

With thoughts as slow as molasses twisting in and throughout her head, Jenny began to realize that this young woman was waiting for Jimmy. This same young stranger reached into the car, grabbed a cell phone which had rung, and talked, animatedly. Quickly hanging up, she took out a pack of cigarettes from her purse and lit up. A few minutes passed, and just as she flicked it away, Jimmy came running out and hopped into his car. The girl entered the passenger side of his car and both sped off as though they were fleeing from a fire.

Jimmy didn't seem at all happy. His face looked almost angry, yet he wasn't yelling. Jenny wondered if she was his sister or possibly a cousin since they had the same hair color. Yet, there was something which told her that their relationship was not a familial, but a familiar, one. There was something more between them. Maybe it was the way she looked at him with such sad eyes. This was all very confusing and difficult for Jenny to grasp.

Jenny stared at the empty, oil-stained spot where Jimmy's car had been parked. He was gone and there was nothing she could do about it now. She couldn't ask him anything. She would just have to wait until tomorrow. With a hollow heart and a frustrated mind, Jenny walked back into the building to find her parents and siblings before heading home.

Friday came and went without seeing Jimmy. Maybe he had become ill last night, which would have explained his hasty retreat from the concert. She wondered how she could get through the weekend without talking with him. Not that they had talked a lot before. But, leaving for the weekend without clearing up the confusion seemed to make the weekend feel more like a year. There was nothing she could do about it now. *At least I'll see him next week before we go on Christmas break,* she thought.

But, she didn't. Jimmy had not attended school Friday or any time over the next week. Then came their two week Christmas break, which would seem like a lifetime or two.

Her parents noticed that Jenny's moods had returned, but each time they asked her about what might be the cause, Jenny answered with the fewest number of words possible that would satisfy them and get them off her back.

"Whew! I knew the teenage years would be rough, but this is ridiculous," Cathey whispered to Randy. Their friends, who had already walked the thorny adolescent years with their children, had tried to gently warn them beforehand about that wee bit of a fine line between smothering them with kisses and smothering them with pillows. Not literally, of course. Such a delicate line! And, it moved daily, if not hourly.

But, Randy and Cathey had just laughed them away, saying that they were going to do everything possible to prevent their children from suffering through adolescence the way theirs did. Ha! Famous last words from naïve parents.

Returning to Liz, their therapist, for help, Randy and Cathey came away with a plan to address their questions. They were to gently push Jenny to talk more instead of letting her take the easy way out with one-word answers. "Parents, in general, tend to give up too quickly." She suggested using phrases such as, "I'll give you a minute to think about that if you need it;" or, "I've got all the time in the world to listen, I really want to understand." Over the years, Liz had used this with her "more reluctant" clients. And, it had usually worked.

"Once she knows that you're not gonna give up so easily and that you genuinely care about what she's going through, she may open up a bit more and at least give you *some* clue as to what's going on," Liz had told them.

"Also," Liz had advised, "Ask her open-ended questions instead of closed-ended ones. Instead of asking, "Was your day okay," it might be more productive to ask, "Tell me about your day," or, "What was the best and worst things that happened today."

Liz always ended with encouragement. "Keep your patience, exercise your compassion, and give it time. And, of course, you can always call me or come in."

Cathey was anxious to put Liz's suggestions into practice. So, that same night, when Jenny was in bed, Cathey knocked on her door.

"Yeah? C'mon in," Jenny offered.

Inhaling deeply, Cathey entered.

The conversation became more productive than any others. Cathey was able to use Elizabeth's examples, which elicited more information from her than any previous exchange.

Jenny took a risk and allowed her mother a brief glance into her heart.

"Boys! Relationships are very tough, Jenny. Heartbreaks are so hard to get through."

She and her mother successfully talked for quite awhile until she asked the dreaded question.

"Sounds like you've been through a lot, Jenny. Do I know this boy? Who is it? Have I heard you talk about him before?"

The hesitation from Jenny triggered suspicion from her mom.

"You're not talking about that Jimmy, are you?" Fear and anger rose within her, regardless of Cathey's attempt at controlling them.

Jenny hung her head and stared at her pillow.

"JENNY! We already talked about this. Months ago! You are NOT to be involved with him. Is this who you've been talking about?"

So much for productive conversation!

"But, Mama, I haven't been *d-a-t-i-n-g* him. I mean, it's not like we've gone out. How am I supposed to control my heart? I really, REALLY like him, Mama," Jenny announced sitting up.

"Well, maybe you're not dating, but you said earlier that "this guy" had kissed you. So, you were talking about Jimmy? Jimmy was the one who kissed you? Okay. That's it. You're not to see him anymore. You're not to touch him. You're not to kiss him. You're not to get in the car with him. You're not to ride on the bus with him. Nothing! Understand?"

Bang! That was the sound of the door to Jenny's heart slamming shut.

As she walked out of Jenny's room, her mother turned for one last comment.

"I'm serious, Jenny. No more of this Jimmy."

"GOT IT, MOM. Heard you the first time. You don't have keep saying it."

Shaking with fear, Cathey walked out and closed the door. She had no idea that Jenny had been talking about Jimmy all this time. She reminded herself that he was far too old for Jenny. What if something would have happened to her? What if they would have been dating without her even aware of it? What if they'd been in a car already? What if she would have gotten pregnant? Her panic thoughts swirled around in her head. The conversation they had just had could have been completely different. Cathey continued to shake for the next few minutes and only began to calm down after she spent some time in her bedroom praying.

Jesus, thank you for protecting my little girl from all kinds of things that could've happened. I can't imagine how I'd be feeling if . . . well, You know. I just want to say thank You. And, please calm my heart. Give me Your peace, Lord. Thank You.

After some moments, Cathey's racing heart began to slow its pace. But, as her thoughts slowed, she began to feel unsettled about the downward turn of her conversation with Jenny.

Okay, back to prayer.

Arguing with the Lord in prayer seemed so silly, yet she knew she was right about this one. She couldn't just let her young daughter wander off with some senior. No, she was certain she was right about this.

Come to Me, my daughter.

Cathey was very familiar with the Voice of the Spirit inside her heart. How could she feel so wrong when she was so right about this?

After remembering that "being right" in a relationship always comes with high price, Cathey reconsidered. She knew it was a good thing to be protective and have good boundaries, but not in the way she approached it. However, she continued to mount her defense for her actions, "But, but . . ." but she knew that this was not the stance to take when speaking with the Lord God Almighty and Creator of the Universe! But, after all, she *was* right. Right?

Train your child tenderly in the way of the Lord, but do not irritate or provoke her to bitterness.

"Okay, okay, Lord. I get it." Cathey popped off, still wanting to enlighten God as to why she had spoken so passionately to Jenny. It *was* "passion," she reminded herself? She realized that Jenny had just spoken those same words to her—with the same attitude.

I'll wait.

Finally, more humbly, she added, "I know. I'm so sorry, Lord. Even my good intentions can't undo the harm I did to her. I hurt You and I hurt my little girl. I'll go apologize."

"Apologize to whom," Randy asked as he entered the room. "Who are you talking to?"

Cathey snickered at herself. "Well, at first, I was talking to God. Then, He was talking to me."

Picking up on her tone, Randy smiled. "I see. I know that one real well!"

"Yeah. He had a few things to say to me."

Cathey explained the situation to Randy while he listened attentively. He had concerns about Jimmy, especially about his age, but admitted that he didn't know much about him.

"Randy! There's no point in knowing him. He's simply too old for Jenny."

"Hey, take it easy, Babe. I'm right with ya. I'm not in favor of letting them date. I'm just sayin' that we don't know him as a person. And, *how* we view him will come across to Jenny. And to God. We don't judge, remember?"

It took awhile before Cathey could calm down enough to even think of apologizing to Jenny. Wondering if she was still asleep, Cathey gently knocked on her door.

"Jenny? You awake?"

Oh, yes! Jenny was still awake. She certainly had not been able to fall asleep, given the heightened levels of adrenaline coursing through her veins. Jenny was so angry at her mom that she felt like throwing something across the room. Instead, she had grabbed her journal and begun writing. Initially, she couldn't get the words out fast enough. But, given enough time, the flow took on a slower pace. *Maybe in her old age, Mama had forgotten what it was like to fall in love.* She guessed she could excuse the "ancient aged" card, but her mom had acted like she didn't trust Jenny at all. *What does she think I am, anyway? I'm not some kind of slut who goes around sleeping with every guy I can get in bed with!*

Jenny finally answered. "Yes, mother. I'm awake." Jenny always used the more detached term, "mother," when she was upset with her.

"Can I talk with you a minute?"

"Sure," Jenny said reluctantly. "What do you want?"

Cathey heard the slight sarcasm and tried to ignore it.

"I came here to apologize. I am so very sorry, Jenny. I let my anger get the best of me and it just took over the conversation."

Jenny wasn't moved.

"Honey, I really liked how we were talking before I ruined it. It's been a long time since we could talk like that."

"Yeah, I know," Jenny said poutingly.

"I'd really like it if we could try again. It didn't end at all the way I wanted it to. I'm just sorry for being so abrupt and walking out instead of talking it through."

By this time, Jenny's heart had softened. Scooting nearer to her mother, Jenny apologized, too, for her secrecy. She really wanted her parents' trust. And, really hated the times her parents were angry at her.

Basking in the warmth of reconciliation, Jenny allowed her mother to stroke her hair and face.

"So, can I still talk to Jimmy?"

Cathey inhaled deeply before answering.

"Look, sweetheart. I love you with all my heart. I want to protect you from the world's pain out there. But, I need your cooperation. We don't need to fight against each other when I'm trying to save your heart and feelings."

"So, is that a yes or a no?"

"It's a no. But, I don't want you to hide things from me, and I really don't like it when you think you have to face things alone. Daddy and I are always here for you, even though sometimes you see things differently than we do."

Feeling the pang of defeat, Jenny quickly lay down, facing away from her mother.

Cathey was disappointed, but knew that she and Randy had set an appropriate boundary against seeing Jimmy.

"Okay. Well, I guess we'll just leave it at this for tonight. I know you're sad and disappointed about our decision. Just remember, I love you. Daddy does, too. Now, try to get some sleep."

That was the last thing Jenny wanted to hear.

CHAPTER 22

"Hey, Jenny," Monica yelled from across the parking lot. "What planet are you on? You're not even paying attention. Did you hear what I said?"

Jenny shooked her head after acknowleding Monica's presence.

"What is wrong with you? Why haven't you returned any of my calls? Are you sick or something?"

Stopping dead in her tracks, Jenny turned to address her best friend.

"I just didn't feel like it, that's all. And, no, I'm NOT sick. Well, not a disease kind of sick anyway. Sick of being at home with my parents, maybe."

"Why? What's happening on the ol' home front?" Monica replied with levity to ease the heaviness of Jenny's mood.

"My parents are . . . well, they're just stuck back in the time of Moses, that's all."

Aware that her lame attempt at humor had failed, Monica waited for more information.

"We had this big fight over the weekend. About Jimmy. They won't even let me talk to him now. They're all like, telling me that it doesn't matter that I like him a lot. Said they were trying to *protect* me from him."

They began walking into school.

"But, you guys aren't even dating," Monica reminded Jenny, as if she didn't know already.

"I know! They're just being stupid. Well, maybe they can keep me from going out with him, but they can't keep me from talking to him. That's against my civil rights—one of them anyway, I think."

Monica repositioned her heavy backpack and headed for her locker.

"Call me later, k? And don't blow me off again either!"

Jenny just shrugged her shoulders and headed in the other direction.

The rest of the day went by without incident. Students were back in school from the break and assignments began again. Transitioning back into the structure of school was never one which Jenny enjoyed. It always took her several days to get back into the swing of studying again.

Concert band class finally arrived, and her first chance to see Jimmy. She rushed downstairs into the band room and hurriedly glanced around until she saw him already in place back by the drums. He looked good, she thought. Good blonde hair day, nice dark jeans, and a green, long-sleeved, striped shirt that made his eye color pop. He had those eyes which seemed to change color to match whatever he wore. Today, his eyes were green.

Their eyes locked and she smiled first. He returned the smile, but it seemed to be tinged with sadness. Shoulders bent over slightly, Jimmy looked as if he was carrying the weight of the world on his thin shoulders. He gently nodded his head and mouthed, *We'll talk later.* She nodded and he winked. Plan set.

Over the course of the hour, they continued their exchange of glances and smiles. As the end of class approached, Jenny's stomach began to knot. She and Jimmy were going to talk soon. What would she say? What had been wrong with him? Well, she was going to find out.

Jenny pushed her way into the room where the woodwinds were stored. Placing her flute on the third shelf, she ignored those who had been calling her. She was focused solely on finding Jimmy.

As she re-entered the band room from storage, Jenny's heart sunk like the Titanic in frigid water. There, standing next to Jimmy, was the same girl who was with him two weeks ago. The pretty, tall blonde girl had her hand on his arm and was whispering something in his ear. Jimmy smiled, but not a full one. It was more like a slight upturning of the ends of his mouth.

Attempting to take it all in, Jenny stopped dead in her tracks, as though her naive, tender heart had hit a tall, sculpted iceberg. This girl who leaned into Jimmy wore a black, long-sleeved turtleneck with a black-and-purple striped jumper over it, complemented by black leggings and boots to match. As she turned sideways, this "friend" of Jimmy's exposed her truth.

This girl was pregnant. Very pregnant.

CHAPTER 23

Blinking several times, Jenny could hardly believe her eyes. In that split second, everything made sense—her familiarity with Jimmy, the sad look on his face, the distance he kept from Jenny, his absences from school—all of it.

"Hey, Jenny," a clarinet player said impatiently. "You gonna move, or what?" Students tried to pass this stationary statue blocking the door frame.

The commotion commanded Jimmy's attention and his eyes met Jenny's. Her face had frozen in an expression that could only be defined as stunned. Though she hated it, tears spilled over Jenny's smooth, chocolatey cheeks. Jimmy's sad and troubled face re-emerged.

Knowing that this would crush Jenny, he mouthed the words, *I'm sorry*, which only increased her searing pain.

"Oh, God. I think I'm gonna throw up," Jenny said aloud as she dashed out of the room. Where could she go? Where could she have a meltdown in solitude? There were people everywhere! Students crammed in every hallway. Heart racing. Palms sweating. Her panic told her to run! She had to get out of here!

Then, Jenny remembered that school had just let out for the day. Dashing towards the bus, Jenny forgot her backpack in the bandroom. She could never return to retrieve it. Not now! It would have to sit there until morning, or next year, or whenever she decided to return, if ever.

Jenny went to bed early that night, drenching her pillowcase with her wet tears. Thoughts swirling in her mind. *How could I have been so stupid? Why didn't I see this coming? See, nobody should trust men. Men shatter hearts and they leave you.*

Her own thoughts were difficult enough to battle, but Satan threw out his lies and half-truths with the hope that she would take the bait.

You're right; you can't trust men. Besides, who are you to think that Jimmy would have wanted you anyway? Given your childhood, you'll have to just settle for what you can get.

WITH PERFECT TIMING, Randy climbed the stairs in search of his princess who had been uncharacteristically somber at dinner.

"Well, here you are. You alright? I've been worried about you." He could see that she had been crying. With shoulders dropped, Randy rubbed his forehead and smiled softly before heading over to wrap her up in a bear hug.

"What's wrong with my girl, huh?"

Jenny melted in her daddy's strong, engulfing arms.

In that moment, no words were needed.

And, Satan's lies? Vanished. On the spot.

NEITHER TEMPTATIONS NOR DARK WHISPERS FROM SATAN COULD HOLD UP in the presence of this kind of love. A father's adoration of his daughter. The kind of love that whose origins are from Father God Himself!

In absolute amazement, Jenny looked up at her father and remembered this sacred type of love which had redefined her early experiences in life. A father's love. Her daddy's love. Pure, unconditional, absolute, enveloping. How grateful she felt in that moment to have been given a father like this. If a father could love his daughter like this, how much more so could God love us? It boggled her mind.

"Daddy?"

"Yes, Princess," her father whispered.

"Why does love always have to hurt?"

Randy had known that this conversation would soon come. How would he handle it? How could he explain the difference between a flawed man's love and God's perfect love to such a young soul? First, though, he must find out what happened.

As Jenny explained to her father what had wounded her so badly, Randy's eyes began to water from both relief and sadness. Relief that Jenny had not been the one to have been seduced by Jimmy and become pregnant; and, an overwhelming sadness that his daughter had to experience the dark side of life. Again.

Her father's tears fell from his red eyes and splashed onto the depth of her pain and soothed its injury.

"Most boys don't intend to hurt you, Jenny. Often, they're just too young to know how to love others in the right way. Even Christians, sometimes, don't know how to love others, even though we claim we know Jesus." Though wanting to say much more, Randy stopped due to a check in his spirit. A thought spoke to his heart: she doesn't need an explanation; she needs love. And, so, in silence, Randy held her while she cried out her hurt and betrayal.

Later that evening, while Randy and Cathey were preparing for bed, they discussed the situation with Jenny. Though Cathey had been previously angry that Jenny had continued her relationship with Jimmy, she felt no anger at this moment. No, she felt only sadness for her daughter.

"That kind of pain hurts like no other," Cathey said knowingly.

"Hmm," Randy teased with one eyebrow raised. "Sounds like you speak from experience. Who was the guy?"

"*Was?*" Cathey asked flirtingly.

While hitting him playfully with a pillow, Cathey gave no explanation. Just raised her eyebrows and giggled, "I'll never tell."

Insightfully and more somberly, Randy said, "Maybe it would help Jenny to know that there is life after a devastating blow like that. What do you think?"

"That's a good idea, Mr. insightful one!" Cathey continued her mischievous mood.

"No, I'm serious, Cath. She's hurting and I don't want her to feel that there's no hope from ever escaping it."

"I know, I know. I'll talk with her in the morning. It's too late now to carry on a serious conversation. Just let her rest, get some good sleep, and things will look better in the morning."

Randy seemed satisfied.

"Now, turn off that light, and get over here!"

Immediately, Randy's low spirit was lifted and he, too, came up with a few ideas of his own on how they could spend the rest of the evening.

CHAPTER 24

Spring semester sped by with a blur for Jenny. Automatic pilot became her modus operandi which helped her through the daily, arduous tasks. *Just keep on walking,* was her motto. *One foot in front of the other, and don't look back.*

Never before had Jenny experienced a hurt such as the blow dealt by Jimmy. Through word of mouth, she heard that Jimmy's girlfriend gave birth to their baby around mid-February, though no exact date was ever disclosed.

Oftentimes, Jenny wondered how she completed that semester. Though daylight savings time lit the evenings, the hurt dimmed Jenny's heart.

At some point in the unforeseeable future, Jenny would admit to her mother that she was right about Jimmy. That he, in fact, had been too old for her and had an entirely different focus than she. Her parents had tried to warn her that she was too naïve to understand the differences between sexes at that age, but Jenny had not had the ability to comprehend.

April and May fared better for poor Jenny's heart. She had heard the old saying, *Time heals all wounds,* but she knew it would take more than time to mend this girl's heart.

Summer arrived, thank God! She would not have to see Jimmy every day in class, and could focus on other activities which would keep her mind otherwise occupied.

Traditionally, the first week of summer allowed Jenny to catch up on some much needed sleep. The second week was spent preparing to spend the third week at Monica's grandmother's house. Jenny loved the two-and-a-half-hour trip to Arkansas. The Beasley's were always so nice and comfortable to be around. After spending so many weeks at Grandma Beasley's, Jenny was now considered "extended family."

Of course, it didn't hurt that Grandma Beasley's neighbor was the very nice-looking Tommy, the one who had rescued them from the car accident.

Though Tommy was twenty-two years old, he still lived with his parents, which wasn't unusual for country inhabitants. Since Tommy's father, Tom, was getting older, he needed his son, more and more, to work the farm and take care of their horses.

An only child, Tommy was a hard worker and seemed to enjoy the farmland and animals. He seemed dedicated to his parents, friendly, helpful, and down-to-earth. And, to the girls' knowledge, unattached! Single; as in, not dating anyone special. They didn't know for certain, but in all the times they had visited, they had never seen him with a girl. Which made him fair game, as far as they were concerned. Even if he did date, all they wanted to do was look, not touch. However, it would certainly increase the richness of their fantasies if he was unattached.

In fact, Jenny admitted she was solely interested in the "no-touching" fantasy, since her heart had already been broken by one several years older. But, Monica was interested in more. Hers was more of a hands-on plan; one in which she would inspire feelings in Tommy that he had never before felt.

"And, I'm just the one who can do it," Monica proclaimed.

"Just be careful, girl. Lookin's one thing, but touchin'll get you hurt."

Monica became defensive and irritable at Jenny's comment.

"You don't know any such thing, Jen," she sassed with hands on her hips. "You're just jealous because I'm going after him, too. Well, we'll just see which one he picks."

"I told you, I am NOT, repeat n-o-t, going to make a move toward this guy. My heart's still broken from Jimmy. You can have free reins with Tommy. Besides, my parents'd kill me if they found out that I was interested in another older guy. And, I'm not goin' there again." For laughs, Jenny added, "All I ask is that you just let me look!"

The tension was broken with this last comment and both girls giggled as best friends again.

While still laughing, a too-familiar unsettling in Jenny's stomach suddenly and silently materialized.

THE TRIP FROM OKLAHOMA TO the Arkansas hills occurred without incident. It was the perfect day to travel. Temperature in the low nineties and an all-blue sky announced the beginning of their summer vacation.

They arrived safely as Grandma Beasley watched them back into the driveway. The girls popped out of the car, running over to hug the seventy-two year-old beloved woman. Jenny's pillow spilled out onto the gravel.

"Wait, girls. Come back and get your stuff and take it on into the house," Mr. Beasley called.

After the girls settled into the smaller guest/sewing room, they went to the kitchen to see what there was to eat. Grandma Beasley always baked things for their visits, like soft, gooey, chocolate chip cookies or a freshly baked, yellow cake with chocolate icing. But, the beaters had already been washed and placed in the drainer to dry. They hadn't arrived in time to lick them, which was a huge disappointment to the girls.

Mr. and Mrs. Beasley planned to stay for dinner before heading back home. The girls were staying the week by themselves this time.

Oh, the plans they had!

CHAPTER 25

The dinner smells lingered after Mr. and Mrs. Beasley's departure. Pot roast with onions, carrots, and small red potatoes filled their stomachs and nourished their brains for their plan-making session later that evening.

Popping into their pajamas early, the girls sat on their twin beds, pens in hands, ready for the ideas to come pouring out of their thoughts and sweeping onto the pages. They brainstormed ideas about what they were going to do with an entire week without parental surveillance, where they would go, and who they might meet in the process.

"Well, we can't just show up over at Tommy's, looking guilty and dumb," Jenny offered.

"Fine, then. We'll go with the original idea of baking him something and taking it over to him."

"Why do we have to bake something? Why can't we just go over to say hi?"

Monica stared at Jenny as though she had lost her mind.

"You can't just *show up*, Jenny. That would look too stupid and immature. We're not kids, Jen. Besides, older men always like food. Actually, all men like food, no matter their age."

Jenny looked down at her paper and began to doodle.

"What's wrong, Jen? You're not acting right."

The doodles had become circles within circles; like a maze with no way out.

"I don't know. I just . . ."

"What? You just what?" Monica demanded.

"I guess . . . . I just don't have a good feeling about all this. Maybe we shouldn't go over there. Let's just steer clear of guys in general and just have a good time, just you and me."

"Are you sick or something? Have you lost your mind? For weeks, we've been talkin' about this visit. You never once said that you've had a funny feeling."

"Yeah, I know. I was excited, but . . . now, not so much."

"Oh, for God's sake, Jenny. Lighten up! We're not goin' over there to get married and run away from home. You're actin' like we're doing something totally spastic."

Jenny looked at her friend with a hesitation.

"So, what are we gonna talk to Tommy about, Monica? Don't you think we'll look just a little goofy, two girls going over just to say hi?"

"Well, then, we'll place ourselves outside at the right time, when Tommy's out workin' and then we'll just play it by ear from there. It doesn't have to look goofey, silly. We'll look totally natural. Quit going all serious on me. Let's just have some fun, okay? Isn't that why we came, to have fun?"

Trying to diminish the niggling sensation in her stomach, Jenny shrugged off her concerns.

"You're right," Jenny laughed half-heartedly. "We came here to have fun. There's no harm in lookin', right? We're just enjoying the moment. And, even if we do go over to say hi, it's really no big deal. I mean, he may not even want to talk to us anyway. I'm sorry for being so, um, so cautious. Let's make some plans and have some fun."

FUN IS EXACTLY what they had in mind.

The next morning, the girls slept until ten o'clock, ate cereal with bananas and two slices of coffee cake, and then dressed with the hope of seeing Tommy in the back field.

Their hope met with success!

Tommy, sweaty and shirtless, was fixing a section of their barbed-wire fence which had been damaged and loosened over the harsh winter. Their horses and cows could not have broken through without being hurt.

Pretending to be on a mission of gathering the branches downed by the last storm, the girls wandered over to the fence.

Tommy heard the noise (more accurately, giggles) and turned to greet them.

"Oh, hey girls. Wha' 'cha doin'?"

Neither Jenny nor Monica could keep their jaws closed as they watched him stand up. This was the first time in awhile that they had seen him that closely. His medium-long, brown hair was tussled by his work, with bangs covering one side of his forehead. His chest, bare and shiny from sweat, was tanned from working outside. The girls had not before considered him well-built. More slightly built than anything. But, something must have happened over the winter. Tommy had obviously bulked up over the last few months, and had developed firm muscles and washboard abs probably as a result from working out.

Monica, being much more outspoken, spilled words before her mind could reel them back.

"Wow! You're ripped!"

Jenny thought she would die from embarrassment. Hitting her friend on the arm, Jenny chastised Monica for being so rude.

"Geez, Monica. Tommy, I'm *so* sorry. My soon-to-be-ex—friend shouldn't have said that. She can be so rude sometimes."

Obviously embarrassed, Tommy shook his head and reached for his tools to continue work on the fence. His ever-deepening reddened face was not solely due to his hard work and the sun.

The girls had not had much contact or conversation with Tommy before so wouldn't have noticed his shy streak which now radiated. Good-looking, ripped, and shy? Oh, this was just too good to be true!

Having ignored Monica's last remark, Tommy continued as though nothing had ever been said.

"So, what are you girls up to today?"

"Jus' hangin' around," Monica said in a flirty way. "Oh, that looks like really hard work you're doing there. What's it like to take care of a farm?"

Jenny suddenly felt the urge the slap her friend again. Monica was acting stupid and oogling his biceps.

"C'mon, Monica. Let's go. Can't you see he's got work to do?"

Monica jerked her arm out of Jenny's hold.

"Not yet," Monica squeezed out of her tightened jaw. "We're just gettin' started."

Just about the time Jenny turned on her heels to make a break for the house, a second young man appeared from the barn. With boots and jeans covered in dust and straw, the shirtless man wearing a cowboy hat, swaggered over.

"Well, h-e-l-l-o, ladies," he sang. "Wha' 'cha got here, Tommy ole boy?"

"Quit, Dagger. These girls are visiting their grandmother next door. Be nice."

"What'd I do? I didn't even say nothin' yet," Dagger defended, never taking his eyes off the girls. Monica especially seemed to capture and hold his attention.

Having noticed Dagger's stare, Tommy turned his back to both girls so as to more firmly address Dagger's unspoken, and no doubt lewd, comments. With a stern look and locked jaw, Tommy addressed his worker.

"Hey, Dagger. Looks like I don't have enough nails to finish this project. Run back and get me some more, would you?"

"Get 'em yourself," Dagger spewed with a crooked smile.

Dropping his hammer, Tommy's hands tightened into fists. Dagger, acknowledging that Tommy was his boss, broke stance first.

"Fine. Geez, Tommy, chill out, man. I'll get 'em." Turning towards the girls, Dagger smiled.

"I'll be back soon, ladies. I can take you on a tour of the ranch then, if you'd like."

"Oh, that would be great! I'd really like . . ." Monica offered enthusiastically before being interrupted by her friend.

"Well, we can't right now. Thanks, but we have other plans, don't we Monica?" Jenny stared firmly at Monica.

"Um, sure, Jenny. Whatever." Being undaunted, Monica wrapped up the conversation with a flirty response directed to Dagger. "But, we'll come back tonight after dinner, which will be at a god-awful, early time. Maybe we'll see you then. That is, if Miss Serious here will let me."

While Monica walked toward the house, Dagger headed for the tool shed, leaving Jenny and Tommy looking cautiously at each other. Jenny's legs wouldn't move, no matter how much she willed them.

Sensing Jenny's fear, Tommy offered a comment made to sooth it.

"Don't worry about him. Dagger just likes to talk big, that's all."

Jenny wasn't so sure, though. She felt far from comforted by Tommy's statement and made a mental note to herself: *Take Monica and run!*

Several nights passed and the end of the week was quickly approaching. The week had been filled with eating, giggling, talking, and flirting. All in all, quite a successful trip. And, as far as Monica was concerned, one to be repeated. And, soon.

Monica's parents were coming to pick them up Saturday morning and take them back to *their ordinary houses and their ordinary lives,* as Monica put it. But, they still had Friday!

Plans were in the making, but they were certain of one thing—the plan would, no, **must,** include the young men next door.

For the last few days, Monica had flirted her little heart out with Dagger. Actually, with both of them, and was lapping up the attention.

On the other hand, Jenny felt a bit more stand-off'ish. Feeling the need for a slight bit of protection, she allowed herself to have a little fun, but certainly not to the degree that Monica enjoyed.

By nature, Monica was more extroverted than Jenny. Monica could feel at home in front of an auditorium filled with people, but Jenny preferred a small group of friends whom she knew quite well before opening up. In the safety of good friends, Jenny could act as silly and funny as any known extrovert. Maybe more so. But, Jenny hadn't felt that comfortable with their "friendly" foursome.

Part of her concern was that the boys were older by several years. She could hear her mother's warnings echoing across the miles in her mind. The guys were certainly cute enough. But, there was an atmosphere of danger which surrounded Dagger, like dirt surrounding Pigpen, the Peanuts character. Pigpen was young, innocent, and uncontaminated, quite unlike Dagger whose colorful past had been the topic of discussion the last few nights.

The other part of Jenny's concern was the secrecy which engulfed this situation. Monica's grandmother knew nothing about their nightly meetings. She ate dinner early and went to bed early, leaving the rest of the evenings open to "additional" plans. Though Monica's parents had informed Grandma Beasley of the girls' crushes on Tommy, they hadn't thought that the girls would be sneaking out of the house after Grandma went to bed.

With a pained-infected heart from the Jimmy incident, Jenny had felt very disconcerted about the whole "secrecy thing," though Monica had gigged her about being Miss Serious. To be perfectly honest, though, Jenny kind of liked the adrenaline rush which rode on the coattails of concealment. It certainly added flavored flair to an otherwise boring life!

Fortunately, Jenny did not have a concern about her crush on Tommy. Yes, he was very good-looking, friendly, and nice. But, more importantly, he was genuinely shy and sensitive about her caution. He had never said anything nor hinted that he thought she was being stuffy or straightlaced. On the contrary, Tommy seemed to really understand that caution needed to be exceedingly exercised, especially when dealing with underaged girls.

When left alone during the times while Monica and Dagger were "touring the farm," Jenny and Tommy had developed a friendship and ease with each other which had come as a pleasant and welcomed surprise. They had discussed many different topics. She had come to understand the reasons why Tommy was still living at home. He had said he was helping out his father, learning how to farm, and biding time until he could gather enough money for college. He was in no hurry, saying, "There would be time enough for everything." Further, Tommy admitted that he had squandered away his teenage years and didn't pay close enough attention to how his father ran the farm. "It's all in the details," his father would say. But, Tommy hadn't listened and now he was spending his time learning things he should have already known.

Matching Tommy's level of sharing, Jenny had told him her experience with Jimmy and how that friendship had led to such heartbreak. She also shared her adoption story, how it had ended in tragedy for her birth mother, and, her hopes of attending college and not repeating any of Natasha's mistakes. "The stupid stuff stops with me," she had told him.

Two nights ago, they had discussed their beliefs about God, favorite ice cream flavors, and which dogs best reflected their personalities. Their discussions had been salt and peppered with flavorful bits of the "meat and desserts" of life. All in all, they had seemed to enjoy each other's company, but friendship had been their only destination. No "extras" for this couple. No "friends with benefits." Just good old-fashioned friendship.

Unfortunately, she could not say the same for Monica and Dagger.

CHAPTER 26

By the time the girls crawled into their beds, both were exhausted. They had stayed up later than usual that night and had every reason to be tired. The day had been filled with laughter, running errands, and putting pieces of a jigsaw puzzle together. And, of course, the evening (meaning after Grandma's bedtime) had matched the day's laughter.

"So," Jenny asked, "what did you two do tonight? You guys disappeared for a long time. I was beginning to get worried."

"No need to worry about us. We got along just fine," Monica responded with a big grin. "I was laughing so hard he had me in stitches. He's very funny. Don't you think so?"

"Yeah, I guess. Really hadn't thought about it much."

"Don't go gettin' all serious on me, Jen. What is the matter with you? Are you just jealous because you're not having as much fun as I am?" Monica was clearly frustrated with her friend.

Monica's cruel comment wounded Jenny deeply. Tears stung her eyes. Sitting up in bed, Jenny turned angrily to Monica saying, "I can't believe you would say that to me. And you ask what's wrong with ME? Well, what's wrong with YOU? I am not jealous, you stupid idiot. I'm just scared for you, that's all. I'm your *friend*, Monica, not your enemy. You have no right to say that to me! I can't believe you said that to me."

Clearly hurt, Jenny lay back down and covered her head with the white sheet and turned her back towards her ex-friend.

Silence hung in the air like a thick fog. Neither was going to be the first to give in. Determination was certainly a trait they held in common, which often bloomed into stubbornness. Stubbornness could be silly, but when coupled with hurt feelings, it could deliver a lethal dose to a relationship.

Neither spoke, but neither would call time of death on their friendship either.

Monica finally broke the silence with words she thought could ease the distance between them.

"Dagger kissed me tonight," Monica said slowly, but excitedly.

Monica heard the sheets ruffle. And, then a big sigh. Finally, Jenny picked up her pillow and flung it across the room into Monica's face. Ah, the gift of laughter!

"So? How was it?" Jenny was dying to find out.

Monica bounded over to Jenny's bed. "Well, I can tell you this much. No guy has ever kissed me like that before," she said in a shrill voice. "He kissed . . . . I don't know. Can't describe it. He kissed . . . older, I guess."

"What do you mean, older?"

Monica searched the bedroom air for more words, but could find none which could express the physical response she received from the touch.

Silent for only a moment, Jenny finally spoke.

"Um, anything else?"

Suddenly, Monica became very uncomfortable. Quickly rising from Jenny's bed, she determinedly waltzed over to her own and dove into the covers.

"What do you mean? Like sleep with him? Is that what you're asking? Is that what you think of me, Jenny? Like I would really do that. Can't believe you would think that, f-r-i-e-n-d," Monica answered very defensively. "I'm tired now. I'm going to go to sleep."

Caught unaware, Jenny blinked several times fighting off stinging tears again.

"I didn't mean anything by it, Monica. I was just askin' if there was anything else you wanted to tell me about your time with Dagger. Sheesh, can't I just ask a little question?"

No response.

WITH ONLY A FEW WEEKS LEFT OF SUMMER VACATION, Jenny tried to savor each day. As much as she did not want to admit it, though, she was bored. She had not spoken with Monica much since they had returned from their week in Arkansas. She missed her and didn't understand why their friendship had taken a turn for the worse. Whenever she broached the subject, Monica deflected the conversation away from any personal feelings about what had happened between them and just spoken about daily details.

Jenny

So, Jenny had decided to leave her alone until this "whatever-it-was"
passed and they could get back to friendship as usual. Until then, she spent
most days with her siblings at the neighborhood pool, which they had done
every summer since being adopted by the Abbott's. The pool was huge with
two diving boards in the deep end, one low and one high, and a separate
baby pool. The snack shop was small, but displayed all their favorites like
pop, laffy taffys, popsicles, nachos, and on special occasions, hot dogs when
they didn't want to walk the few blocks home for lunch.

Never before had they had such fun as a family! Jenny and her siblings
had never had a pool before—certainly not when living with Natasha. She
had memories of a small, nasty pool with green water in their apartment
complex and the pumps had always been broken. So, being able to swim
in a pool like this was remarkable.

Swimming at the pool was the family's main source of entertainment
and enjoyment, and was well appreciated during the hot summer months
in Oklahoma.

Jenny appreciated much more than just the pool. So much more!

ONLY ONE MORE WEEK HAD PASSED before Monica called, frantic to
speak with Jenny.

Her tone was urgent.

"Jenny! You have to come over right now."

"What's wrong, Monica? Slow down. Did somebody die or something?"

"No, don't even . . . just . . . . I have to talk to you. Right now."

"Okay. Let me ask my mom if she can bring me over," Jenny responded.

Monica, barely able to contain herself, counted out each second that
Jenny was gone, which seemed like hours.

Finally, Jenny returned to the phone.

"Yeah. Mom can bring me over, but only if your mom can bring me
back home. Is that good?"

"That's fine," Monica said hurriedly. "Just come now!"

Jenny couldn't imagine what was so important that she had to go
right over. She wondered if she and her mom got into a fight, but quickly
dismissed that as an option because they rarely fought.

By the time Jenny arrived, she found Monica crying upstairs in her
room.

Rushing to her side, Jenny ran over and flung her arms around her
friend.

"What's wrong, Monica?"

"My life is over! I can't believe it. I just can't believe it. I'm dead meat. Just kill me now!"

Barely able to make out a word, Jenny told her to slow down and explain what she was talking about.

Monica quickly showed her something which was in her hand.

"I'm pregnant!"

CHAPTER 27

Looking at the home pregnancy test, Jenny confirmed what it said.

Then, glancing up at Monica's tear-filled eyes, Jenny hugged her friend unsure of what to say or do next.

"What am I gonna do?" Monica managed to ask.

"Let's just stop and think," Jenny said to buy some time. "Maybe the test was wrong. Maybe you should get a couple of more of those stick things and see what those say."

Pointing inside her dresser drawer, Monica showed her the two other tests she had taken. All said *positive*.

"My life is over, isn't it?"

"No, no, no," Jenny said reassuringly. "We'll figure out something. We just need time to think, that's all." After a small pause, Jenny continued, though cautiously. "You know, you're gonna have to tell your parents."

"No, I can't. They're gonna kill me. You know how they are."

"Is it, um, it's Dagger's baby, isn't it?"

"Well, whose else would it be, Jenny?"

Collapsing into a heap of shame on the carpet, Monica nodded. Remains of Kleenex strewn around the room told the story of a young, frightened girl, engulfed in secrecy and embarrassment, who had not shared with her best friend even the least of details about the incident. Until now.

Jenny was partially hurt that Monica had not told her about having sex with Dagger. Over the years, they shared everything with each other. They had a way of sharing that carried with it no judgment. Frustration maybe, at times, but certainly no pointed finger.

Wondering whether she should have pushed Monica for more details back when "it" had happened, Jenny began to feel guilty. Maybe she could have prevented it from happening in the first place if only she'd known what was going to happen that night. Jenny could have kicked herself for not paying enough attention to what Monica and Dagger were doing, or where they were going that fateful night. The only thing she could remember was that she had experienced a bad feeling in her stomach.

But, hindsight was 20/20 as the saying goes, and there was nothing she could do about it now. Jenny had to keep her wits about her so that she could help her friend manage this horrifying position. Fifteen years old and pregnant. These were words that should not be used in the same sentence. Pregnancy, at this age, was certainly something which happened only to someone else. Not someone who's close to you. Very close!

THE TRUTH WAS NOT ADMITTED TO MONICA'S PARENTS that night. Nor the next. But, both knew it needed to be divulged soon. Procrastination had choked out any motivation to address the situation. Though Monica's parents could tell something was wrong, they certainly would not have guessed that their family's world would be rocked soon.

However, having made a plan, the best friends would help each other face the situation instead of avoiding it. Tonight was the night. Nothing would stop Monica, thanks to Jenny's staunch support. Once Jenny put her mind to something, she always followed through with the plan—a determined young lady, for sure.

"See ya tonight," Jenny said to Monica over the phone. "After dinner. And, if I don't hear from you, I'm coming over anyway. So, just expect me there about 7:00pm. I have it worked out with my mom."

"You didn't tell her, did you?" Monica was almost speechless with the thought of Jenny's parents knowing her secret.

"Calm down, girl. No, I did not! That's not the plan. Did you forget already? The plan was that you would tell your parents first and then I'd tell mine. I am NOT changing the plan now."

Feeling nauseous, Monica felt procrastination knocking at her stomach.

"And, we are *not* backing away from this, Monica," Jenny said more sternly than she preferred. More softly, she added, "It'll be okay. You'll see. They love you and will see how upset you are. You'll feel better just getting this thing over, too. I know *I* will. That's for sure!"

NOTHING COULD HAVE PREPARED MONICA'S PARENTS for the words which stumbled out of Monica's mouth that night. *'I'm pregnant'* had never even entered their minds about what might have been disturbing her lately.

At least it was over. Everyone cried. That is, after feeling shocked and stunned. Monica had to leave twice to vomit before she could pry the words out of her mouth. But, with Jenny's soft glances, Monica was able to do the unimaginable, though she felt like she was floating above her body.

That earth-shattering night was now part of their family's history. The walls of the living room, if they could speak, would tell of silences too loud to endure, sentences too difficult to say, and reactions too pained to view. But, it was done. The hard part was over, or so Monica thought. Little did she realize that the real work was about to begin.

OVER THE NEXT FEW WEEKS, Ben and Amy Beasley, Monica's parents, stopped by to visit "reality's" home. Not able to stand much of its company, they stayed for only brief periods of time, and only in the company of each other and close friends. Randy and Cathey Abbott, Jenny's parents, were two on which they could rely.

Though the Abbott's were shocked as well, they knew Monica's heart, which was good, nice, yet young and naïve. Because of having adopted Jenny and because Cathey was involved with Crisis Pregnancy Outreach, she was the perfect person to help in this sticky situation. Though on the receiving side of adoption, Cathey had attended the CPO support group for pregnant girls for years and had become well-acquainted with the accompanying issues. She had seen their tears and heard their fears; she had understood the anger and frustration from the girls and their mothers.

Cathey would, indeed, be a welcomed prayer warrior and knowledgeable support person. When needed, she would remind Ben and Amy of God's promises: that He is always with us, that He has a plan for this baby, that all things are possible with God, that Jesus hears our prayers and pleadings, and that He will give us His own peace and comfort in our darkest hours.

This was going to be a rough road for the Beasley's. Each will grieve from different perspectives. A parent's anguish was considerably different from a young girl's sorrow. Though all hearts would be broken, all would have the opportunity to mend. That is, if they stayed within God's plan for this unborn baby.

Cathey promised herself that she would keep them lifted up and continually bathed in prayer. Nothing but the best for this cherished family!

CHAPTER 28

"What is wrong with you?" Mr. Beasley demanded to know of his daughter.

Silence in the household had quickly given way to anger.

"I don't know, Dad. I've already told you, I just don't know," Monica practically screamed. "What else do you want me to say?"

"Just tell me the truth, Monica. That's all I ask."

Monica hated it when her parents were disappointed or angry with her. Though she could withstand anger a bit better, it was painful, nonetheless.

"No, Daddy. He did not rape me," she pleaded again, tears streaming down her ashened face.

"I don't know what I was thinking, not wringing his neck when I had the chance. Did you know you were pregnant when I picked you and Jenny up from your grandmother's? Oh, God! Does she know?"

For some reason, her father's last comment struck a discordant nerve within her and suddenly she turned indignant.

"Leave Grandma out of this," Monica yelled.

"Well, Monica," her father said sarcastically. "I'd love to, but she happens to be a part of this family. At least for now anyway. Need I remind you that your little rendevouz happened on her watch when I trusted her to keep you safe?"

Amy had been present for their entire conversation, that is, fight. But, she had stayed quiet until now. Having been caught in the middle between them for the last several weeks, she felt that her new command post was the role of peacemaker—and it was not for the faint of heart. Not in this arena.

"Ben! Stop it!" Amy had more to say on her end. "Your mother knew nothing about this. It's not her fault. Besides, blaming her won't change one single thing about this situation—about this baby."

Taking a moment to calm down, Amy continued after breathing deeply.

"I'm just as upset as you, but we're not going to resolve this by yelling at each other. So, can we all just calm down and talk about what we're going to do about this?" Amy had sounded off more forcefully than she had intended, certainly catching the attention of the other two.

But, Ben, being undeterred, made his final point, though in a more subdued tone, and Amy knew what was coming.

"This boy has not heard the last of me. I'm going to press charges. Statutory rape. And that's final!"

Feeling as though she would die from parental stupidity, Monica turned and ran upstairs to her room, slamming the door and locking it. She wondered how her father could be so insensitive. How could he want to do that to her?

Fixing her gaze upon Ben, Amy stared at her husband—a man with a side of anger to him that she's never before seen. Of course, she agreed with Ben that this older boy ought to be brought up on charges, but there was certainly a better way of presenting this to their daughter. In a delicate situation like this, timing and presentation were everything!

EMERGING FROM THE THERAPIST'S OFFICE, the Beasley family finally felt a ray of hope. Feeling emotionally desperate, Amy had called Liz, the therapist from CPO, who had twenty-five years of experience with the girls and families. The hardest thing for Amy to accept was hearing Liz refer to Monica as "birth mother." Though she had heard this term used in support group for years, it was always used to describe somebody else's daughter, not her own.

However, Liz had told them that their responses were entirely normal and that they could expect a roller coaster of emotions over the next eight months. They listened as Liz told them that, because she had acted outside of God's will, there were no pain-free options. Monica had acted impulsively and without consideration for the long-term, serious consequences. Neither she nor this boy had used any protection and now faced pregnancy and possibly a sexually transmitted disease.

The choices were few, yet very painful. She could either parent this baby or make an adoption plan. Each choice would bring its own set of difficulties to face, but that with help, they would be able to reach a decision that was right for their family.

Before ending the session, Liz had prayed with them and informed them that she would most assuredly continue to lift them up in prayer.

They would all need it. Further, she had assured them that she prayed every morning before seeing the girls and families for that day.

Of all the things said that day in the session, Amy heard this one the loudest. She felt the touch of comfort, hope, and the presence of Jesus who would help them through this. God was always present. He promised that He would never leave them.

Monica had seemed to connect well with Liz, whose mildly sarcastic sense of humor had won her over. Ben had appreciated Liz's insight and experience with these situations, and Amy had just felt eternal gratitude for all of the help from her and CPO.

Behind her locked bedroom door, Monica retreated from reality into the much friendlier world of denial. Life was too difficult and her father was not making it any easier. But, friends could.

"Seriously, Jenny, can I come live with you and your family?"

"Why?"

"Because *Daddy dearest* is out of his mind! Everyone over here is angry, and I just can't take it anymore," Monica pleaded.

"Are you kidding? It's not any better over here. My parents have grounded me forever and the silence from them is very loud."

"Why are you grounded? I'm the one who's pregnant," Monica said protectively.

"Yeah, well, I snuck out of your grandma's house, too, ya know? My parents are way pissed off."

"Oh," Monica said in a slightly diminished tone. "Sorry. Guess I've been a little too caught up in myself lately. So, do your parents hate me?"

"Nah. It's just weird right now. They don't want me hanging out with you because of what we did. But, it's not just you. They don't trust *me* with anyone right now. They think that since you had sex with ol' stupid guy, my parents think that I had sex with Tommy! I mean, they wanna believe that I didn't, but now they just don't know. I shouldn't have even gone with you to visit your Grandma, then none of this would have happened. You wouldn't be pregnant, my parents would trust me, and we wouldn't even be having this talk."

After a brief pause, Monica sighed. She could feel the ugly cry coming on, as Oprah always put it. The ugly cry was not just a tear drop here and there, or eyes filling up with water. No, the ugly cry was the sob-until-the-mascara-runs-and-the-eyes-and-nose-gets-red type, which requires a lot of repair work when it's over.

"Oh, Jenny, what am I gonna do?" Monica sounded pitiful.

Frustrated with Monica's tone, Jenny's mood suddenly worsened from frustration with her friend to rage. Monica's pitiful, helpless, victim-sounding voice triggered a memory of how Natasha used to sound and it made her crazy!

"I have no idea. I never wanted you with Dagger in the first place. I knew something bad was going to happen. I just *knew* it. You should've listened to me!"

Monica's sting of tears transformed into spears of anger directed back.

"So, *you're* starting in on me now? Ya know, if I wanted to feel worse, I'd just go back downstairs. I called you because I needed a friend, not another parent."

"Well, if you consider me a friend, then why didn't you listen to me in the first place? Friends listen to friends, Monica."

"I did listen," Monica yelled. "But that doesn't mean I have to do what you say."

Jenny's intensity now matched Monica's.

"But, that's exactly what I mean. If you'd have listened to me when I told you something wasn't right, then you wouldn't be in this situation. And, now, because you didn't listen, you're gonna have a baby!"

Having reached her limit, Monica defiantly said the one thing she knew would end their conversation.

"I don't have to have this baby. There is another choice, ya know!"

Jenny was stunned at Monica's hurtful words and couldn't help but reply.

"Are you talking about abortion? No, no, I KNOW you can't be talking about getting an abortion. Why would you even say such a thing? You know how I feel about tha . . ."

Monica hung up and that was the end of that discussion.

For now.

CRAWLING INTO BED, JENNY PULLED HER COVERS up to her chin. The air conditioning felt really good on her raging, white-hot cheeks. She couldn't believe what her ears had heard. Sickened by Monica's words, Jenny's heart flared with anger and darkened with sadness.

This darkness felt like black ash and hot lava from an erupting volcano which sprayed to all corners of her small frame. Just when she was on the verge of exploding, a strange vision of a heart filled her head.

Initially, this vision showed an outline of a heart, but many things about it were all wrong. The heart was not red, nor was it full and whole. No, this one appeared as a thin slice of Swiss cheese—dingy white in color and bulleted with multitudes of holes of varying diameters.

This vision was a stark contrast to the erupting volcano and one which stopped Jenny's mind instantly. She wondered where this odd and, seemingly, random vision came from. No sooner had she finished that thought when something even more odd happened.

A voice spoke. But, it wasn't exactly audible. She "heard" this voice through her insides and it was speaking in English, using ticker-tape-like phrases.

The first message her insides "heard" made absolutely no sense to Jenny.

"This is a picture of your heart," said the voice.

She figured that, somehow, this voice had just witnessed her raging thoughts yet didn't seem deterred or distracted by them.

Feeling quite odd with the situation, Jenny wondered whether or not she should speak to the voice or just ignore it. She decided that, with nothing to lose, she would correct the voice.

"Um, NO," Jenny spoke with a tinge of sarcasm. "You must mean my heart is like a volcano. Can't you s-e-e that I'm really, really mad?"

And, as if on cue, the voice spoke again.

"No. Your heart is like the Swiss cheese I showed you."

Weirdly, Jenny became aware that she was engaging in a discussion with an "inside" voice. Feeling bolder for some reason, Jenny tried to persuade the voice again.

"What? You are NOT getting this. I'm so mad at my friend that I'm about to . . . to . . . explode."

"Look again," the voice said calmly.

"I don't get this. Am I just arguing with myself here? This is crazy," she pronounced. Certain that she would see an erupting volcano, Jenny placed her hands on her hips and closed her eyes to concentrate when, suddenly, the vision of the Swiss cheese appeared again. Now, this made no sense to Jenny whatsoever.

"What are you talking about?" Jenny asked, becoming more agitated. "How is my heart like a stupid lump of cheese?"

"No, not just any cheese. *Swiss* cheese," the Voice corrected.

Sitting up in bed quickly and throwing off the covers, Jenny's tone became enboldened yet still sarcastic.

"Okay, then, I'll bite. Pun intended. *Swiss* cheese, then. How is my heart like Swiss cheese?"

Along on the way, Jenny had noticed that this voice had richness to it. Like it was as smooth as . . . as . . . melted chocolate which, despite her desire, was having a calming effect on her rage.

As she was left hanging for a moment in silence, Jenny's heart began to soften. Though she didn't know why, her defensive stance changed to one which seemed more open to trying to understand what was happening; one which was going to allow this conversation to continue.

Responding to the serene tone, Jenny decided to lie back on her pillow, to get in a more relaxed position.

The more Jenny thought about it, the more she realized that she did not know who this "voice" was that was talking in her insides. Feeling a bit suspicious, she began to wonder if she might be going a little cuckoo, like people who believe that their televisions or trees are talking directly to them. Fear came upon her.

"W-who are you?" Jenny asked hesitatingly. There was a brief pause before she "heard" yet another response.

"I AM WHO I AM."

For a moment, Jenny thought she misunderstood. But, before she could open her mouth, the Voice spoke again.

"YOU KNOW ME AND I'VE ALWAYS KNOWN YOU."

Sitting straight up in bed again and with eyes popping open, Jenny's face and entire body became strangely warmed. There was something about this Voice, His tone, and the words that reached out to Jenny in a way she had never before experienced. It was strange, but not in a bad way. Then, she suddenly experienced an awakening.

"Hey, I know You!" Shouted Jenny. "And, I know those words. They're from the Bible." She couldn't believe her discovery. "Are you G-god?"

"I AM."

"COOL!" Jenny popped, grinning from ear to ear. "How awesome is this," she exclaimed with a child's innocence. "But, why are You here? And," she questioned, "Why are You talking to *me*? I'm just a kid. Shouldn't you be off parting the Red Sea or healing somebody or ascending to Heaven or something more important like that?"

"I AM DOING SOMETHING IMPORTANT. I AM TENDING TO MY SHEEP."

"Y-you mean me?" she asked with a nervous stutter. "Am I-I one of Your sheep?" Jenny could barely contain her heart within her chest.

But just as quickly as she felt warmed, she began to doubt herself. *What if I'm just hearing my own voice? Wouldn't she feel really stupid then? Maybe I am just going psycho. What if . . . .* Her thoughts were interrupted.

"YES, YOU ARE ONE OF MY BELOVED SHEEP."

"B-but, why?" Jenny asked, cocking her head in confusion. "I'm nothing special. I mean, there are a ton of people out there better than me. Why aren't you talking with them?"

God's voice took on an especially soft tone and a smiling one at that!

"AH, MY CHLD. YOU ARE SPECIAL BECAUSE YOU HEAR MY VOICE."

"So, that makes me special?"

"YES, YOU ARE MOST WONDERFULLY MADE BY ME. I HAVE COUNTED EVERY HAIR ON YOUR HEAD."

Unable to make sense of this recent information, Jenny frowned but continued to try and make sense out of this most unusual encounter.

"But, You said that I was just cheese," Jenny confirmed before quickly adding, "I mean, *Swiss* cheese."

"I GAVE YOU A VISION OF HOW YOUR HEART HAS BECOME—I DID NOT MAKE IT THAT WAY. YOUR HEART HAS BEEN WOUNDED, LEAVING NOTHING BUT THE DARK SHADOWS OF HOLES WHERE LOVE USED TO BE."

Jenny looked again at the vision God had placed in her head. The folds on her forehead gathered due to the intensity of her concentration. Jenny's shoulders drooped. Minutes passed before Jenny's expression changed. Her eyes did not open but, rather, leaked tears which raced down her cheeks.

"I'M WITH YOU."

Sniffling, Jenny said, "I know what the Swiss cheese means."

God's gracious silence allowed her to speak in her own time, gaining insight at her own pace.

Jenny used the top sheet of her bed to wipe away her tears. And her runny nose.

"I can feel You. You're still here, aren't You?"

"I AM."

Plopping both arms at her sides on the bed, Jenny began to explain, more to herself than to God.

"The holes in the cheese are from all the times I got hurt. Like, when Natasha left me alone and scared, and I had to take care of the boys; or, every time she yelled at me; or, like every time I thought of my dad and how he left me. He just up and left and I don't even know why. I don't even *care* why anymore. He should never have done that. I mean, what kind of father leaves his child? Who does that?" Clearly, Jenny was becoming more agitated. And, clearly, she wasn't done.

Streams of tears ran down her cheeks and onto the sheets. Angry thoughts about her father whirled round and round in her head. "I just don't understand . . . never even knew him . . . never even knew ME . . . if he were here now, I'd . . . who does he think he is . . . leaving my mother that way . . ."

A lifetime full of hurt and anger spilled out of her mouth and directly into the ears of her Heavenly Father.

Drenching her pillow with tears, Jenny sobbed. And sobbed. And sobbed. It hurt so badly that she feared her heart would implode. She thought she might now have an inkling of how people felt when experiencing a heart attack. This was, truly, a heart *attack*. Dropping to her knees beside the bed, Jenny cried out for God.

"Ple-e-ease, Lord," Jenny cried. "My heart hurts so bad. Take it away. Do something. ANYTHING!"

Jenny's sobs were gut-wrenching. Her chest burned. Her eyes stung. Her cheeks blazed. Wailing into her pillow, she feared the pain would never stop. Jenny dragged the sheets down with her to the floor and engulfed herself in them. The womb-like, self-created environment felt safer to her than being exposed to the air.

Just when she thought her tears had run out, a new source of them got tapped into. Memories flooded her mind. Unable to stand it any longer, Jenny, again, cried out.

"God, WHERE ARE YOU? You left me, too, didn't you?" Gripped with fear, Jenny felt completely alone on the floor of her bedroom. "I can't feel you anymore. WHERE ARE YOU? PLEASE, DON'T LEAVE ME!"

The Voice spoke strongly to her spirit.

"I AM WITH YOU. I WILL NEVER LEAVE YOU OR FORSAKE YOU. I LOVE YOU WITH PERFECT LOVE, MY DAUGHTER. I SENT MY ONLY SON TO DIE ON A CROSS FOR YOU. FOR YOU!

TO SAVE YOU FROM DEATH, SO THAT YOU COULD ALWAYS BE WITH ME. YOU ONCE ACCEPTED ME INTO YOUR HEART; NOW ACCEPT MY GIFT OF SPIRIT."

Warmth swathed her heart and softened her sadness as she collapsed onto the floor. Liquid light poured over her soul like oil on a lamb's nose, protecting and soothing it. Her heart was finally at peace.

This was a state of being like nothing she had ever before experienced. She didn't want to think or talk; she just wanted to be. To accept. To allow. She didn't really feel like she was a part of this world, yet she was in the world.

Minutes passed, but Jenny was unaware of time. She basked in divine love that was offerered. Overwhelmed by the intensity of perfect love, Jenny was moved to tears. But, not tears of sadness and hurt. No, her eyes were moistened with delight and relief.

She knew that nobody could offer a love such as this. It simply wasn't of this world or of human understanding. She did not initiate it nor could she control it. She simply had the presence of mind and willingness of spirit to embrace it.

Lying face up yet still entangled in her sheets, Jenny became aware that she had dropped her death-grip on the sheets. *Good thing sheets aren't alive, or they'd have been dead by now*, she thought as a grin creeped over her mouth.

Jenny certainly needed tissues after that wailing. The sheets would no longer be enough. She arose from the floor, retrieved the box of tissues from atop her desk, and sat down cross-legged in the chair.

In a small, child-like voice, Jenny finally spoke.

"I've got a red, stuffy nose now."

Having blown her nose a number of times, the soft-brown tone of her nose had morphed into Rudolph-the-red-nosed-reindeer red.

"I LOVE YOU."

"I actually *know* that now. I feel it. Man, you sure know how to love right!"

Slowly, Jenny began to reflect on her experience. Her nose was already sore, but it didn't matter. Little else mattered to Jenny at this moment. Finally able to piece together the Swiss cheese thread, Jenny repeated what the Father had already known.

"So, all those times that somebody hurt me, they actually took a bite out of my heart, one by one, right?"

"YES," came the softest response.

"Ya know," she continued, heaving a huge sigh, "if people hadn't taken so many bites out of my heart, it might still have been red rather than dead, pasty white, like year-old cake frosting. But, with each bite, I lost more red, didn't I?"

"YES," came the response.

After throwing about twenty tissues into her trash can, Jenny had made enough sense out of her childhood that she was able to face the next part with more strength and clarity.

She had once believed the lies Satan had fed her. Lies about how unimportant, how unlovable, and how unworthy she was. But, Truth annihilated those erroneous beliefs. Truth said she was His daughter; Truth said she was lovable; and, Truth said she was special. But, there was still the matter of the holes in her cheese. Sitting back down on the bed, Jenny paused a moment to collect her thoughts. Having done so, she lifted her chin and spoke.

"So, what do I do now with all the holes?"

"GIVE THEM TO ME."

His response seemed so simple, yet she wondered how something like that could be done with the Almighty in Heaven.

"How am I supposed to do that?"

"CLOSE YOUR EYES."

As she did so, Jenny's imagination focused on the vision of the Swiss cheese which had now returned.

"Okay, Lord. Now what?" she asked in anticipation.

"GIVE THEM TO ME. GIVE ME ALL YOUR WOUNDS."

Using her young imagination, Jenny pictured herself holding the Swiss cheese in the palms of both hands. *Such a sad-looking heart,* she noticed.

Holding out her heart-shaped cheese, she suddenly saw a vision of Jesus standing before her and He was smiling. Of all the important matters He could be tending to, He was, instead, here with her and reaching for her cheese, her wounded heart. She watched Him gently take it from her and hold it for what seemed like hours, yet time seemed to stand still.

Jenny couldn't help but be awestruck at the sight of her Savior. The One who had been so horribly wounded on the Cross now took her own wounds. While He held it, something happened. She paid less attention to that, though, than on the details of Jesus. She was mesmerized. The Son of God. Enthralled at His sight, she drank in His soft gaze, yet rugged face; His long, brown hair and beard; the brilliance of His robe and the simplicity of His sandals. Truly, He was the humble King about which the Bible spoke.

As she gazed into His face, words seemed to be an unwelcomed distraction, especially since she was in the presence of The Word.

But, a bright light caught her attention. It was coming from His hands. Pure, stark-white, concentrated light which then radiated streaks of brilliant light into her room, reminding her of how the sun often looked as it breaks through dark clouds.

The room seemed to warm, but not uncomfortably so.

Reaching out her hands to take what obviously Jesus was trying to give, Jenny took hold of the object she had originally surrendered—her hole-filled, beaten-up heart. But, the holes had vanished. The holes in her Swiss cheese had disappeared and, in its place, He gave her a restored, beautiful, deeply red, bursting-at-the-seams, young, and vibrant heart. Her heart had been instantaneously transformed! And, due to no effort of her own. How incredible!

Jenny's face lit up, amazed that her heart could look so striking. Suddenly confused, she looked to Jesus for answers.

"So, what does this mean?"

"YOUR WOUNDS ARE HEALED. I HAVE MADE YOUR HEART ANEW!"

Looking at Jesus unbelievingly, Jenny seemed still unsure of what this meant, exactly, other than it was a fine work of divine art.

"So, what do I do with it?"

"TAKE IT. IT IS A GIFT FROM MY FATHER," said Jesus. "SHARE IT WITH OTHERS."

"Wow! I'm n-not so sure how to do that," Jenny said, feeling pressed.

Showing nothing but patience and kindness, Jesus smiled and explained.

"WELL, YOUR MOTHER, NATASHA, HAD WOUNDS, TOO."

A lightbulb went off inside Jenny's head.

"Her heart was Swiss cheese, too, wasn't it?" she said excitedly.

Smilingly, Jesus responded with delight.

"YES," said Jesus. "ONLY SHE HAD EVEN MORE HOLES THAN YOU."

Jenny thought about it for a moment. *Hurt people have Swiss cheese for hearts. Pain from others shoots holes through their cheese.* She wondered just how many holes Natasha's heart had received over her years, where they came from, and who put them there. Feeling a sudden stab of fear, Jenny forced herself to ask the question.

"Is s-she . . . is my mother fixed now?"

"SHE HAS NO MORE TEARS," Jesus gladly offered. "SHE KNEW ME AND I KNEW HER."

This assurance brought tears to Jenny's eyes. She remembered that her mother had been baptized, in a lake as a matter of interest. Jenny and her brothers had been present that day and had watched their pastor dunk her. Jenny especially remembered the child-like expression of delight on her mother's face as she came up out of the water. It was the happiest she had ever seen her mother.

Suddenly, Jenny's feelings seemed different toward Natasha. Gone was the anger, the hurt. In its place, she felt compassion for her mother's wounded heart.

Her birth mother had certainly made more than her fair share of mistakes over the course of her interrupted life. Natasha could have chosen abortion when she was pregnant with Jenny, but she hadn't. She had not compounded one bad decision with yet another painful one.

Natasha had given life to Jenny not once, but twice. She had given birth to Jenny but had also given Jenny a new start in life when she made the grueling decision to make an adoption plan for her and her siblings. Twice she had given Jenny the chance for a beautiful life.

Jenny teared up at the thought of the sacrifices Natasha had made. Until this very moment, Jenny had never before understood the depth of love it took to make that decision—to sacrifice what she wanted. Natasha had been sixteen when she had given birth to her first child—only two years older than Jenny. *How frightening that must have been for Natasha,* Jenny thought.

This last realization startled her. Feeling that familiar sense of warmth from deep within, Jenny sat up in bed. This warm, tingling awareness somehow made her heart feel full. Not a stuffed-on-pepperoni-pizza type of full, but a fullness nonetheless.

"I GET IT! I GET IT!" Jenny exclaimed. "I don't have the anger anymore and I see Natasha differently. I can see beyond *what* she did. I can see *why* she did it. It didn't have anything to do with me. It had to do with her wounds, her Swiss cheese, right?"

Jenny was smiling big now, her bright teeth showing. Understanding this made her heart want to sing and dance. She hadn't felt this good in . . . a very long, long time. Ever, maybe. She felt . . . well, she felt free! Yes, that was it. She felt light as a feather. Unchained. The heaviness in her heart was gone. It had vanished. She couldn't have forced herself to feel badly at the moment, even if she had tried.

Looking upward, Jenny clasped her hands together.

"Thank you, thank you, thank you, Jesus! I get it now," Jenny yelled excitedly. "How cool was that! You are awesome, Jesus! I love you!"

Suddenly, Jenny felt a strong urge to tell her mother about all that had happened. Actually, she felt an urge to speak with her birth mother as well, though impossible. Even knowing that Natasha had died in the car wreck years earlier did not stop the desire to somehow connect with her. But, even this couldn't burst her warm bubble. She didn't care about anything right now except telling her adoptive mother about this wonderful experience.

Throwing back the covers, Jenny raced out of her bedroom calling after her mother.

"Mom. Mom!"

"Back here, honey," her mother called back. "I'm in the utility room taking out my contacts.

Racing out of her bedroom, Jenny suddenly stopped as she remembered Jesus. Sticking her head back in her room, Jenny addressed Him.

"Sorry, Jesus. Didn't mean to leave you hangin'. I'm just so excited. Um, do you mind if I go now and tell my mom?"

"I'M ALWAYS HERE."

"Cool!" Jenny exclaimed before resuming her original goal.

Flying downstairs and across the kitchen's slate-gray tiles, Jenny reached the back of the house where her mother stood at the sink.

Standing at the doorway, Jenny took a moment to observe her mother. Unexpectedly, she saw a different side of her. Cathey was her mother, of course, but it was as though Jenny had been given the ability to see, really *see*, Cathey as seen through God's eyes. And, what Jenny perceived practically made her weep.

Though she saw Cathey doing a mundane task, physically, she was spiritually bathed in the color of love. Softly lit hues surrounded her mother, engulfing her. Not in a confining way, but in a defining way. This definition did not seem to restrain her. Quite the opposite, really. It seemed to release in Cathey more love, more commitment, more devotion, and more beauty than Jenny had ever seen.

Jenny stared for what felt like only a few seconds, but enough time had lapsed which caused her mother to turn towards her.

"Jenny? You okay?"

Needing a moment to answer, Jenny then quickly answered, filling in the awkward silence.

"Oh, um, yeah. I am SO okay."

Looking oddly at her, Cathey observed, "You look excited about something."

More silence filled with anticipation.

"You look beautiful, Mom," Jenny offered genuinely.

"M-m, well I can't see without my eyes in, so I'll just have to trust you on that one. But, thank you. So," Cathey asked suspiciously. "Why such a nice compliment? Is there something you're wanting? No, you can't go to Monica's house to spend the night."

Jenny acted as if she had not even heard her mother's doubt. "Can I talk with you about something?"

A medium-sized knot quickly formed in Cathey's stomach. Turning slowly to face Jenny, yet with hands holding onto the sink, she asked slowly, "What's wrong, Jenny? Are you alright?"

"Nothing's wrong. I just had this . . . this weird, no great . . . no, wonderful experience and wanted to see if you've ever had this happen to you before?"

Seeing the smile on Jenny's sweet face and the shine in her eyes relieved Cathey from sensing that something catastrophic was about to hit. Cathey's emotions were still raw from Monica's situation. She had felt such anguish and pain for everyone in Monica's family. Watching Monica's mother, Amy, weep with fear and grief had struck a deep fear in Cathey as well. Her heart ached for all of them, but especially Monica, whose life would never again be the same no matter what decision she made.

But, Cathey could now see from Jenny's glow that she had no bad news to share. A look like this could only be a deliciously warm gift.

When Jenny had finished sharing her experience with her mom, she noticed that the hour was late. Time had flown by without them even realizing it.

Midnight had come. Jenny looked forward to slipping in between her yellow sheets and thinking about the night's experience.

Meanwhile, Cathey patted back to her bedroom, feeling her own warmth about Jenny's encounter with Jesus and her infilling of the Holy Spirit.

Though Randy had already gone to bed, he was not yet asleep. Rolling onto his back, he groggily acknowledged his wife's presence by gently touching her arm.

"Oh, sorry, honey. Didn't mean to wake you," Cathey whispered.

"That's okay. It got too late for my eyes to stay open any longer," Randy admitted. "But, I wanted to know if everything was alright with Jenny. You guys talked a long time. Anything I need to be worried about?"

"Actually, no," Cathey said quietly and slowly. "Nothing to worry about at all. You go back to sleep."

Randy could sense that Cathey was smiling as she spoke and wanted to understand why.

"So, tell me. What's the deal? Don't keep me in suspense. I can listen with my eyes closed."

Excitedly, Cathey filled him in on all the details of their conversation. As she lay on her side facing him, and with folded arm supporting her head, Cathey awaited his response.

Meeting her gaze, Randy considered these things and became tearful.

"God is so good, isn't He?" Randy offered after a brief pause. A nicely blended cocktail of reverence and awe comforted them both.

Sleep embraced them all that night allowing a particularly deep, restoring slumber for their stressed bodies. Truly healing.

And, though they knew Jenny would be changed by her encounter with the Lord, they had no idea just how extensive her transformation would be!

CHAPTER 29

Stuffed with pepperoni pizza and pop, Jenny and Monica sat on the floor in Monica's room. It wasn't often that she was allowed to eat in her bedroom, but rules had been somewhat suspended since Monica's moods began to swing far and wide.

Monica's parents had been walking on eggshells lately, unsure of how to proceed in this decision-making process. But, one thing they knew for sure was that Jenny's presence lately had helped calm the stormy waters at home. Unable to pinpoint exactly what it was about her that was different, Monica's mother didn't spend much time figuring it out. She was just exceedingly grateful that Jenny's friendship was helping her daughter.

Weeks had passed with Jenny and Monica holed up in either Monica's or Jenny's room. Mrs. Beasley had known that they had been in an argument a few weeks ago, but it seemed to have blown over, or they worked it out in some way.

Amy would have loved to have been a fly on their walls, she thought.

"I'm over-the-top full. I should have stopped two pieces of pizza ago," Jenny blurted.

"Yeah," Monica said leaning back and rubbing her stomach. "I didn't really need that last one either. Lately, I've been feeling like a beached whale."

"You're pregnant, silly! You're supposed to feel like that."

"Yeah, my jeans and shorts are already getting tighter. If I feel this way now, how much worse am I gonna feel when I'm nine months pregnant? Ohh, it makes my stomach hurt to even think about it."

After some moments of silence, Monica broached the topic of several of the recent discussions—forgiveness.

"Jenny? Now, don't get mad at me, okay?"

Jenny groaned. "I'm too full to get mad at you. Even if I did get mad, I couldn't move to do anything about it. So, go for it."

"Okay, so, do you really forgive me for spewing off about getting an abortion? You know, I didn't really mean it. I was just so . . ."

"Excuse me," Jenny interrupted. "We've already talked about this, remember? If not, then let me recap for ya. We talked, I realized that you were not really serious about having an abortion, you said you were sorry, I forgave you, and that's it. Were you not there for that? I mean, I saw you lookin' straight at me."

"Quit," Monica giggled. "Yes, I was there for that and I remember what you said. I guess I just feel so badly for sayin' it. You gotta hate me or somethin' for even thinking it much less saying it. You can't say that it's no big deal."

"I understand venting," Jenny announced boldly. "I really truly don't feel the sting of it anymore. I can try to dig up some good ole' rage, but I'm just not feelin' it. So, it's done. Over. Gone. Kaput. At the bottom of the ocean, okay? So, quit bringing it up. Deal?"

Starting to object, Monica gazed into Jenny's determined eyes and decided to drop it. It really had seemed to Monica that Jenny no longer held it against her at all. In their recent discussions, she had never again referred to it or even made a sarcastic comment about her flippant remark.

"Okay, deal," Monica reluctantly conceded.

"I don't know how else to explain it to you. It went away that night, you know, when Jesus healed me. All my anger . . . it just vanished. Actually, a lot of things changed that night. No, wait, that's not right," Jenny said. "I can explain it. That night, Jesus took all my bad stuff away. He just . . . . He spoke and healed it. Just like that! And, that warm feeling. It was . . . just so awesome. I've never felt anything like that before."

Jenny drifted off in thought for a moment, recalling the details of that night.

Struggling to put it into words again, Jenny continued. She discovered that it was actually impossible for her to keep from speaking more about that night.

"He wiped the slate clean, like erasing black marker writings off of a dry-erase board. With one swipe of His hand, all of it was gone . . . including your stupid comment," she concluded with a smile. "The one you won't EVER say again."

Monica nodded her head in agreement, and then wrinkled her forehead in confusion.

"I get the part where Jesus wiped it all away, but," she continued with head hung in shame, "d-do y-you *see* me differently now because I said that . . . because I said it?"

Jenny considered Monica's question carefully before answering.

"Actually, yes. I do see you differently."

Feeling the dam of tears about to break, Monica quickly glanced at her tissue box.

Seeing her friend close to tears, Jenny quickly explained.

"No, goofhead, not like you're thinking," Jenny said reassuringly while reaching over to tussle her hair.

"I love you! Look, we've been through a lot together, you 'n me. So, nothing, I repeat, NOTHING can hurt our friendship—that I KNOW for sure!" Grabbing about ten tissues and sticking them into Monica's hand, Jenny continued, though Monica's tears of relief began to flow.

"I guess you can say that I see you like Jesus saw me—you got Swiss cheese holes in your heart, too!"

The girls laughed together at the vision of Swiss cheese again. Monica playfully tossed a pillow at Jenny hitting her in the head.

"Alright, sista, the war is on!" Jenny grabbed her ammunition. Monica may have fired the first salvo, but Jenny was determined to end it.

Downstairs, Monica's mother paused with fright at the noise. Initially, she worried that her daughter was having another meltdown. But, after listening for a few seconds, Amy was relieved to hear that she had, in fact, heard *laughter*! Of late, laughter had been loudly absent from their house. But, a smile slowly emerged over Amy's face, like the sun gently rising over God's creation. In that moment, hope was born. Its absence had been sorely missed.

When the dust had settled from the pillow fight, and each had declared victory, Jenny and Monica resumed their discussion. Monica broke the silence first.

"So," Monica began, "since you know me so well, tell me about my Swiss-cheesed heart."

The expression on Monica's face signaled a slight warning sign, entitled, *Walk softly, for she throws a mean pillow.*

"I don't know what to say about your cheese holes."

"You mean, *Swiss* cheese holes," Monica giggled through her tears.

"Fine. Have it your way. Actually, it was God's way. I don't know what to say about your *S-w-i-s-s* cheese holes then. Mine were caused by the hurts people did to me. So, I'm assuming that your holes came from your hurts."

The first thing Monica thought of was her pregnancy and all the anger she still had towards Dagger. Her mouth spewed before she could close it.

"Oh, you mean, like that loser Dagger and what he did to me?" Sarcasm covered her words like an umbrella.

Monica's face turned red and she lost her need for tissues and her desire for further conversation. Her mind raced with cursings and evil thoughts about revenge. Suddenly, Monica stood and began to pace.

Jenny was sorry she even brought up the subject. She wondered whether or not Monica could ever reach a point where she could forgive Dagger for what he did. She knew one thing for sure, thought—it wasn't going to happen tonight. Monica made it clear that this part of the evening had just ended.

"C'mon," Monica demanded. "Let's get Mom to take us for ice cream."

Between Monica's sessions with the therapist and daily talks with Jenny, Monica's mother was beginning to feel left out.

Liz had told Amy to allow some sessions so that she could connect in some way to Monica. Liz needed to get some background information and history first, while allowing Monica to tell her, in her own words, why she was there, what she liked about her life, her dreams, goals, activities, family, friends, faith, and what she wished she could change about her life. Liz had given Monica some paperwork and writing assignments to assist her in thinking, seriously thinking, about her life.

The gift of listening, genuine listening, to clients was one of the most important skills a good therapist could offer. That, and the ability to be an objective party without personal or emotional involvement. Objectivity, coupled with prayerful discernment and true caring for the client, presented a perfect intersection for the client to face the reality of her situation and her feelings and beliefs about her choices.

There was much work to be done in therapy. Amy wanted to do this the right way, whatever that was, so she waited to be included in the therapy discussions. However, Amy and Ben had emotional work of their own to do and an assignment to complete before their next family session.

Liz had stated how vital it was that Monica be allowed to make decisions about her own and her baby's life, but this did not mean that the parents had no say at all in the matter. "A girl this young could not possibly parent a child without extensive and lengthy dependency on her parents," Liz had said. The parents' assignment was to discuss what options (adoption or parenting) would look like in their family's life. Basically, they were to decide what they would be willing to provide and *not provide* to Monica in this situation which would, then, give guidelines to her so that she could make a well-informed decision.

Additionally, Liz had informed them that this process, however long it took, would feel like a grieving one—much like the process one goes through when experiencing a death. But, instead of mourning the death of a person, they would grieve the loss of dreams, the loss of innocence, and the loss of what used to be their reality.

Amy had recalled Liz's repeated warnings that, because of these circumstances, there would be no pain-free decision. "Each would bring its own degree of hurt, sadness, and fear," Liz had said. "Each option would bring its own blessings and grievances to their family. An unplanned pregnancy was a huge upheaval to the entire family, not only Monica. And, this situation included additional complications, like Monica's young age, the age of the birth father and whether or not to press charges; all would have to be considered in their decision-making process."

"There are too many things to think about," Amy had cried to Ben.

"Well, one thing's clear to me," Ben had exclaimed. "This boy is going to jail. I'm pressing charges on him and that's it."

Amy was tired of feeling caught in the middle between the two of them. She had her own grief work to do, but had been so distracted by their arguments, that she rarely had any time to think about her own feelings.

At least the long talks between Monica and Jenny had provided some relief in this area over the last two weeks. Jenny's presence in their house had not allowed the opportunity for many fights.

Being a mother meant that Amy's heart would hurt in a way that no one else could understand or comprehend, not even Ben. The depth of a mother's pain knew no limits. She would grieve in a way no one else would. She had once heard Dr. Phil say that 'a mother's heart is only as happy as her saddest child.' Amy was intimately familiar with this truth. Ask any mother and they'll tell you that their children carry their mother's heart in their pocket and never know it.

But, Amy had taken some comfort in knowing that there was one Person who knew the depth of her cries; One Who sacrificed His own Son for all. God, and God alone, knew the breadth and width of pain. Of love.

This truth reminded her of yet another truth. God provides hope. He grants strength enough to get through anything, if we but allow. If she could let go enough to permit God to take this situation, if she could pry her fingers off and keep them off, if she could release her fingernails from the mesh of this ordeal, only then would there be hope.

Until the moment she chose to take her hands off, Amy's mind would continue to run an endless marathon, like a hamster on his wheel. She was reminded of the saying, 'that you never know that Jesus is all you need until Jesus is all you have.'

How her gut ached! How her stomach churned. She felt so alone. And broken. A seemingly lethal crack had broken through Amy's spiritual foundation. In the weeks since discovering her daughter's pregnancy, she had cried rivers of tears, and had doubts that God had a plan for this. She had questioned, more than once, if she was even on His radar. Was God listening? Was He hearing her cries of help in the late hours of the night when life seemed at its darkest?

For weeks, the family had been entrenched in deep grief, just as Liz had warned. Amy had tried to lift her own spirits. She had been faithful by listening to music, reading Scriptures, praying, journaling, attending support group, and talking with friends—all the tools that Liz had made sure to suggest to utilize. Some days had been better than others, but Amy had repeatedly wondered if she could face months and months of this. She had wanted so badly to run—to just get in the car and drive. But, to where? She had no idea. Someplace where she didn't have to *feel*. But, she couldn't run fast enough. Where was the 'off' button to turn off the pain? If not an off button, then at least a dimmer switch.

Amy could not escape the fact that she had left her heart in a most dangerous place—in her daughter's pocket.

Suddenly, a Scripture verse came to her: *He is before all things, and in Him all things hold together.* All things hold together, she thought to herself. Okay, since God can hold together an entire cosmos, then doesn't it seem likely that He can hold together my reality, my moods, my tears, my life, and my child's life? He has a plan for this, doesn't He? For my child? My baby?

Another wave of grief crashed over her. *Oh, God, my baby is having a baby.*

Questions flooded her mind again and she began to pace. How did it come to this? How did we get here? I don't know who she is anymore. I don't even know how to talk to her. How did she get so lost and will she stay lost forever?

Trying to resist Satan and stop this line of downward thinking, Amy changed her perspective, and spoke aloud to the empty room.

"I know it's not as bad as it could be. I mean, she could have murdered somebody, she could have contracted a fatal disease, and she could be in a wheelchair, any number of things. So, why don't I feel comforted by this? God, please help me! I believe the Bible where it says that You are the beginning and the end, and in everything You have Supremacy." Doubting her memory, she continued. "Or, did it say that You *could* have Supremacy. I'll have to look up that verse. Oh, where is my Bible?" Suddenly, she was frantic to know the Truth of that verse. She needed hope and a place to put her fears. She needed to know that God would never leave her. She needed so many things. Putting her head in her hands, Amy began to cry. Again.

Blowing her nose with yet another tissue, she straightened up, walked into the dining room, looked in the mirror and boldly told herself, "The only way through this is to hold on to your faith, Amy Beasley. And, never let go! That's exactly what you're gonna do."

Wiping her eyes one last time, Amy turned and went upstairs. She wanted a family meeting with her husband and Monica. She was determined that they would get through this with faith and family intact. Satan would not get a foothold in this family. Never.

With a final cheer and unwavering heart, Amy spoke, "No, sirree, I will *not* be moved."

CHAPTER 30

While Amy was out in the living room pacing, Ben was back in their bedroom lying down nursing yet another headache. Ben had noticed that a pattern had been emerging. Normally, he seemed fine during office hours at the bank where he was a loan officer, but along about four o'clock—about an hour or so before leaving for home—he would begin to experience a dull throb behind his left eye. Within thirty minutes of that, a similar ache would develop along the back of his neck which would slowly crawl up and around until it covered the entire back of his head. The small, pint-sized throb would, then, grow into a full gallon-sized headache by the time he'd arrive home.

For weeks, Ben had thought of nothing else except his daughter's pregnancy. Putting the words, "daughter" and "pregnancy" in the same sentence made him nauseous, almost to the point of vomiting, but he hadn't yet.

A crisis of this magnitude brings a family to its knees. A daughter breaks her mother's heart and her father's trust.

Wrestling with an intensity of emotions he didn't know existed had kept Ben counting sheep every night. He couldn't stop his racing thoughts. Always running, seldom productive.

Of late, his bedtime routine had consisted of comforting and reassuring Amy, praying together for strength and direction, and holding her while she wept and he suppressed his anger. There would always be plenty of night left to deal with his feelings after she fell asleep.

Alone with his thoughts last night, Ben's mind began to wander again. The family needed him more than ever, especially Amy, but nobody knew what to ask for or how to ask for it. He was trying to be the strong, spiritual leader of the family, but it seemed to him that no one at home wanted to be led. Amy seemed to be either in a tearful state all the time or in a zombie-like zone. And, Monica, his little girl-no-longer, seemed to stay in her room, by herself or with Jenny, resisting any and all regular family time or normal interaction.

Ben needed things back to normal, but what was normal anymore? There had been none at the Beasley house since . . . well, since Amy dropped the bomb. He and Amy seemed to be guessing at what to do, what to say, and how to say it, much less trying to lead it!

At work, his job was so simple compared to this giant abyss of mixed emotions. Ben knew how to lead as a loan officer. He knew how to facilitate meetings and plug numbers into spreadsheets. He had the power in his hands to change people's lives. And, if he didn't know an answer to a client's question, he would simply research until he discovered it. But, in a situation such as this? His daughter's pregnancy? Wondering how to maneuver through this maze of emotions kept Ben grabbing at straws and guessing what would come next.

Longing for family familiarity and comfort, Ben sought their company, but it wasn't the same. For Ben, normal interactions provided predictability, not chaos. Predictability provided an order—a sense of control. A family routine would be such a welcomed change from this . . . whatever it was.

The "protector" in Ben could not rest or even close his eyes. His awareness was on high alert. Continual code blue! He felt like he was a soldier on the front line without even so much as a lunch break.

Tossing and turning in bed the previous night, he had realized that someone had stolen his family. His beautiful, perky wife had vanished the moment the bomb had exploded, along with his brilliant, unstoppable teenager who now refused to go outside, go places with friends, or even talk with the neighbors when the evening cooled off a bit.

Ben wondered where he had lost control. How had it happened? And, did it happen slowly or had it been going on for months? Was this a grab-gone-bad theme? The kind where somebody had quickly broken and entered their house and kidnapping the old Amy, their former innocent daughter, and his entire world? His family had been taken hostage and he didn't know what to do. There was no ransom he could pay to get them back. No guns, no weapons. No crime. Wait! He quickly corrected himself. Yes, there HAD been a crime and Mr. Dagger whatever-his-last-name is, is gonna pay a price for what he had taken from his daughter and family. He's not going to get away with this, he thought with intense determination.

Ben felt like a failure. If truth be told, he felt ashamed. Inadequate. But, the only emotion that ever emerged was anger. He was a man; he knew how to be angry. Angry at himself that he never saw it coming. Angry that he wasn't prepared for it. Angry at Monica for breaking his trust. He angrily thought, "A father should be able to trust his daughter," only to be haunted in shame by, "But, a family should be able to trust the one who is supposed to keep them safe from harm." Emotions would roll from anger to shame and then back to anger again.

Poring frantically over Scriptures alone at night in the wee hours of the morning, Ben kept obsessing over a verse: "Children, obey your parents in everything, for this pleases the Lord." But, of course, the next verse is, "Fathers, do not embitter your children, or they will become discouraged." Ben felt trapped. Was it okay to be angry or not?

Over the last few weeks, Amy had asked him if she had been a good mother, and if so, then why did this happen. Ben had assured her that she had been the best of mothers. It angered Ben that she had to struggle with her doubts. Yet, he wrestled with the same thought. This niggling uncertainty spread like cancer to other areas of his life. If he wasn't a good father, then maybe he really wasn't a good loan officer either. He hated all this questioning. It was painful. Heartbreaking. He wanted their old reality back.

When he couldn't stop his brain, Ben would quietly slip out of their bed and go stand on the back porch. Somehow searching for and staring at the Big Dipper gave him solace. During these summer months, the stars were in the same place at the same time. They were predictable. No guessing. No wondering. Just steady and stable.

Standing outside in the dark one evening, Ben's mind had begun to entertain an un-Christian-like fantasy about what he'd like to do to Dagger. Thinking about Dagger's action, Ben had found himself a load shy of a truck full of grace.

These fantasies had pulled him back to his own teenage years. Never one to start a fight, but never one to walk away, Ben had been known for his wild side. A quarterback on the high school football team, Ben had spent more time on the field than he had at home. Between working out at the gym and attending daily, exhausting practices in the sizzling Oklahoma summer heat, made Ben buff and tough, with insides to match.

The man in the mirror may have packed on a few pounds over the years, but Ben was still in good shape and could quickly, if necessary, get in touch with that tough kid inside. And, this would be the perfect time.

While staring at the constellations, Ben had started a game out of which "bag of tricks" he could use on Dagger, to help him more "fully" comprehend what he had done to his little girl and to his family.

First out of the fantasy bag had been the obvious. One word had come to his mind. Castration. Using an unusually dull kitchen knife. Should the act be completed with a single, quick slice, or should it be done with a slow, see-sawing movement, he wondered. But, the more he thought about it, the more he realized that this was entirely too easy for such an important moment. Besides, it had previously been done, a decade or so ago, by a scorned wife.

Maybe, Ben had thought, he should consider the second option as opposed to the first. How about a brief, meaningful, outdoorsy fishing trip using Dagger as bait? He could wind fishing line directly around specific sections of his anatomy, attach it to a fifty-pound weight, and then shove him overboard.

Having smiled at the visual in his head, Ben's mind had begun churning out a yet third idea, crowding out the rod-and-reel routine. One of his favorite colors was gun metal gray. He began to wonder what he could possibly do with a color such as that. Oh, right. Get one of his shotguns. Shoot, (pun intended as he smiled), he didn't even need one of his better guns. He could use his old BB gun from his childhood and get in some good and lengthy target practice for the day. That could certainly be a slow and rippling conversation to have with the young man who'd knocked up his baby girl.

Ben could barely fulfill that fantasy before others had begged for acknowledgement. The following fantasy had included the use of rusty nails, a sling shot, and a tall tree. But, the moment he had burst out in laughter, a new and sobering picture filled his mind—one which contained a visual of Jesus, nails, and a tree in a setting some two-thousand years ago.

If he could find a way to make his brain focus solely on his fantasies, then he wouldn't have to be gripped with such guilt. Nope. Ben couldn't do it. He couldn't continue to think of ways to purposefully harm a young man, no matter how stupid he was, while being confronted with the face of Christ before him.

Faced with a critical choice, Ben considered his options. He could either keep on sinning by entertaining these crazy thoughts, or he could stop, turn around, confess, and ask Jesus to heal his hatred.

Ben returned to his bedroom.

And knelt.

CHAPTER 31

As Amy headed upstairs, Ben gently called to her to come back downstairs.

"Oh, Ben, I was just calling you—actually Monica, too. I am tired of not facing the elephant in the room. We need to sit down and discuss this."

Taking her hand in his, Ben guided her into the study.

"What are you doing, Ben?"

"I want to talk with you a minute," Ben answered.

"Well, can't this wait until after we've all talked?" Amy was clearly becoming impatient.

"No, honey, this can't wait," he said while bringing her over to the sofa.

"First, we're going to pray, and then we'll go up and talk with Monica. This is too important to do without Jesus," Ben said firmly.

Surprised at Ben's sudden change of heart, Amy could find no words to combat his plan. He was right. This was too important to rely solely on their words.

Silence surrounded and engulfed them in its perfect serenity. With closed eyes, both took a deep, cleansing breath as though screening the air for peace particles.

"Father, God," Ben began to plead. "You are merciful and mighty. You are our life and reason for living. We praise and thank You for your Word, for it helps us to know Your Son, our Savior. You sent your Holy Spirit to guide and give us wisdom when we need it. Well, Lord, we certainly need it now. We need You now. Our family is in trouble and we have lost our way. But, we know the way to You. Your Word tells us that all things work together for the good of those who love you and who have been called according to Your purpose. We give you our hearts and lives and, particularly, this situation. Give us your words to say to Monica, and open her heart to receive them. We thank You for Your unending grace and Your mighty power. We pray this in Jesus' name. Amen."

Amy stared at Ben for a long time trying to adjust to his transformation. Clearly, both of their hearts had been touched by his prayer. She saw Ben's eyes water and noticed her own, wet with moisture and bathed in hope.

Holding his hands within hers, Amy leaned into him and rested. His prayer had reminded her that this world was not solely about her daughter's pregnancy. Widening her perspective allowed Amy to be reminded that God uses any and all situations to bring lost sheep into the fold, especially ones which have strayed from the fold. No, this was about God, not them. A miracle needed to be acknowledged in the midst of their pain—the miracle of a child.

The hairs on this baby's head have already been counted. God, Himself, has ordained that this life that would soon be living in this world among them.

In the time it took for them to say the prayer, the world seemed to right itself on its axis. The air seemed lighter, their burden lifted.

"I am humbled," Amy said quietly.

"So am I," Ben agreed.

"Then, I believe we are in the right frame of mind for a family meeting. Let's go find Monica," Ben said rising from the sofa.

EPILOGUE

The conversation between Monica and her parents had gone very well that hot, August night, almost a year ago, though they should not have been surprised—especially since God had been in the mix.

The softening of Ben's heart coupled with his bold, spiritual confidence had initiated a desperately-needed time of healing which the family had not previously experienced. The Holy Spirit's guidance, combined with Ben's newly recovered leadership, as well as family therapy with Liz, attendance at the support groups, and hours upon hours of family discussions, allowed the Beasleys to manage their way through this web, and had become one of CPO's most beloved families.

Never before had Monica's father, Ben, traversed such a dangerous and complicated mine field as the one he led his family through this last year. The firey rage toward Dagger that had burned so hotly inside Ben had lessened considerably after they had made the decision to press charges. Witnessing fairly immediate justice had allowed Ben's temper to lessen which, in turn, diffused everyone's anger on this subject and sparked far more productive meetings.

Though Monica's heart had not been fully healed, she eventually had been able to see that Dagger had used her for only one purpose. It had taken a couple of months before she had gained clarity, but Dagger's consistent lack of interest in her, the pregnancy, or the baby had finally convinced her that he had been just an immature, stupid, impulsive "player." He had finally been caught with an unavoidable consequence that he couldn't wriggle out of this time. Not once in those emotionally-ladened weeks after she had told him about the pregnancy had Dagger called her. Not once. Feeling desperate and alone, Monica had called him six or seven times, but had always been directed to his voicemail. The last time she called, she had become crystal clear about him. No more phone calls had been made.

Unfortunately, Tommy had not been surprised by Dagger's disturbing antics. He had been aware of Dagger's bad reputation and had, therefore, tried to steer the girls clear of him. But, Monica had been young and naïve and had fallen for Dagger's smooth lines. She had not been the first to fall prey to Dagger and would, unfortunately, probably not be the last, though it would be awhile before he could get to anyone else.

Tommy had found out about Monica's pregnancy from Dagger whose pathetic, apathetic attitude toward Monica and the situation had infuriated him. Of course, Tommy had immediately reported the information to his father who, in turn, fired Dagger but not before first planning how he'd wanted it to play out.

Tom, Sr., had called the police and reported the incident about Monica, and had asked that they do Tom the favor of picking him up on Tom's property when Dagger would be at work. During this phone conversation, Tom had learned that the police had an existing warrant out on him for his arrest, but that they had been unable to find him.

Though the police had been unable to tell Tom the nature of Dagger's previous charge, they had been more than willing to accommodate Tom's request to pick him up on site. Tom had hoped that it would have made a bigger impact on Dagger if he had been arrested at work in front of his employer, but Tom had been wrong. Turns out that Dagger had taken apathy to a newer, lower, sub-basement level. Showing his true lack of character and thought process, Dagger had initially smirked at the police when they picked him up, then had turned and winked at Tom. But, the tables had quickly turned as they watched Dagger being taken into custody adorned in shiny, metal handcuffs, and without a smile.

Dagger had been charged and found guilty of engaging in sex with a minor. This charge, along with two others, had insured his place behind bars and in a cold cell for years to come.

On a brighter note, this past March, angels had ushered in a fine, strapping baby boy, son of Monica Beasley and firstborn grandson of Amy and Ben. Born with a full head of dark hair and rivoting blue eyes, he weighed in at eight pounds, four ounces, and measured twenty inches long.

At first glance, baby boy Beasley had resembled Ben's childhood picture, making this occasion even more sentimental, yet painful. Within weeks, this angelic cherub had reflected many of Monica's features, including her dark hair, long toes, and small nose. Other characteristics had eventually mimicked his birth father, Dagger, much to the dismay of everyone, though it was a reality they would have to accept.

On that cold March evening one year ago, after fourteen long hours of labor, Monica had welcomed her baby, held him tightly, and kissed his face before handing him over to his adoptive parents, Glenn and Pam Oosterhaus.

Tears had flowed from everyone present. Not a dry eye in the house, including the nurses and doctor. This had not been an easy journey or decision for Monica and her family. The long, winter months had held a roller coaster of emotions—fear, sadness, happiness, relief, anger, and joy. But, with the help of their support system, the Beasleys had managed their way through the winding, twisted road of grief and had come out on the other side of it intact.

Amazingly, and not surprisingly, Jenny had played a key role in the open adoption process because of her own childhood. Hearing the details of Jenny's experience of having been born to, and parented by, Natasha for six years, and then adopted by the Abbott family had made the Beasley family much more comfortable with the concept of open adoption. It had offered them the unique perspective from a child's point of view, which had been a critical component of Monica's decision to make an adoption plan.

Though it had been Monica's deep desire to keep the newborn baby, she had come to grips with the reality that she had been far too young to consider the option of parenting. Someday, she would become a parent, but she had vowed that this would happen within God's perfect timing and in His holy way. She had paid the cost of this decision by escorting in rivers full of tears and nights of disturbed sleep. Monica had not known that it was humanly possible to feel the depths of this type of love and anguish, but had become accustomed to pain's presence while simultaneously being uplifted by God and sustained by her family, CPO, and friends—most of all, Jenny.

Acknowledging the special bond and friendship between Monica and Jenny, Glenn and Pam had decided on a name for the baby which would, in fact, honor this relationship. Baby boy Beasley had been named Jonathan David Oosterhaus, referring in the Bible to the deeply-felt loyalty between Jonathan and King David. Additional tears had ushered that name into existence, and Monica had felt cherished for the selection of names. Having been convinced that the adoptive parents had truly understood the nature of Jenny and Monica's friendship, Monica had received it just as it had been intended—a gift of honor—but she felt the true place of honor had been Jenny.

God had worked through Jenny in powerfully healing ways throughout Monica's pregnancy. In response to holy nudgings, Jenny had spoken timely nuggets of truth and words of wisdom to the Beasleys. As a result of offering her unique perspective about her childhood, she had affected the direction of the Beasley family's discussions, moods, and ultimately Monica's decision to make an adoption plan.

Jenny's healing enounter with the Holy Spirit a year ago had transformed her emotionally scarred heart into a vibrant, bold, and spirited young soul. God had taken the years of her youth and the tears of her heart and had used them to mature Jenny in a way which would bless the lives of others. Though she had been abandoned by her earthly father and others, she had never been dismissed by her heavenly Father. On the contrary, God had showed Jenny that He had a plan for her life. An exciting one.

Unmistakeably, Jenny had been a gift. She had been able to *be* a gift because she had *received* a gift. The gift of pain. Followed by the gift of healing. Jenny had never considered that wounded hearts could be washed clean and used in a plan which would show God's love and glory. Jenny had felt rejected and abandoned by Natasha and her father so many times. Every time Natasha had chosen to run those "late-night errands" with the slimebag-of-the-week, leaving her, alone, to care for her brothers for hours, it had taken a bite out of her heart. Yes, Jenny's unhealed heart had looked like Swiss cheese—dingy-white cheese bulleted with multitudes of holes. Some bigger, some smaller, but, filled with holes nonetheless, leaving nothing but bitterness and hurt. In her youth, Jenny had often wished for emptiness instead of such pain, which she had (mistakenly) thought would be easier to manage. What she had discovered was that all pain, regardless of form, leaves deep, dark, desperate and continual longings for something or Someone.

But, God had eventually restored it (using Cathey and Randy at first) having used a love more pure than she had previously known. But, God had not left it there. When the time had been perfect, He had sent the Holy Spirit—Jesus' spirit—to touch her in such a powerfully quiet way as to capture her attention.

Cathey had developed a relationship so close to Jesus for so many years that she couldn't help but reflect the holiness of His love and extent of His grace. Jesus' love had been the only one that could heal her wounds and restore her to wholeness (and holiness). In turn, God had used Jenny's obedient spirit and her more perfect love to pour onto her friend, Monica, when she needed it most.

In the Bible, Jesus says, "Blessed are those who mourn, for they will be comforted." Looking back, it's easy to see that Natasha had been broken, producing a broken Jenny. But, Jenny had also received the touch from the holy hand of the Redeemer Himself and had been saved and healed. And, she had no doubt that Jesus would heal Monica's heart, whenever she was ready. In the meantime, He would wait and continue to knock.

In the past year, many families have come to CPO needing a loving heart and wise direction. God had used this young woman to speak the truth into the lives of many. She had shared experiences of having been damaged by a mother who, herself, had been damaged.

Not only had the other girls at CPO support group been touched by the entirety of Jenny's testimony, but the adults as well. All had been amazed that God had so mightily pursued a girl who had existed in such sadness early in life. By society's inaccurate measurements, Jenny's life with Natasha had been substandard. But, God's ways are vastly different from society's ways—as far as the east is from the west. No, God had looked at the *heart* of His princess, not the conditions of her environment.

During those early childhood dark times, God had never left her side. Nor had He left her in it. The Creator of the universe had zeroed in on the heart of this cute, velvety chocolate—skinned girl whose bright eyes and sensitive heart had been open to the spiritual workings of the Lord. He had sung over her and taken delight in His relationship with her.

God had chosen her. In His perfect time, He had filled her with the power of the Holy Spirit for her ministry. The world was now open to her to touch lives in a way that she could not do in, and of, her own strength.

Oh, what miracles Jesus can do through the power of a heart. A heart fully opened and surrendered. A willing heart.

Jenny's heart.

TO THE READERS

I hope you have enjoyed this fictional piece of work. It is my desire to bring to life the troubles, issues, and agonizing decisions which face young, unwed, pregnant women. Their road is emotionally treacherous and fraught with searing pain. As a therapist with over twenty-five years' experience in the field, and who has worked with Crisis Pregnancy Outreach for over twenty, I feel honored that CPO allowed me to be a part of their healing and decision-making process.

Though the characters in this series are fictional, Jenny's life portrays a likely scenario of one who has found herself in a seemingly impossible situation. If you find that you are in a similar circumstance, remember that you are never alone. God is always with you and He will never forsake or leave you. Hope always accompanies God, and His love will lead you there.

My personal desire is to educate the public on the benefits of open adoption. Though open adoption may be impossible in some situations where safety is an issue, my hope is that, wherever possible, you consider the benefits and blessings it could offer the child and family.

For more information about open adoption, please visit the Crisis Pregnancy Outreach website at www.crisispregnancyoutreach.org

OTHER BOOKS BY JANE WATERS

ARMS WIDE OPEN: Realistic Expectations of Birth Mothers
ABIGAIL, the first fictional novel in the Nine Month Series about a birthmother
BUILDING BLOCKS OF CHARACTER—Applying the Book of Proverbs in daily, realistic life. It includes a Study Guide for individual, small, and large group discussions. Especially written for teenagers and adults.

NATASHA, the second fictional novel in the Nine Month Series about another birthmother.

You can purchase all of these books through www.AuthorHouse.com.

I'd love to hear your story. Feel free to email me at courage2heal@cox.net.

Thank you,
Janey

ABOUT THE AUTHOR

Jane Waters is a Licensed Marriage and Family Therapist and former certified alcohol and drug counselor who has worked in the mental health field for over twenty-five years. A large part of her clientele has been teenage pregnant young women who are faced with making the most painful decisions of their lives—whether to parent the child or make an open adoption plan. Jane is a Christian and is married to Chris. She has four adult children and three grandchildren and lives in Owasso, Oklahoma.